JULIE AND DAVID WATCHED AS THE KIDS POURED OUT OF the lodge. Brenda, one of the girls, squealed, "Ew, Chad, you're all sweaty!" She dodged the boy as he tried to put his arm around her, running into Julie and knocking her off balance.

Before Julie had the chance to think, strong arms caught her and held her fast. She looked up, and David's tender grin took her breath away. He lowered his head slowly, and Julie thought her heart would stop. Was he going to kiss her? Right here?

But his lips stopped next to her ear. "I think you should tell Brenda she doesn't know what she's missing, don't you?" The whispered question sent shivers through her. Before she had a chance to pull away, he simply set her back on her feet and stepped back, that infuriating, teasing smile still in place.

♥ *Palisades Pure Romance*

SUMMIT

Karen Rispin

Palisades is a division of Multnomah Publishers, Inc.

SUMMIT
published by Palisades
a division of Multnomah Publishers, Inc.

© 1999 by Karen Rispin
International Standard Book Number: 1-57673-402-1

Design by Andrea Gjeldum
Cover art by Tom Antonishak

"Spring" by Gerard Manly Hopkins

Scripture quotations are from: *The Holy Bible,* New International Version (NIV)
© 1973, 1984 by International Bible Society,
used by permission of Zondervan Publishing House.

Palisades is a trademark of Multnomah Publishers, Inc., and is registered in the U.S. Patent and Trademark Office.

Printed in the United States of America

For information:
MULTNOMAH PUBLISHERS, INC.•P.O. BOX 1720•SISTERS, OREGON 97759
Library of Congress Cataloging-in-Publication Data
Rispin, Karen, 1955–
    Summit / by Karen Rispin. p. cm.   ISBN 1-57673-402-1 (alk. paper)
    I. Title.   PS 3568.I68S86   1999   98–49979   813'.54—dc21   CIP

99 00 01 02 03 04 05 — 10 9 8 7 6 5 4 3 2 1

OPM

For Phil,
my partner in adventure

For we are God's workmanship, created in Christ Jesus to do good works, which God prepared in advance for us to do.

EPHESIANS 2:10

GLOSSARY

Anchor: A solid point to resist the pull of a fall. It can be anything from a sling around a tree to an elaborate placement of chocks and bolts in cracks in the rock face.

Belay: A system of using a rope to stop a climber's fall if one should occur. Belaying works like magic, but like any good magic trick, it takes a lot of practice to do well.

Belayer: The person who manages the rope and is ready to stop the climber's fall.

Carabiners: (Or "biners") Metal snap links used to connect almost anything and everything in the climber's world.

Chocks and bolts: Metal devices that can be wedged into cracks in the rock with a sling to link the metal piece to the rope.

Crux: The most difficult point in any given climb. The place a climber is most likely to fall.

Pitch: One rope length of climb up a cliff. Climbs can be multipitch—these are longer than the climbing rope—or single pitch, shorter cliffs that are only one rope length tall.

Protection: The anchor and also the chocks and bolts inserted into the rock by a climber as he moves upward. These less elaborate anchors are connected to the rope by slings. A lead climber will fall twice as far as her last piece of protection. Placing protection well so it will save the climber's life is an art in itself.

Scree slope: The steep, tumbled rock debris at the foot of many cliffs.

Prologue

JULIE THREW BACK HER HEAD AND LET THE MOUNTAIN wind play with her hair. Kurt had actually agreed to come hiking with her. Maybe there was still a chance. Hope made her feet light, and she danced ahead of her fiancé, skipping from rock to rock. She hesitated, not wanting to get too far ahead. A rough gray boulder twenty feet high leaned over the path. It would be fun to wait on top.

Quickly she felt for handholds on the limestone. Perched like a pixie on top of the rock, she watched Kurt climb toward her. His stocky, muscular body looked good as he plodded deliberately upward. And yet, as she watched him, Julie felt her smile fade. Kurt was a good man. The kind of man her family expected her to marry. Mom and Dad had been so happy when she showed them her ring....

Julie's stomach tightened and she fought an urge to move away from Kurt, up the mountain toward the blue sky. She should be happy. In a month she'd be married to this wonderful Christian man. Instead her eyes suddenly stung with tears.

Kurt's head was down as he doggedly picked his way up the tumbled rocks. Just below her, he stopped. His face red with exertion, Kurt scanned the path ahead of him with anxious eyes. "Julie!"

"I'm right here, Kurt."

His head snapped back as he looked up too quickly. He staggered backward, trying to catch his balance.

"Careful!" Julie's warning was too late. Kurt caught his heel on a stone and sat down hard.

Julie was already moving. She climbed quickly down the face of the boulder.

In seconds she was at his side. She knelt and touched his arm. "I'm sorry; I didn't mean to startle you."

"Are you insane?" Kurt pushed her hand away and got to his feet in one sharp motion, glaring from her to the spot she'd been waiting.

Julie stepped back, her hand falling to her side. "It was an easy climb and not that high."

"You could have been killed. That's how much you care about our commitment? So little that you'd risk it all to perch on the top of a rock like some fool bird?" Kurt's fist chopped at the air. "One wrong move and you would have fallen! Been seriously injured, or even killed."

Julie reached out her hands to him. "Kurt, I wasn't in danger. This climb was easy, no more than a 5.7 level of difficulty." His eyes narrowed at her use of a climbing term, and she bit her lip. "I've been climbing at a much higher level for years, and I was careful. I made sure of each hold. I'm not foolish."

Kurt studied her, then shook his head. He reached out to take her hands. "I just don't want you hurt." His eyes held nothing but sincerity. "Julie, you are not a child anymore. You're an adult and we have a life to plan together. We should never have come here. The mountains are bad for you."

"No!" The word was forced out of her in a gasp of pain. In a flash of insight, Julie was sure of what she'd been fighting for months. She'd been trying to remake herself in a pattern that would please Kurt. But that was wrong. She couldn't do it anymore.

He tugged on her hands, drawing her into his arms. "Julie, sweetheart…" His mouth came down on hers. For a second she longed to stay there, safe in his arms. Safe as his wife. It would mean security, safety, the kind of life everyone wanted.

A vivid image of that life brought a rush of panic. It would mean many more endless months of working the job he'd found for her, then years of staying home with children in his stuffy suburban bungalow. Years of pretending to be another person.

Suddenly Kurt's arms and mouth seemed to suffocate her. She pulled away, twisting in his grip. Kurt released her so suddenly that she almost fell. Catching her balance, she backed away from him.

"What is wrong with you, Julie?" His eyes were anxious, confused. "I thought you gave up all the childish, risky rock climbing stuff."

Julie kept backing up. Her throat was so tight with emotion it was hard to get the words out. "Guiding rock climbers is not childish. It isn't! I worked hard to get the qualifications to do that. It was a difficult and responsible job."

Kurt shook his head. "You agreed it was right to give all that up. A Christian wife shouldn't take those kinds of risks. She belongs with her husband in the home. We looked the verses up together, remember? Like the verses in Timothy that say a wife should be a keeper at home."

Julie clutched at the boulder to steady herself. "I tried, Kurt. I really did. I denied it, even to myself, but working in the bank has been stifling. God didn't make me to do that." She knew that was true. Knew it as sure as she knew her name. Conviction steadied her voice. "The mountains are good for me, not bad. I belong here, taking risks, teaching people the skills they need to be here. I feel God smiling at me when I climb. How can I stop being me?" She met his gaze, begging him with her eyes to understand. "Today when you said you'd come hike with me I was hoping..." She half reached out to him then dropped her hand helplessly.

Kurt shook his head. "Hoping what? Hoping I'd say it was fine? That my wife can go risk her life with strangers? Julie, that's crazy."

"Does it have to be?" Tears were streaming silently down her cheeks.

Kurt gave a little grunt of pain—she knew how it hurt him to see her cry—and moved toward her. Julie dodged him, but he caught her arm. "Julie, stop it. I love you. You're going to be my wife. You'll get over this."

Julie tried to shrug out of his grip. "How can I get over who I am? I can't marry you, Kurt. I can't be the person you want." Sadness swept over her. "No matter how much I wish I could."

Kurt's grip on her arm tightened. "No! Don't say that! You can't say that. You're mine, Julie Miller. We're getting married. The wedding is planned. Everyone would laugh at me."

Julie's vision blurred as her tears flowed more freely.

Kurt looked at her, then let go of her and turned his head away. "I've been afraid of this. I could sense you slipping away. Why, Julie? Why can't you grow up and settle down?"

"It's not a matter of growing up." She wanted to help him understand.

"Of course it is!" Kurt slammed one fist into the palm of his other hand. "Women are supposed to grow up and settle down. What I want from you is what the Bible says a wife should be. Any man would want that. So what are you going to do, never get married at all?"

Julie stared at him, her throat tight and burning. Was he right? "I—I don't know." And she didn't. All she knew was that she couldn't take this conversation—or the feelings that were overwhelming her—one moment longer. She spun and ran away from Kurt. She ignored his voice calling after her as she sprinted hard up the mountain trail until she couldn't see through her tears. Stumbling to a stop, she leaned her forehead against the cool rock. She listened, but Kurt didn't come after her. Pain rolled over her, choking her, forcing itself out in deep sobs.

Kurt was right. She could never fit in the kind of marriage he'd described. His words rang in her ears, over and over. *"Any man would want that...Any man would want that..."*

She was going to be alone for the rest of her life.

She wanted to pray, to beg God for answers, but all that came out was one low, whispered sentence: "Father, help me."

After a long time her heart quieted. She looked up

at the peak above her, gleaming against a deep blue sky. Its beauty sang to her of God's love. Julie stood and let the mountain wind cool her swollen eyes. If climbing was to be her world, then so be it. Maybe she couldn't honor God by being Kurt's wife, or by being anyone else's wife for that matter, but she could honor God by being an excellent climber and guide. She would focus on that with all her strength and accept the cost.

Men simply would not be a part of her future.

One

≋ ≋

"I'M GOING TO FALL!" RON'S VOICE SHOOK WITH FEAR. HIS elbows angled out like wings as he tried to hang on to the cliff face.

Dealing with her clients' fears was something Julie could handle. There were other things in her life that weren't so easy. She had thought she was getting better, but she'd had a jolt that morning that made her less sure. Julie shook her head and focused on Ron.

"Reach up. There's a big hold just above your right shoulder."

Ron didn't respond. He just hung there about forty feet above Julie's stance at the base of the cliff. His legs were shaking with fatigue from the unnatural crouched position he'd held since he started the climb.

He was powerful, with a chunky, compact body, but he wasn't using his strength well. Julie made sure the rope that kept him from falling was snug and tried again to communicate with him.

"Look up. Look at the hold. Do you see it?"

Ron gave a jerky nod.

"Okay, concentrate on it. Then stand up and get it." She tried to impart confidence with her voice.

"Come on, man. You can do this!" Murry called from just behind her. He and Ron played hockey together in a recreational league and talked about adventures. Deciding to try rock climbing, they'd found the Big Foot Outfitters ad in the yellow pages. As Big Foot's rock-climbing guide, Julie had ended up with the job of taking them on the day's climb.

Julie schooled her tone to be both firm and reassuring. "Stand up and get that hold, Ron. You can do it. If you fall, I've got you." A gust of wind picked up some of last fall's leaves and spun them up past Ron. A lull in the wind let Julie hear his harsh breathing. He crouched slightly, then made a desperate lunge for the hold. Scrabbling, he managed to find footholds and keep his grip.

"All right!" Julie and Murry cheered.

Julie took up the slack. "You're past the hardest part of the climb, Ron." He kept moving upward in an uncoordinated scramble. He was obviously tired and was climbing badly. The climb was not difficult. At first he gained ground quickly. Then, just below the top, his hands slipped. With a strangled bleat of terror, he fell.

Automatically, Julie's right hand moved down and outward, locking the rope in place. The stretch in the rope and the friction where it ran through the anchor at the top took some of Ron's weight. Even so, Julie sat hard in the harness to keep her feet on the ground. Her full concentration stayed on the climber.

Ron swore in a shaking voice. "I want to come down."

"You're almost there," Murry protested.

"That's right," Julie said. "You can do this, Ron. Use your head, and climb carefully. That fall wasn't so bad. I caught you."

"Yeah, yeah—I guess."

Julie nodded in satisfaction as Ron started moving again. "He's a brave guy," she commented to Murry. "That fall scared him badly. A lot of people would have quit."

"So what does that make you? Some kind of super-woman? You went up that cliff like it wasn't even there when you put up the rope."

Julie cringed. Murry's voice was close to anger. His attitude toward her skill touched on open wounds. "This is my work, okay?" Hearing her defensive tone of voice, she took a deep breath. "This level of climb will be an easy walk up for you, too, in a bit if you keep at it."

"You're saying you're stronger than Ron?"

"No, I'm not." Her hands moved rhythmically as she took up slack, keeping the rope to Ron's harness taut. Now she focused completely on Ron as he hauled himself up the last few feet of the climb.

"Way to go, man!" Julie took the last bit of slack

out of the rope. Ron whooped with exhilaration as he slapped the tree at the top of the pitch.

"Now, put your feet on the rock and walk backward. I'll let you down."

"People who do this are crazy," Ron called as he complied.

"Isn't it the best?" Julie's voice was full of enthusiasm. She loved everything about climbing: the height; the roughness and beauty of the rock itself; the isolated wild places where she worked; the strength, grace, and discipline it took to learn a new face; and the self-reliance it demanded. Most of all, she loved the way the wild country spoke to her of God. His power and awesome beauty were very close in the mountains.

"It's a rush! Murry, you've got to do this." When Ron's feet were back on the ground, Julie noticed he was sweating and shaking, but his grin was incandescent.

"I will as soon as you get off the rope." Murry sounded irritable. Julie watched him cautiously. He was even more tense than Ron had been, but she couldn't blame him. The May wind had an edge to it. Julie reached to pull a fleece jacket over her head.

After he was tied in, Murry looked up at the cliff, then rubbed his hands together. "Okay, so if it's not strength, what does it take to make a climb like this a walk up like you said?"

19

"Not strength?!" Ron's eyebrows shot up. "My muscles are trashed."

"Yeah, but you did it the hard way," Julie said. "Think about balance. If you push yourself up with your legs instead of mostly pulling with your arms, it's easier. The first time up, most people don't feel secure, so they won't straighten their legs. Ron hauled himself up almost totally on arm strength. It gets very tiring moving like this." She illustrated a crouched walk reminiscent of a Ukrainian dance.

Both men laughed. Ron flexed his biceps. "I made it anyway. Murry, let's see you do the same thing."

Murry wasn't smiling. He took a deep breath before he started climbing. Twice Julie saw him remember to straighten his legs and stand up. He was moving very well for a first-time climber. In minutes he was at the top. During the entire climb, he hadn't looked down once. Even now, he didn't look down.

"Okay, sit in your harness and back over the edge."

Murry glanced down, then quickly up again. His eyes were like dark holes in his pale face. Backing over the edge was the scariest part of the whole experience for many first-time climbers. It just didn't feel natural to sit back with one's weight over the abyss. Julie could still remember the sharp thrill of fear the first time she'd done it.

"Murry, listen, this rope would hold a minivan. Put

your feet high up in front of you, and let it hold your weight."

Ron also called encouragement, but Murry seemed frozen. Julie was beginning to think she'd have to climb up to him, when he began to obey. She lowered him very slowly. She stopped his descent and asked him to use his legs to push off the wall. He did so, timidly at first, then with more confidence. By the time he reached the ground, his grin was as big as Ron's. They whooped and gave each other high fives.

Julie watched them with a half smile on her face. It would be nice if she could feel that same exhilaration, that sense of victory with her problem, but she had no idea how to do that, or even if it could be done. After all, she had found herself unable to cope once. As far as she was concerned, the problem was with her. And it wasn't going away anytime soon.

If it had turned out that either Ron or Murry was unable to climb, it wouldn't have wrecked their lives. They could get on with life just fine without climbing. Julie intended to get on with her life as well. It was much better to concentrate on enjoying the moment at hand. She flipped her long dark braid over her shoulder and pulled out candy bars to aid the celebration.

She looked at the two men. "So, do you guys want to climb here again to consolidate the things you've learned, or shall we move to another climb? Moving will take a few minutes."

"I want to try this climb without the Ukrainian dance style." Ron grinned as he stood and stretched.

Watching him, Julie's mouth tightened. When Ron had gotten out of the car that morning, she'd thought for a second that he was someone else. She'd realized almost instantly that the resemblance was only superficial. As the morning went on, she'd almost been able to put it out of her mind. But the way he'd moved just now as he stood and stretched was so painfully familiar....

Ron hesitated. "Hey, don't look at me like that. If you want us to move on, that's fine with me."

"Sorry, I was thinking about something else." Julie handed him the end of the rope. "See if you can tie yourself in."

Murry came closer as Ron took the rope. The two men bent their heads in concentration as they tried to remember the correct knot. Julie watched the men work, furious that she'd let her memories intrude. She couldn't go on brooding forever.

The two men stepped apart displaying the knot. "Taa daa!" Ron's face creased in a proud grin. "We got it right, right?"

"Right." Julie made an effort to smile. She watched as Ron climbed the route again with more confidence. He fell once but showed none of the panic he'd shown the first time. Already he was trusting the rope.

As she lowered Ron down the face, Murry said, "Okay, I'll try again too."

Julie was checking Murry's knot when the sound of approaching footsteps turned their heads.

"There you are, Julie." Brent's smooth voice couldn't be mistaken.

"Hi, Brent." Julie watched her boss warily. A tireless self-promoter in his late thirties, Brent radiated good will as he introduced himself to Ron and Murry as the owner of Big Foot Outfitters.

"I just wanted to make sure Julie was treating you right." Brent thumped Julie on the back. He looked through the screen of trees at the base of the slabs and motioned expansively. "David, come here. I want you to meet these people."

It was only then that Julie realized another man had come with Brent. Brent must have brought a climber to join her party, though it was odd that Brent would bring the person himself. She looked at Ron and Murry, wondering if they'd mind, then back at the newcomer. She hesitated as the man's eyes met hers. Confidence and calm. That's what she saw in that level gray gaze. He was lean and wiry, more than six feet tall with curly dark hair.

"David, I want you to meet Julie, and Ron and Murry, who are climbing with her."

"It's a pleasure." David's English accent surprised

Julie as he held out his hand. She realized she'd been staring and reached to shake his hand. It was unexpectedly hard with calluses. She glanced down and saw that the back of his hand was marked with scars and scrapes: a climber's hand. His sinewy forearm was ridged with muscle. This was no new climber.

Julie glanced at Brent in puzzlement as David shook hands with her climbers. Apparently responding to David's accent, Murry began to talk about a friend he had in England.

Brent caught Julie's curious look and came to stand beside her. "He's Big Foot's new climbing guide," he explained in a quiet aside to Julie. "He just got in this morning. I was showing him around and thought we'd stop to meet you."

Julie had been watching David, but her attention came back to Brent with a jerk.

"You hired a full-time climbing guide? Why?" She was supposed to be Big Foot's guide. Brent knew as well as she did that there were lots of guides whom he could hire for a day or two if Big Foot had extra work. In fact, he had already done that several times. So why was he hiring this man?

Brent's expression had hardened, so Julie forced her tone to be calmer. "Um, are you planning to expand the sport climbing?" Big Foot did mostly mountaineering climbs. Brent and the other mountain guides or assistant guides he hired on contract led those. There were ten guides who more or less worked regularly for Brent. Most of them did other work as well. The sport climbing, for which Brent usually used her, had not been a big part of the operation. She needed her contract work with Big Foot if she ever wanted to move from assistant rock guide to full guide. "Is this guy internationally certified as a climbing guide?"

"That's right. Remember when I went to England last summer? David Hales was my guide, and I told him he had a job here if he ever came over." Brent shrugged. "Well, he came. He'll be here until mid-September."

"You must have been doing paperwork for months to get work permits and stuff. How come you never said anything?"

Brent frowned. "Don't get in my face, Julie. You're good with clients, but replacing you wouldn't be hard. David is a world-class climber, and those aren't thick on the ground. He's supposed to be a good teacher. You should be glad for the chance to work with him occasionally."

Occasionally! She was going to lose work. She blinked and tried to focus on what Brent was saying.

"Besides, you should be happy to have him around. His nickname is the Vicar."

"What is that supposed to mean?"

Brent didn't answer because David and the other

two had quit talking. Julie watched Brent turn on the charm full bore for his clients. "So, what do you think of climbing now that you've tried it?"

Both men responded enthusiastically to Brent and in a few seconds were talking animatedly about their experience.

Julie and David weren't part of the interchange. She found him looking at her.

"Your name is Julie; is that right?"

She nodded.

"I'm looking forward to working with you. I'm sure you can teach me a few things about climbing around here."

Brent looked over and laughed. "You'll teach her a few things, more like. Julie, I'll need you tomorrow after all. I'll send someone to get you at 6:30 A.M. Come on, David, let's go. Julie has some climbers here who want to get on the rock."

David hesitated, his eyes still on Julie, but Brent motioned impatiently. Julie watched them walk off, two long, lean men striding together. Brent was limber enough, but David moved like a dancer.

Julie set her jaw. It was no use admitting that the Englishman was attractive. There was no room for men in her life. Besides, unless Brent gave her a chance to work with this David Hales, having him take over the available rock climbing work with Big Foot would

26

likely mess things up for her.

Julie wanted to finish her certification with the Association of Canadian Mountain Guides. Working for Brent she didn't get the kind of training and supervision on harder climbs that she knew she'd need to take the full-guide test in the fall. If she did get to work with this Brit, it could be a very good thing. But if she lost all her work with Big Foot, she'd be in big trouble.

"So that's Brent Wilson, your boss," Murry said. "I heard he was a famous mountain climber."

Julie brought her attention back to the climbers. "Yes, he's done some amazing Alpine climbs."

"You didn't look too pleased when he told you to come to work tomorrow."

Julie shrugged. "It messed up some plans, but guides are like mercenary soldiers. We take work wherever and whenever we can get it. Anyone who won't do that just doesn't survive in this business. How about we get climbing?"

"Yeah, quit stalling and get on the rock so I can have another turn." Ron danced around, eager to go.

"Okay, I'm climbing already."

Julie was pleased to see that Murry wasn't as tense this time up. The wind dropped, but the pine-scented mountain air had a spring bite to it. As they moved on to different pitches, Julie was careful not to push Ron and Murry too hard. No use in making them so sore and battered they never came back.

If only all of life could be as simple as a long, lazy afternoon spent teaching two people to play on the sun-warmed cliffs.

Two

JULIE MOVED QUIETLY AS SHE GOT HERSELF BREAKFAST. Laurel, the woman with whom she shared the little two-bedroom apartment, wasn't up. Julie had just finished eating when she heard a car in the drive. Glancing out, she saw Big Foot's van. She grabbed her pack and ran to get to the door before the doorbell rang. Upon opening the door, Julie stepped back. The lanky Asian teenager on the step was new to her.

"Hi, I'm Tommy Oshikawa. Brent Wilson hired me to drive for him and buy food and do some other stuff. You're Julie Miller, right?"

"Right." Julie hefted her pack and headed for the van. "Brent seems to be expanding in all directions."

The boy's grin brightened his whole face. "Yeah, I met the Englishman. I guess Big Foot is going international. I grew up here, so I don't exactly count, but he hired me partly because I speak Japanese, which Brent said would come in handy at times with international climbers."

"So are you going to climb with them?"

Tommy shrugged as he started the van. "He didn't say. Mostly I'll be driving, buying supplies, maybe sorting gear when I learn what everything is. I'd like to, though. I don't think there are many groups coming from Japan, so it would just be something different once in a while."

"Have you ever done any mountaineering before?"

"Just little stuff, but I'm in pretty good shape."

Julie smiled at his confidence. He'd learn soon enough. People were interesting. She liked to draw them out and find out what made them tick. During the short drive to the Big Foot office, she found out that Tommy had just finished his first year of political science at the University of Calgary and wanted to go into law. He seemed a wide-open book.

"What kind of law?" Julie asked.

"Corporate law. My dad wants me to do that, and it's interesting enough."

"The dutiful son?"

Tommy shrugged. "I guess. How about you? Did your folks want you to be a guide?"

Julie laughed. "Not at first, but they helped pay for the training anyway. They're getting used to it, sort of. So what's your family like?"

Thankfully, he launched into his response. Julie didn't want to think about her parents' opinion of her job—or her life. They had been so pleased when she'd been engaged.... Mom had talked about how nice it would be to have grandchildren nearby.

She mentally shook herself and tried to focus on what Tommy was saying. Bright, glib, and talkative, he described his traditional grandmother who lived with the family in a way that had Julie laughing in no time.

"If the ability to talk makes a lawyer, you ought to be a good one."

"Whatever." Tommy grinned.

"So why did you take this job with Big Foot? It doesn't sound like wilderness activities have been a big part of your life."

Tommy gave her a quick, sliding glance. He fell silent, and Julie got the distinct impression the shoe was on the other foot now, and he was the one who didn't want to answer a question. Then he shrugged. "Just something different to do for summer break." At his bland response, Julie shrugged. She must have imagined the tension in his manner.

"I've got to pick up supplies for a bunch two guides on contract are taking up Mount Robson." They pulled up in front of the Big Foot office. "It was nice meeting you, Julie."

"Likewise, Tommy."

She slid from the car and headed inside. It never ceased to amaze her that Brent could run a business in what amounted to little more than a storefront. Brent's office was in the back, along with another room that served as storage space for food and gear. Brent's office and the reception area out front were covered in big photographic prints, mostly of Brent standing on the top of various peaks.

Sheryl looked up as Julie walked in. "Hey, Julie. I didn't think you were coming in today."

"Me either. You don't know what Brent wants me for?"

Sheryl shook her streaked blond head. "There aren't any rock-climbing groups booked that I know of. Maybe he wants you to take the new English guy around. He and Brent should be here any minute."

"What's with Brent hiring all these new people?"

Sheryl's perfectly made-up face went cold. "Brent knows what he's doing." Sheryl turned back to the computer.

"I'll wait in Brent's office," Julie said to Sheryl's back. *When will I ever learn?* She should have known better than to say anything Sheryl might construe as criticism of Brent. When Brent first hired Sheryl, she and Julie had gotten along fine. Things fell apart when Julie realized Brent was moving in on Sheryl. Julie had tried to warn her that Brent was a casual opportunist. That had only made Sheryl angry. She'd moved in with him not long after.

It was hard to believe that had only been a couple

32

of months ago. Twice in the last week she'd come in to find Sheryl suspiciously red eyed, though she was as loyal to Brent as ever. Julie wrinkled her nose. Brent had made a play for her when he'd first hired her, too. Fortunately, he'd taken Julie's rejection with a teasing good humor, but she still felt bad for Sheryl.

Sitting at Brent's computer, Julie logged on to the Internet to check on the weather. She had just printed a weather map when she heard Brent and the Englishman come in.

"Julie!" Brent called, ignoring Sheryl's greeting. "I want you to take David to Acephale. Let him get onto the climbs there."

Julie swallowed. She knew she couldn't consistently handle many of the harder pitches there. She was also aware of David's compelling gray eyes on her. She was surprised by the intensity of her desire to look competent in front of him.

"Are you sure, Brent? Could Acephale still be seeping from the snow melt?"

"Not after the last few weeks."

"Right, we go to Acephale, then." Julie lifted her chin, vowing to climb better than she ever had in her life.

"Take the pickup. You can pick up lunch on the way out." Brent abruptly turned to Sheryl and started talking about meeting the Robson group at the airport and getting them connected with the guides he'd hired to lead them.

David walked over to Julie. "I assume there's gear to load."

"Just some stuff from the storeroom." Julie shouldered her day pack and headed in that direction. She picked up a spare rope and grabbed a bag full of slings, quick draws, and carabiners. There was something about David Hales that definitely got under her skin. The last thing she needed was to let this Englishman put her off balance. Julie took a deep breath, prepared to be as polite and professional as she knew how. She had found that almost everyone liked to talk about themselves. As she drove the battered Ford crew-cab down the Trans-Canada Highway, Julie turned to David.

"Have you climbed mostly in Europe, you know, since you're English?"

"Actually, I'm not English." There was a disturbing twinkle in his eyes.

"Not English! With that accent you couldn't come from anywhere but the British Isles."

"Oh, I am, indeed, but Britain is made up of England, Wales, Scotland, and Northern Ireland. You shouldn't call a Scot English if you don't want a black eye."

"You're Scottish? You don't sound…I mean, I thought I knew what a Scottish accent sounded like."

"Oh, aye, ye probably do, lass." He laid on the accent with a trowel. "But ye see, I've been corrupted

34

by living among the foul English. So I'll forgive ye this time, on account of your ignorance." The twinkle was pronounced now, and the edges of his mouth tilted up in a teasing smile. "I must tell you, though, I had to lay aside my kilt when I took up climbing."

In spite of herself, Julie laughed. "How about the bagpipes?"

"Oh, they're an essential part of my gear. The skirling is sure to demoralize opponents at any climbing competition. Without my bagpipes I would never have done so well on the competition circuit."

"It was all due to bad music?"

"Aye, that's why I had to leave. I fled to the New World just ahead of furious music critics. They wanted to hang me by me own rope."

"Seriously, if you were doing as well as Brent says, why did you come over here? Sport climbing is much bigger in Europe than it is here. You must be missing critical events."

"Seriously?" David's gray eyes turned steady and questioning, and he dropped the exaggerated accent.

She looked away, disturbed by how he seemed to look right into her soul. "Never mind. I didn't mean to pry."

"I've got nothing to hide. My reasoning may sound a bit odd, but I left because climbing was getting too important to me. I was in danger of the sin of idolatry."

Julie gave him a startled look. He had used almost exactly the same archaic-sounding words that her father had used the last time she'd been home. Dad had been warning her against making climbing her god, the thing she followed above all else. When her father had said those words, it had made her feel misunderstood and betrayed. Dad had known her since she was born. How could he misread her so badly?

Just because she couldn't make her relationship with Kurt work didn't mean she had quit putting God first. God's Word and his glory in creation continued to be the bedrock on which Julie built her life. God came first. He was her Father, her anchor, her comforter. The real hurt came from her confusion about what God expected of her. Had he made her a person who was meant to be always alone? The topic was too raw for comfort.

The silence in the cab grew longer and felt awkward to Julie. David didn't seem to be bothered. They'd already passed Hart Creek. Julie pulled off by the guardrail where she always parked for the hike into Asaphale. The sky was overcast, and a sharp wind blew through the pass. Her seat belt jammed as it often did in this old truck. She had to fiddle with it before she could get out. David was already securing one of the ropes to his pack. She did the same with the other rope; then they set off.

Julie wanted to break the tension but could think

of nothing to say that didn't sound silly. She thought of saying that it was a forty-five-minute walk to the walls, but Brent had probably already told David that. Admiring the scenery seemed trite. Especially since David was already looking around in obvious appreciation. They moved into the trees and out of the wind.

Julie watched David out of the corner of her eye as they walked. His undefended directness about why he'd quit climbing intrigued her. Now he seemed untroubled by the lack of conversation as he strode easily over the rough ground. Julie bit her lip, wondering if anyone could be as comfortable with himself and others as David Hales seemed to be. They crossed the groomed trail to Quaite Valley and started up the cleared area under the power line. There, where the sun had warmed the ground, crocuses were out, their fuzzy purple blooms dancing in the wind.

David gestured toward the crocuses. "Do you know what these are called?"

Julie was glad for an excuse to break the silence. "They're crocuses, the first flowers that come up in spring." She pointed. "And that tree is a lodgepole pine. Behind it is a white spruce. There are deciduous trees here too. Mostly aspen poplar like those. Birch trees are part of the ecosystem, but I don't see any right here—"

Why do I talk so much? Why was this man making her so nervous?

The sound of falling water grew louder as they approached and climbed past a waterfall. By the falls, the damp, cool air felt good on Julie's cheeks. She looked around as she hiked, letting the beauty of the woods steady her. A few minutes later, Julie stopped to fill her canteen at a gushing spring.

"Alberta has so much wild country." David bent down to fill his own water bottle. "That's what's really struck me since I got here. I hope you realize how fortunate you are."

Julie nodded. "We really are lucky."

"Lucky? I'd call that blessed of God."

"I guess that's what I meant. Are you a Christian?"

"That's why they call me the Vicar."

"Brent said something about that, but I didn't get it. I still don't."

David gave her a puzzled look. "Vicar, padre, parson, priest? What do you call the man in charge of a local church?"

"Oh, you mean like a pastor? That's your nickname?"

David laughed. "Don't look so surprised. I got the name because of the way I talk. I used to edit most references to God out of my speech, but then I thought, what's the point? There are lots of verses that say we're supposed to give God glory, and I'm into that. Didn't Brent tell me you are a Christian too?"

"Yes." Julie shouldered her pack and headed up the

path. Her stomach had coiled itself into a tight knot. David seemed so unafraid and open. She'd been like that once, but not anymore. Once they were at the cliff, Julie stopped to look back at him. "Do you want to warm up on a moderate climb before we tackle some of the harder stuff?"

David had been looking up at the rock with concentration. "I don't mind where we start."

Julie let out her breath in relief. At least she could start the day by looking competent. She dropped her pack at the base of a climb called Keys in the Car, then pulled out her guidebook to double-check.

"Could I have a look at that?"

Julie gave it to him, open at the appropriate page, and began laying out gear.

David moved closer to her. "We're here, at the lower wall, right?"

Together they bent over the book. Julie was uncomfortably aware of his proximity. Quickly she pointed to the climb and took a step back. "It's rated a 5.10b climb. Do you want to lead?"

"No, I'd like to watch you climb first."

Julie swallowed. "Sure, whatever."

Usually climbing was a refuge from life's other complications, but now she could feel that her whole body was tense. She put on her harness and her glove-tight climbing shoes. David was ready to belay. Right from the start she could feel that she was climbing badly. Instead of her normal smooth rhythmic moves up the rock, she was rattled and awkward. Five-ten was no big deal. She'd done this climb before. She set her jaw and hurried, not wanting to look as if she were near the edge of her climbing envelope.

Hurrying was always a mistake. In her rush, she placed her foot incorrectly. When she reached to clip into a bolt, that foot shifted. She compensated by pinching the hold in her left hand with all her strength. She could feel the little muscles in her forearm tiring as they took her weight at an awkward angle. She fumbled the move. Clenching her teeth, she tried again to clip in. Her foot slipped, and she fell. Yelling with frustration and fury, she twisted like a cat and put up her legs to take the impact as the tightening rope swung her against the rock.

The temptation to swear was almost overpowering.

"You okay?" David's question drifted up to her.

"Yes, just fine!" Julie added under her breath, "Humiliated, but just fine."

She paused, taking time to breathe deeply and collect her wits, and decided to try to block out the fact that David was watching. Methodically she found handholds and got back onto the route. Climbing slowly, she double-checked her grip on each finger- and toehold. This time she reached the top smoothly enough, but her stomach ached with humiliation as she set up the anchor and let herself down. Losing work at Big Foot was no more than justice if she couldn't do any better than this.

"I can't believe I fell!" Julie's feet hit the ground. "It was sheer stupidity."

"I don't know. It looked like an interesting climb."

Julie bit her lip. The last thing she wanted at that moment was kindness from David Hales. She would do better on the next pitch. She had to! Her attention was taken off herself as she watched David climb. He moved with an easy, fluid grace that left her open-mouthed with admiration. Watching him, Julie could see why so many who loved the sport called rock climbing a vertical dance. It was beautiful when it was done well.

"Wow, that was pretty!" Julie couldn't keep from smiling at David as he rappelled back down.

He gave her a quick grin. "Thanks. You didn't look too bad yourself. After you fell, you climbed with much more collection."

"Thanks." Of course, he'd only said that to be nice. She hadn't climbed up to her own standards, so there was no way someone of David's skill could think she'd been anything but clumsy—or even worse, amateurish. Automatically she reached to re-coil the rope, fighting against the lump in her throat. This man wasn't likely to want to work with her, not after watching that climb.

Besides, unless something changed drastically, Big Foot didn't have work for more than one climbing guide. And it was painfully clear who was best qualified for the job.

The next two pitches were near the limit of Julie's climbing ability. She asked David to lead them, then watched him with a mixture of admiration and chagrin. He was so beautiful on the rock. Her stomach sank as she tried to memorize the moves for her own climb.

Using every atom of strength and balance in her body, she climbed the first pitch without falling. By the second climb, she began to tire and fell repeatedly at the most difficult section. Pushing herself to her utmost, she finally made it past the crux. The pitch was still steep and unrelenting. Several times she was within milliseconds of falling before she was able to transfer her weight to a new set of tiny holds.

"Good for you!" David's enthusiasm was contagious as she reached the top of the climb. She was close to him on the tiny ledge. Feeling humiliated and sticky with sweat, she pushed herself away. She hung in her harness in midair, breathing hard and waiting for her arms and legs to quit shaking. Julie set her jaw. She was obviously out of shape from guiding on easy pitches. From now on, tired or not, she'd be back on the rock in the evening, honing her skills.

Back on the ground, Julie untied herself with aching hands. A few seconds later she looked up to see David gracefully rappelling down the cliff. But this time she didn't feel the same admiration she'd felt earlier. For a split second, she intensely wished he would disappear from the face of the earth.

Three

THAT EVENING JULIE PUSHED OPEN THE APARTMENT DOOR and dropped her pack onto the floor with a thud. Shedding her boots, she headed toward a much-needed shower.

"Hard day?" Laurel called from the kitchen as Julie came in, her head wrapped in a towel.

"You're not kidding!" Julie said. "At least I get the day off tomorrow. How about you? Are the mama and baby bears behaving?"

Laurel was throwing together a salad since it was her night to cook. Now she looked up, her eyes excited. "I saw Samantha and her babies. She's got triplets."

"Triplets?! Wow. That should help the black bear population. So are they all as light as their mother?"

"One is. Hey, if you're off tomorrow, why don't you come with me? Maybe we'll get lucky and see them up close."

"Hey, thanks. I will. Bears are better than the company I kept today."

Laurel laughed. "That's not hard. Bears are nicer

than people.... Well, most bears are nicer than most people anyway."

Julie had met Laurel at church a month ago. Laurel had come out to Canmore to start her thesis on cub survival rates. Rooming with her, Julie had learned quite a lot about black bears. Laurel started to talk about Samantha and her cubs, then paused in midsentence.

"Julie, you're looking straight through me. What is it?"

"Brent hired a full-time climbing guide. He's English, well, Scottish really. I spent the day with him at Acephale being humiliated."

"Humiliated?"

Julie made a wry face. "He made me look like a total putz."

"How? You're an excellent climber."

"Ha! I couldn't even climb decently on the easier pitches. I haven't been practicing climbing at that level. Besides, the man climbs like an angel."

Laurel had put the salad on the table. Now she dumped spaghetti noodles into a colander.

"Put some plates out, and we'll eat, spaghetti à la Boyardee. The sauce is in the microwave. Humiliation always feels better if you're not hungry too."

"Sounds good to me."

After they said grace and began to eat, Laurel settled in her chair. "So tell me about this man who climbs like an angel. Does he look like one too?"

"If angels are tall, lean, and muscular with penetrating gray eyes," Julie said between huge bites of spaghetti. "That's not the point. The thing is, I'll probably lose any work with Big Foot, and I don't know if I can find enough other work."

"Maybe Brent is going to expand the rock climbing. You've talked about wanting to work with good climbing guides, so this could be good, right?"

"If I get to work with him. I doubt I will after today." Julie shook Parmesan cheese onto her spaghetti and banged the container down. "I don't care! I'm going to start climbing every single evening no matter how tired I am. There is no way I want to climb like I did today in front of him again."

"He climbs like an angel, and you care what he thinks of you? Hmm..."

"No! Not that way. The man is really weird. He is supposed to be a hot item on the European competition circuit. When I asked him why he came over here, he said he left because he was in danger of idolatry. People call him the Vicar, like a pastor."

"What is so weird about that? It sounds like he's a serious Christian, and a climber too." Laurel liked to tease, and her eyes were still twinkling.

Julie laughed. "Laurel, don't. David Hales makes me feel like he's looking straight through me. I don't

46

like it. Not all of us are going to get lucky enough to find a man like your Ian. Leave it be."

Laurel was suddenly silent. Julie sucked in her breath. "Me and my big mouth. I'm sorry." She'd forgotten that Ian hadn't called or written to Laurel for two weeks. The tense, miserable look on Laurel's face hurt Julie. "Men are not worth the trouble they cause!" Julie hit the table.

"Quite the pair, aren't we? Me moping because I haven't heard from Ian for a whole fifteen days, and you treating men like some sort of deadly virus."

"I, for one, am going to Calgary to work out at the climbing gym and forget men. Want to come?" Julie jumped up.

"Not tonight." Laurel glanced at the phone, and Julie knew she was hoping Ian would call.

"If that's how you want it. Leave the dishes. I'll do them when I get back. Oh, wake me up in time to go with you tomorrow, okay?"

Laurel nodded, and Julie ran upstairs. She threw her harness and climbing shoes into a day pack. Seconds later the door slammed behind her and she was on her way to Calgary. It felt good to pit herself against uncomplicated physical difficulties. Soon she was shaking with exhaustion. When she could no longer grip the smaller holds, she moved to easier sections until even there she couldn't hold her weight.

When she finished, she felt exhausted and exhilarated all at once. It had felt so good to climb hard. She threw her pack over her shoulder and headed out of the bouldering area.

"Julie."

She jumped slightly, then turned to find one of the gym's staff members standing there. He indicated the boulder. "That was quite the workout. Have you ever thought about competition climbing?"

Julie laughed. "No, but thanks for the compliment."

In spite of the fatigue left from her day of climbing with David, Julie knew she'd climbed well. The man's comment topped off her evening. Once she was back in her car, she wondered if she should have worked quite so hard. Her hands would not grip the steering wheel properly. She drove home still smiling, with her wrists hooked over the wheel. She didn't get back to the apartment until almost midnight.

Something was making a knocking noise. Julie rolled over and pulled her pillow over her head.

"Julie? Julie?"

"What is it?" She pulled the pillow off her head and tried to focus.

"If you want to come, you'd better get up."

Julie squinted at her clock. "Okay, I'm coming."

Within minutes she was singing in the shower. On her way down, she took the stairs two at a time. "Have you looked outside yet? It's a gorgeous morning. Thanks for getting me up."

Laurel, proving yet again that she definitely was not a morning person, nursed a cup of coffee. She looked up with sleep-swollen eyes. "It's indecent to come bouncing downstairs sleek, happy, and looking like a million dollars at this time in the morning. You know there's a Bible verse about people who bless their friends with a loud voice early in the morning."

"Yeah, my brother used to quote it at me. Hey, I can't help it if I like mornings." Julie cut a bagel in half and put it in the toaster. "It's the best time of day."

"I've been getting up at five for the last three weeks, and my body still thinks it's the middle of the night."

"Maybe you should get a job that lets you sleep in—be a bank teller or something." Julie loaded her bagel with cream cheese and took a huge bite.

"And sit inside in a box of a building all day? No, thank you!"

"I'm with you there. I'd rather die." Julie halved a grapefruit and cut around the sections in between bites of bagel.

Laurel sipped her coffee and watched. "You know, it's not fair. You eat like a horse and still stay fit. If I just look at food, I gain five pounds. Hurry up and finish

49

feeding your face. I haven't trained the bears to sleep in yet, and I don't want to miss the morning activity."

Once they were in Samantha's territory, Laurel turned on her radio-tracking equipment. The big sow bear wore a collar that gave off a signal that Laurel could track. Pulling off onto a rough logging road, Laurel pointed up the hill. "I saw her just up there yesterday. She was digging roots, positively pigging out."

"After not eating all winter, I'd be hungry too."

Laurel laughed. "You're always hungry anyway." She had leaned forward and was fiddling with the tracking gear. "Oh no. I just picked up Sir Walter."

"Who?"

"Sir Walter, the big boar Alex collared earlier this spring. Julie, if he gets the chance, he'll kill Samantha's cubs. The big boars often kill younger bears. That's one of the major factors in the mortality rates of cubs and yearling bears."

"See, I told you men are bad news."

"Yeah, maybe, but I'm not sure the principle applies to human males." Laurel stopped the old jeep, pulled out a notebook, and jotted things down; glancing at her watch, the tracking gear, and back at her watch. "Samantha is not far away, either. I don't like Sir Walter in this close to her and her cubs."

Laurel shoved the jeep into gear, and they rattled up the track. Julie braced herself against the bucking vehicle. Half an hour later, the two women were moving as quietly as they could toward a mountain meadow when Laurel pointed. "There she is!"

"Where?"

"There. See? Just inside the trees."

Julie finally made out a lighter shape inside the woods, far down the slope. As they watched, Samantha moved into the open, followed by her cubs. She was pulling something off the low bushes with her mouth. Laurel unpacked her camera. Julie could hear the shutter click as Laurel took pictures. The old sow paused and started digging up the ground, throwing earth behind her in fountains. A big paw full of dirt hit the lightest cub full in the face. It sneezed, shook itself, and bounced over to tackle the other two. The three rolled on the ground like puppies.

Julie was spellbound. "They're beautiful!"

Laurel nodded and bent to write in her notebook. As she watched the bears, entranced, Julie could hear Laurel muttering. "Feeding on overwintered berries, attempting to dig up a ground squirrel." Movement to her left caught Julie's attention, and she turned her head in time to see another bear enter the clearing only about twenty feet away.

A very big bear.

Julie poked Laurel—she knew enough not to startle a predator who was that close. Her heart was pounding so hard and fast it felt like her chest was going to explode. A heavy, rank smell came on the wind. This new bear was so black his coat seemed to soak up all the light, making a bear-shaped hole in the world. He was magnificent. He moved steadily away from Julie and Laurel, down the meadow.

"Sir Walter!" Laurel breathed in Julie's ear.

Samantha had seen him now. She gave a warning snort that sent all three cubs scrambling up the nearest tree. With a coughing roar, she turned to face Sir Walter. He hesitated, and Samantha came slowly forward, every hair on end. Sir Walter angled his path away from the light-colored female and back into the trees.

"Now that's the way to treat a man that tries to get into your space." Julie crossed her arms.

"If you're a sow bear." Laurel laughed and began writing in her notebook frantically. "It's not often you're going to see something like that." Both women were talking very softly. Laurel had made sure they approached the meadow from downwind. Neither bear had sensed their presence.

Julie watched as Samantha paced back and forth. It took her a long time to calm down and go back to her digging. She sent the cubs back up the trees twice before she let them remain on the ground. Julie had occasionally seen bears on her father's ranch, but only at a distance. The idea that a boar would kill cubs was unsettling.

Julie shivered. "Maybe I like people better than bears after all."

Laurel shook her head. "I don't, not as a species anyway. Look at the mess we're making of the planet." She put down her notebook and turned, her blue eyes intent. "You know, poachers have been killing bears just to get their gallbladders? With the right contacts, they're worth more on the international market than heroin."

"More than heroin? That's crazy."

"Pound for pound, yes. When they kill a bear, they slice off its jaws and paws to sell, then leave the rest to lie and rot. There are almost no more bears to kill in Asia, so they're starting to go after our bears. A man in British Columbia was caught with thousands of bear bladders in his house. That's thousands of animals reduced to stinking hulks to serve people's greed. No, I definitely don't think people are nicer."

Julie looked at the magnificent animals at the far end of the meadow. "Is it happening here, Laurel? Are people killing the bears you're studying?"

"Not yet. There have been reports from farther north, but the Fish and Wildlife people say there is no problem in Alberta so far."

"I hope it stays that way." Julie watched the cubs wrestling in the sun.

"She got one!" Laurel said suddenly. Julie looked to see the big sow gulping something. "Did you see her jump at that ground squirrel when it ran?" Laurel grinned. "This morning is turning out great. The bears are staying in sight. First we see a standoff, then this kill. I should bring you more often."

"Sitting and watching is fun sometimes, but—"

"I know. You'd go crazy if you had to do it all the time. I don't think God made you to hold still long, Julie."

"How did you ever guess?" Both women laughed. Down in the meadow, Samantha was sitting in the hole she had dug. Propped like a person in a lawn chair, she nursed her cubs. Minutes ticked by, and nothing else happened. Julie knew that as long as a bear was in sight, Laurel was not going to leave this meadow. She moved back a couple of feet and found a tree against which she could lean comfortably.

There were tiny glacier lily plants around her feet. Only two had delicate yellow flowers as yet. She could hear the fluttering leaves of an aspen and the high, sweet calls of juncos and mountain chickadees. Alert and yet full of peace, Julie knew she was surrounded by God's love and beauty.

Around 11:00 A.M., Samantha and the cubs disappeared into the trees. Laurel stood and stretched. "Do you want to stay with me all day or get back? I've got time to drop you off. Most wild animals sleep through the middle of the day."

"I'd better get back. Could we stop by Big Foot's office on the way? I want to check the schedule."

Julie hadn't expected anyone but Sheryl to be at the office, but Brent, Tommy, and David were all there. She hesitated in the doorway, fighting the sudden impulse to disappear. She'd had enough of David Hales yesterday, and she could call Sheryl from home. It was too late, though. David saw her.

"Julie, we were just talking about you."

"You were? Hope it was good."

"I tried to call you three times this morning." Brent sounded indignant. "An Italian couple came in. They want to go out hiking, just an overnighter, in an area where they won't see other hikers. They sound experienced. I figured you could take them in south of Black Diamond. There's not likely to be anyone in there."

"But there are climbers booked. I was supposed to take those two from Colorado up the east end of Rundle Mountain." She'd been looking forward to that climb.

"David will handle that." Brent thrust a contour map of the southern Kananaskis into her face. "Do you know the trail I mean? You used it once last year. You said it was beautiful."

Julie nodded and bent over the map. Already it was turning out as she feared. David Hales was taking all the best climbs away from her. How would she ever be ready for the guide test this fall?

"I want to get a chance to do some hiking while I'm in Canada," David said.

"Want to trade?" Julie was only half teasing.

"Don't be silly." Brent rolled his eyes. "He doesn't have his hiking certification. You do. Besides, he's the better climber."

"That's right. He is." She lifted her chin. "I've got to go. Laurel is waiting for me."

"I told the hikers to be here by 6:00 A.M.," Brent called after her. "Get your equipment and supply list to Sheryl before two."

Julie's heart sank as she moved to obey. Her fears were coming true. She'd lost the exciting climbing work to David Hales. What was going to happen to her now?

Four

THE FIRST MORNING OUT WITH THE ITALIAN COUPLE, JULIE woke very early, as she usually did when she was camping. She stretched luxuriously, sat up, and opened the zipper on the side of her tent. The sun wasn't up yet, but the sky was lighter to the east. Overhead the last few stars were still out. Another nice day—it looked as if the high-pressure weather system was holding. Julie smiled. It was so good to wake up out here in the wilderness.

The other tent was quiet, the Italian couple not moving yet. Julie reached for her Bible and a flashlight. She was reading Ephesians chapter 2. It had been talking about God's grace, then it said: "For we are God's workmanship, created in Christ Jesus to do good works, which God prepared in advance for us to do."

The words sank in. God *knew* her. He had chosen her and had good things just for her to do. Julie sighed. It would have been easier if he'd made her in a more conventional mold.

Dressing in a small tent wasn't easy, but Julie was

used to it and slid quickly into her clothes. By the time the Italian couple woke, Julie had fetched water and had breakfast almost ready. A whiskey jack perched on the lodgepole pine overhead, obviously hoping for handouts as Julie cooked pancakes on the tiny backpacking stove.

"If we are the only ones who come here, how does this bird know to beg?" Paulo asked between bites of his third pancake.

"We're not the only ones. A few hikers come through every year, and gray jays are smart. They've got a good memory. Some of the other hikers must have fed him."

"But it is not correct to feed wild things," his wife, Sophie, protested. "He will become ill, this—how did you call him—gray jay?"

Julie looked up at the sassy bird, who had come even closer and was tipping his head, watching them with bright eyes. "Some people call them whiskey jacks or camp robbers. You're right about feeding wild things, Sophie, but I don't think this guy gets enough human food to do him much harm."

Suddenly the bird darted across in front of Sophie. In midflight he snatched the last bit of pancake off her plate. Sophie squealed and dropped her plate, then laughed with Julie and Paulo. "Camp robber is a good name for him!"

58

Julie led Sophie and Paulo on the last half of a long loop that would bring them to the vehicle at dusk. Yesterday she hadn't been able to stop herself from thinking about David Hales leading the climb she had wanted so badly. Today was easier. The climb was over. She'd already missed it. To her chagrin, she found herself thinking about David himself, his gray eyes and lean, graceful frame.

Apartments in Canmore were as rare as hens' teeth. David had been staying in a motel, and that had grown old quickly. To David's relief, Brent had used his contacts and found a small place for him. After the climb, Brent thumped David on the back.

"Happy customers make for a happy boss. Take the day off, buddy, and get yourself moved in."

He didn't have to offer twice. David headed for his new home. It didn't take long to put the picture of his parents on the dresser and put away his clothing. He sat on the bed and stared at the blank wall of the tiny one-bedroom furnished apartment. He'd come to Canada to do some thinking. What he'd told Julie was the truth.

He could still hear Lance's angry voice, "What are you going to do? Throw away the chance to be the best climber in Europe to go be a pastor or something?" Lance was a fantastic climber and made no secret of the fact that climbing was his god. Most of his anger had been because David was abandoning that god. In fact, Lance's reaction only served to reinforce David's decision. He served the true God and needed to keep his priorities straight.

David shook his head and stood up. What did God want from him? How should he use the skills he had? Should he go back and push to be the best, or was there some other way he should serve? Through the small basement window, sunlight was falling across the floor in wide, bright squares. Staying inside on a day like this was crazy. David got up. He wasn't going to solve his dilemma this morning, so he might as well put the beautiful day to good use and explore his new town.

It wasn't yet ten in the morning when David headed out to look at the town of Canmore. Compared to what he was used to at home, the streets were wide and empty, the houses huge and new. Canadians had so much space that their towns sprawled. No one seemed to walk anywhere except in the small downtown area.

Before noon, David found himself approaching the Big Foot office. He quickened his step. Maybe Julie Miller would be there. From the first time he'd seen her, working with those two climbers, she'd seemed special. Deliberately David slowed down. He was in Canada to make some decisions about what God wanted with his life. He shouldn't let himself be distracted.

Still...Julie's dark, alert eyes and graceful way of moving seemed to haunt him. Maybe she could be part of what God wanted for his life. One eyebrow went up in speculation. *Why not?* But God couldn't steer a parked car, so he'd go ahead prayerfully and see where things led. With that settled, at least in his own mind, he entered the building.

"Hi, David." Sheryl smiled. "Are you all moved in?"

"Yes, thanks. I was wondering if you could tell me of a good hike that starts within walking distance of town. It's such a beautiful day, I can't bear to stay inside."

Brent walked out of his office. "You were at the east end of Rundle yesterday. Do you want to hike the ridge?"

"I'd love to, but it's an hour's drive from here. I can't get there without a vehicle."

"A party just canceled. I'll come with you. I don't want to stay inside, either."

"Brent, could I come too?" Sheryl's expression was eager. "There's not much happening here and—"

"You've got work to do here." David frowned at Brent's abrupt tone, but his boss just went on. "Tell Tommy to be waiting for us at the far end of Rundle by eight this evening." He headed for the door. "Come on, David. If you need anything from your place we can pick it up on the way out."

With one last glance back at the forlorn receptionist, David followed Brent out the door.

As they hiked up to the long ridge, Brent pushed hard. David had the impression he was testing him— even competing against him. David let his long legs stretch into a faster stride. When they reached the crest of the ridge, both men were sweating.

"You can really cover ground." Brent stopped and bent over, panting.

David only smiled. As they started along the ridge, he looked in awe at the scope of the mountains. Coming to Canada had definitely been a good idea.

"What did you think of the climbing at Acephale?" Brent's question broke into David's thoughts.

"It was good. I enjoyed climbing with Julie."

Brent laughed. "Julie is furious that you're here. She figures you'll get all the good climbers and she'll get nothing."

"Is that true?" David stopped midstride and turned to face Brent.

"Naah, she'll still get some climbing. Besides, she could learn a few things from you. She wants to take her climbing-guide test this fall, and I haven't had the time or the work to give her the kind of training and supervision she needs." He pointed ahead of David. "Watch out. It gets really windy by that gap."

Even with the warning, the wind's onslaught nearly

succeeded in knocking David off his feet. Leaning into it, he concentrated on keeping his balance on the smooth, gray limestone. It was only after they were behind the ridge again that the two men could speak and be heard clearly.

"How long has Julie worked for you?"

Brent gave him a sharp look. "A couple of years off and on. If you're fishing for information, she's unattached as far as I know and cute enough with those big eyes and sleek body, but she's way too uptight for me. Not interested in having fun at all."

"Maybe her definition of fun is different than yours."

"Whatever. Anyway, she's too religious, but then you're pretty religious too, aren't you?"

"I don't know that I'd call myself religious. Religious sounds like tradition, rules, and regulations, things one does to get on God's good side. It's not like that for me. God already did all the work. I've just reached out to take his hand."

"Whooo!" Brent shook his head, his grin wry. "I don't know where I find these people. First Julie, then you."

"Maybe God is trying to get your attention, Brent."

He laughed. "I can see why they call you the Vicar. Climbing the mountains is plenty of religion for me. Don't start messing with my fun." He whooped and ran down the ridge. David laughed and followed, running down the ridge with the wind in his face. Brent slowed before a narrow stretch. David dodged past him and danced across, leaping from foothold to foothold. A couple hundred yards farther, he stopped and waited for Brent to catch up.

"You're a maniac. You know that?" Brent was leaning over again, panting.

"It's been said before. I had a T-shirt that said If you're not living on the edge, you're taking up too much space. I figure that's about right."

"I like it! But I don't get how that fits in with you being so religious. You don't seem exactly the stuffy type."

"Does Julie?"

"Nope, so how do you do that?"

"'I consider everything a loss compared to the surpassing greatness of knowing Christ.' To me that's the most radical living on the edge that I do. There is more of real value in living all out for God, more glory, more risk, and more joy. My God is an awesome God. Catching on to some great new truth from the Bible is right up there with flashing a 5.13 climb."

"Get real!"

"I am."

Brent shook his head. "I don't buy it, buddy. There's no way the two can compare."

"There's only one way you'll ever know…. Check it out for yourself."

Brent studied him for a minute, then shrugged. "I

might just surprise you and do that."

"Good." David finished the walk with a spring in his step. He'd been straight with Brent. Learning and talking about God was exhilarating. It left him feeling high for hours. From the ridge of Rundle they could see a huge panorama of peaks spread out around them. The Banff town site lay like a handful of bright-colored pebbles in the Bow River valley—all around them was clear evidence of God's creative power. What was it the Bible said? "Let those who have eyes to see, see..." David grinned. Maybe, just maybe, Brent's eyes were being opened even now.

Brent pointed out various peaks he had climbed and told David a bit about the climbs. Not too surprisingly, in his stories Brent always came out a bit of a hero.

David smiled and listened.

Amid enthusiastic thanks, Julie dropped Sophie and Paulo off at their hotel around five. They tried to get her to come out to dinner with them, but she wanted to get home. After two days out, she wanted a shower more than she wanted food. She faced into the water and let it stream across her body. As far as she was concerned, hot water was the true mark of civilization.

"What is that awesome smell?" Julie called downstairs as she put her hiking clothes into the washer.

"Cinnamon buns. I had a fit of domesticity." Laurel opened the oven to check on them.

Julie shook her head so her wet hair fell into place and took the stairs two at a time. "When are they coming out of the oven? I'm starving."

"Better eat some real food first."

"Right." Julie shoved a couple of potatoes and some fish sticks into the microwave.

"So how was the hike?"

"Super. Paulo and Sophie actually knew how to backpack and were decently equipped. The weather was great. The only hitch was on the first day. I couldn't quit thinking about the climb I was missing. I'd been looking forward to doing Eeor for weeks. How about you? How was your day? All the baby bears okay?"

The timer went off, and Laurel opened the oven, releasing a powerful wave of fresh-bread-and-cinnamon scent. Julie shut her eyes in bliss. Quickly she began to eat her fish and potatoes.

"The babies are okay so far. Alex said there's been rumors of poachers working in our area, though. One of the young-adult females that he used to see often has disappeared."

"Don't the young ones travel to new places sometimes?"

"Males more than females, but maybe. They die for other reasons too, disease and so on. Hopefully it's nothing more than rumors."

Julie had just finished her food when the doorbell rang. Laurel was getting a second tray of buns out of the oven, so Julie jumped up and went to open the door.

"Brent, Tommy, David! You guys sure time things right. Laurel is just taking cinnamon buns out of the oven. Come on in and have some."

"I'm not going to say no to that offer." Brent said.

Julie introduced David and Tommy to Laurel, and in moments the whole bunch was crowded around the tiny kitchen table, slathering butter onto buns and licking sticky fingers.

"We were on the way back from Banff." Brent took another bite. "We were driving right past your place, so I thought we'd stop and see how your hike went."

"It went really well. I think they were happy with me. They talked about rebooking in a couple of years if they come back to Canada again and also took a bunch of your business cards for their friends."

"Excellent!" Brent smiled. Julie knew that any promotion of Big Foot always made him happy.

"Stopping here is the best thing we've done all day." Tommy reached for his fourth bun. "These are amazing!"

"Thanks." Laurel sat back in her chair, clearly pleased by the way the men were enjoying the fruits of her labor.

"This woman may like bears better than people,

but she bakes a mean cinnamon bun." Julie washed her hands at the sink.

"Bears better than people?" David glanced at Laurel curiously.

That was all the opening it took to get Laurel launched on her favorite topic. After a few minutes of enthusiastic explanation of why bears were important and what she was learning about the black-bear population, she jumped up to wash her hands. She came back with a couple of photo albums and spread them on the table.

The men craned to see as Laurel pointed out pictures of different individual bears. "This is Samantha. See, she's got triplets. I took that picture the day Julie came with me. The pictures help me identify individual bears that aren't collared."

Brent asked about exactly where the bears were, obviously wanting to know which ones he might encounter with clients. Even though David said nothing, Julie's awareness of him was intense. He looked from the book to Laurel's face and back, a little smile tipping his lips. Julie felt a flash of jealousy, which she quickly pushed away. She wrinkled her nose. Laurel was her friend, and David Hales was nothing to her. He could smile at Laurel—or *any* woman, for that matter—all he wanted.

Julie glanced at Tommy. He had pulled away from

the circle and stood back with anxious eyes. Laurel suddenly realized he couldn't see her pictures. Leaving one book with Brent and David, she jumped up to show Tommy the other one.

"I never thought of bears as individuals," Tommy said as she pointed out one animal after another. "They aren't rare or anything, are they? I mean, if a few died, it wouldn't really matter."

"It would matter! Black bears aren't endangered, not in Canada anyway. But things aren't easy for them around here. Banff National Park, just the place you'd think would be good for bears, really isn't all that great. We don't have a lot of bears because a lot of the best lowland is disturbed by roads and development. Besides, people have put out the lightning fires that would have opened meadowland for the bears. I guess you could say our bear population is under pressure from lack of good habitat."

Tommy flipped through the book as she talked. Laurel suddenly stopped him, putting her finger on one picture. "Julie, look. These are Samantha's cubs from last year. See this little female? Isn't she great?"

Julie moved over to them and they all looked at the image of a very dark bear with a tiny white mark in the center of her chest. She was sitting on her bottom with a dandelion hanging out of her mouth. Julie laughed. "She's cute. Do they actually eat dandelions?"

Laurel nodded. "What's weed to us is food to them."

"I've got to go." Tommy quickly moved to the door. "I just remembered I'm supposed to be somewhere. If you guys want to stay, I'll walk."

"No, I'm coming." Brent stood up.

David was last out the door. His thank-you seemed to be aimed more at her than at Laurel, but Julie thought she might be imagining that. She had one last impression of kind and direct gray eyes before the door closed.

As soon as the door shut, Laurel turned to Julie. "Hey, your David Hales is nice. I can see what you mean about the way he looks at you, though. It's like he's trying to see your soul or something, but he has a good smile."

"First of all, he is not *my* David Hales." Julie began to clear off the table. "Moreover, he's messing up my summer. I need the climbs David is taking. Oh, well, enough of my problems. Speaking of men, has Ian called?"

Laurel's grin gave Julie all the answer she needed.

"Great! I thought you looked happy. How come he didn't get in touch before?"

"He's just been really busy, but things are going to be okay now."

"I sure hope so for your sake." Julie turned and

70

began scrubbing dishes with a will. She wasn't convinced. No one was too busy to make a short phone call. Maybe Ian had realized the kind of woman he had here and had gotten his act together. Julie splashed another plate into the dishwater. Laurel shouldn't have to get hurt. Julie wouldn't wish that on anyone.

Her eyes closed tightly against the memory of her own hurt.

She shook her head. Things might work out for Laurel, but not for Julie. Never Julie. And it was time she accepted that.

Five

THE PHONE RANG ON SATURDAY MORNING AROUND seven. Julie reached for it. There had been no work for her with Big Foot Outfitters today, though she'd seen David up on the schedule. She just couldn't get him out of her thoughts. His level gray eyes, even the way the hair curled on his temples, had found a solid lodging in her mind. She ought to hate him, but instead she found herself drawn to the man.

Well, of course you're drawn to him. He's an excellent climber. It would be neat to get a chance to work with him, a real privilege to learn from a climber of his caliber.

And *that,* Julie told herself firmly, was the only reason she couldn't stop thinking of the man.

The phone jangled again, and Julie picked it up and heard David's voice. "Speak of the devil."

"Pardon me?"

"Sorry. It was nothing. Uh, how can I help you?"

"I've got two questions for you, Julie. First of all, could you recommend a good church to me, a place where God's Word is taught and Christians pray for each other?"

"Sure. Laurel and I go to Mount Olive Evangelical Church. That's where we met. The pastor makes you think, and there's a good college and career group."

"A what?"

"Oh, maybe they don't call them that in Britain. It's a sort of fellowship group for unmarried young adults. We have Bible studies, prayer groups, social activities, stuff like that."

"Sounds good." She could hear the smile in his voice.

Quickly Julie told David where Mount Olive was and when the worship service started. Already she wished she hadn't been so enthusiastic. There were other good churches in town. Now David Hales would be in her face not only at work but also at church and probably the college and career functions, too. His next words made her wish even more fervently that she'd sent him to another church instead.

"Julie, would you like to go out tonight for supper? There must be somewhere nice in town."

She swallowed hard. Was the nightmare going to start all over again? "No, David, I'm sorry, but I'm busy." Quickly she hung up the phone.

The next morning, instead of getting up for church, Julie stayed in bed and read. David would likely be at church, and she didn't want to see him. She frowned. That wasn't true. She did want to see him, but—

"Julie, hurry up. You're going to be late," Laurel called up the stairs.

"I'm not coming today."

"You never miss church. Are you sick?"

Julie shook her head and didn't answer. There was a knock on her door, and Laurel's dark head looked in. "Can I get you anything, then? Tea, soup, ginger ale?"

Julie grinned. "You really are a mother hen, aren't you? I'm not sick. I just thought I'd stay home today."

Laurel looked at her doubtfully. "Okay, I guess I'll see you this afternoon."

As soon as Laurel left, Julie went downstairs. Laurel was such a worrier, she'd probably ask the group to pray for her. Julie paced back and forth across the tiny kitchen. Why had she let David's presence stop her from going? That was so stupid. Julie grabbed a glass, filled it with water, and drank it down. She took a deep breath. It wasn't David who'd stopped her. He was probably wishing she were there. Julie banged down the glass and started pacing again. She hadn't missed church for months.

Julie flipped on the TV, watched a preacher for a bit, and impatiently turned it off again. She hadn't been home very often since she broke up with Kurt. He and his folks went to the same tiny church that Julie's family attended. She missed her folks, and anything was better than sitting here. Well, it would be after church by the time she got home if she left now. Julie scribbled a note to Laurel and in minutes was on her way.

She walked into her parents' house just as the family was sitting down to Sunday dinner. Her mother's face lit up, and she ran to Julie. Julie hugged her back, feeling bad that she hadn't been home more often. Dad squashed them both in a bear hug, and her big brother, Ben, had a huge soppy grin on his face.

"Hanna, I guess we'd better set another place." Dad's weathered face was all creased into a big smile.

"I'm just doing that," another voice said.

"Amber! You're here!" Julie stepped back from her parents.

Amber laughed. "Ben talked me into coming out for the weekend."

Amber and Ben had met the summer before last. They'd been engaged for most of the time since then and were due to be married at the end of August. Julie was to be one of the bridesmaids. As she watched, Ben smiled, reached out his hand, and took Amber's. Julie fought the urge to shut her eyes. Their happiness and love for each other was so strong she felt burned by it. She swallowed hard. God didn't give the same things to everyone. What

Ben and Amber had was something she'd probably never have. She'd just have to learn to live with that.

In minutes the whole family was seated at the table, happily tucking into Hanna's fantastic pot roast. The meat had been raised right here at home. It was good, and there was plenty of it. Julie bit into her mother's homemade bread. Surviving in an apartment was nothing like this, not even when Laurel got one of her urges to bake.

"So, Julie, how are things going at work?" Her father buttered his bread before taking a bite.

"All right, I guess." She found herself suddenly reluctant to mention David Hales. "Tell me what's happening at home. I'm lonely for this place."

Ben laughed. "It's going to be different in a couple of weeks. Mom agreed to keep Nathan this summer."

"You did?"

"Oh, come on, you two. He's not that bad, just an active six-year-old."

"That's bad." Ben's eyes were laughing. Julie knew that Ben liked their youngest cousin as much as she did.

"Just to get him out of the city?" Julie asked.

Hanna nodded. "Also it will give Elsbeth a break. She's taking some courses at work, upgrading, and finding it difficult to spend enough time with Nathan. I'm home all day, so why not? It seemed like a good idea to both of us."

Elsbeth was her mother's much younger sister. The family had been praying for her ever since Julie could remember. Nathan had been born out of wedlock, and Elsbeth's longtime live-in had left when she got pregnant. Since then Elsbeth had gotten her life straight with God, but things still weren't easy for her or Nathan. Both were often at the ranch.

"Okay," Julie said. "Besides the earthshaking news of Nathan's arrival, what else is new?"

She listened as her father talked about everything from the price of beef to which fences needed mending. Ben brought her up to date with the news in the community. He was a veterinarian and saw many of the other ranchers.

"I thought I'd try something new in the garden." Hanna passed around the potatoes for the second time. "Did I tell you I took a Chinese cooking course? No? Well, I planted bok choy and some other Chinese vegetables."

Julie laughed. "Are they immune to Canadian cabbage butterflies?"

Hanna made a face. "No, caterpillars like Chinese food, too."

In spite of all the happy conversation, Julie felt a tension. In all the news of the community, no one had mentioned Kurt's family. Never one to dodge an issue, Julie put down her fork. "So, how are the Schneiders?"

There was a short silence.

"Albert and Cora were in church this morning—so was Kurt." Her father looked uncomfortable. "Did you want to see him?"

"Why? Are you still hoping we'll get back together?"

"Oh, Julie, honey, no." Hanna got up and came around as if she were going to embrace her. To Julie's relief, she hesitated at the last moment. "We just didn't mention them because we thought it might make you uncomfortable. It's such a treat to have you home. You've been so upset. It's been almost two years and—"

"Mom, I'm sorry. Let's drop it and talk about more pleasant things."

Ben frowned. "It's about time you did the same thing in your life."

"In my life?"

Ben put down his fork. "Yes, drop it and go on to more pleasant things. Kurt has certainly gotten over it. He's dating Sharon Fraser now."

Julie's stomach tightened at Ben's rebuke. She found she didn't care if Kurt was dating someone else. Sharon Fraser was welcome to him. Ben was misunderstanding what was bothering her.

"Ben, don't!" Amber put her hand on his arm.

"Julie needs to know." Ben turned to Julie. "Like Mom said, it's been a long time. Kurt is getting on with his life, and so should you. There are other men in the world."

Gordon chuckled. "I can't say I disagree with you, Ben, but you haven't always been a quick healer yourself."

Julie stared at her plate. Ben sighed. "Okay, you're right." Julie looked up and caught a rueful grin from her brother. "Julie, I'm tired of watching you hurt, but I hereby give you my permission to be miserable as long as is necessary. God brought me and Amber through, and he'll help you too. I just wish he'd hurry up."

Julie swallowed hard. "You're right, Ben. I should get over this."

Gordon pushed back his plate. "Now that we've cleared the air, how about some dessert."

Everyone laughed, and Julie got up to help her mother bring in dessert. Mom put two plates on the table, then stood and covered her mouth. "Oh, Gordon, you forgot to tell her."

"What?" Julie shifted in her seat.

"Your mare foaled during church this morning. I was going to call you after dinner."

Julie squealed. "She did? What'd she have?"

"A nice chestnut colt with two white socks and a blaze."

"Do I have to pretend to be civilized, or can I run out and see the baby?"

"We wouldn't want you pretending." Her father

waved her off. Julie could hear fond laughter following her as she ran for the door. The mare wasn't really hers. The papers were in her father's name, but she'd ridden Dot her last year of high school and whenever she'd come home since then.

She opened the corral gate and stepped in, taking care to move slowly. The gentle mare looked up calmly. She'd always been a good mom, but there was no need to startle her. The little colt was around the far side of his mother. Julie held out a chunk of carrot. Dot's soft whiskered mouth lipped it out of her hand.

"Hey, Dot, you remember me? Can I look at your baby?" Julie rubbed the mare's neck for a couple of seconds, then slowly moved around to her far side. The baby, braced on wobbly legs, stared at her wide eyed. His short, fuzzy mane stuck straight up. Julie stepped forward slowly. The colt pulled back, then, stilt legged, tipped and tilted his way to the other side of his mother. Almost there, he gave a ridiculous little buck and fell in a heap on the ground. Laughter made Julie turn. Mom, Dad, Ben, and Amber had followed and watched from the corral fence.

"Julie, he's gorgeous!" Amber's eyes sparkled.

"Strong too." Hanna pointed. "Look at him get back on his feet."

Ben just stood there with his hand on Amber's shoulder, smiling.

Julie turned her attention back to the foal. "Dad, did you imprint him yet? Can I do it?"

"Sure, why don't you help her out, Ben."

Moving very slowly, Ben and Julie cornered the little colt against his mother's side. Then, gently and expertly, Ben caught him. The little guy struggled and kicked. Ben held him fast, one arm under his neck, the other under his rump. In a few seconds the colt held still.

Hanna turned to Amber. "Do you do this with your colts back east?"

"I've trained horses, but I've never raised a colt. Most of the people I knew figured handling a colt in the first few hours of its life makes it less frightened as a two- or three-year-old when it's time for training." Julie looked up to see Amber smiling at Ben. "They used to argue a lot about the best way to do it. I'll watch Ben and see how it really should be done."

Ben laughed. "I don't know about that, but we'll try."

While he held the colt, Julie ran her hands all over the baby's soft, fuzzy body. Dot stood very close, watching over the whole process. Julie picked up the little round hooves and tapped on the bottom, mimicking the farrier. She gently pressed on the colt's back and hugged his torso like the weight of a rider and girth. Imitating the bit, she put a finger in the colt's mouth. Julie kept doing the actions over and over, calmly and gently, until the little guy relaxed. He sucked on Julie's finger.

"You hungry? I think you're done with the first lesson of your life."

Ben gently let him go and stood up. They laughed as the colt rushed to his mother's side and began nursing, his fuzzy, short-haired tail flipping rapidly.

"Did you name him yet, Mom?" Julie brushed the hay off her knees.

"I haven't had time to really look at him, what with making dinner."

"How about Dash?" Julie leaned back, the rough surface of the corral rail under her shoulder.

Amber laughed. "I like it. His blaze does make a kind of dash across his face. The way he's built, he's likely to be fast."

"Dot and Dash?" Ben raised his eyebrow. "Mom, you'll have to call the next colt Morse."

"Morris? I don't get it." Amber frowned. Julie rolled her eyes, anticipating Ben.

"Yup, Morse code," Ben said, and everyone groaned. "Sorry about that—I couldn't resist. Amber and I are going out for a ride. Anyone want to come?"

"I'd better get the dishes done." Mom started back to the house.

"I'll help you." Julie ran after her. Ben and Amber

would want to be by themselves. Besides, it was hard to watch their happiness. Together in the kitchen, Julie and her mother started to clean up. Hanna put a platter down on the kitchen cupboard. "Julie, I feel terrible that you thought we wanted you and Kurt to get back together. We're not mad at you, honey. We want what's right for you."

"I tried to be the kind of person he wanted me to be. I really did."

"You never told me what happened." Hanna put the leftover potatoes into a container. She looked at Julie, then back at her hands. "There's no need to tell me now if you don't want to."

"Mom, I panicked. I've never felt so trapped in my life."

"Why, Julie? I don't understand."

Julie shrugged and went back to scraping dishes. What was the use? Her mom was so different from her.

"I'd like to understand. Maybe talking about it would relieve some of the hurt."

Julie put down her plate. "He asked me to stop guiding. He said he wanted his wife by his side, not chasing around with other men. He said that right after we got engaged. He said climbing is dangerous, and he wanted his wife to be gentle."

"Oh, Julie." Her mother's voice was sad, but Julie wouldn't meet her eyes.

83

"I thought I loved him, so I tried. I really tried. I worked in the bank for half a year. He was buying a house. He had our whole life planned out. I'd work until we had kids, then I'd stay home in that little house while he worked in the store. I couldn't. I just couldn't." Tears coursed down Julie's face.

Hanna put her arms around her daughter. They stood together for a long moment. Finally Julie stepped back and smiled through her tears. "Anyway, I'm glad I came home and we talked."

"You seemed so happy when you met Kurt here at church. I didn't know he wanted to change you so much. Your dad and I were taken aback when you quit guiding."

"You were? But you didn't like it when I started the training."

"No, we didn't like it that you quit college, not at first anyway. But it didn't take long for us to realize working outdoors was right for you. We're not all made the same, honey. God may have someone for you yet."

Julie just shook her head and turned back to doing the dishes. They worked together quietly for a few moments, then her mother turned to her. "Julie, I've never told you before, but the way you've gone after adventure has meant a lot to me."

Julie stopped and stared at her mother. There was something in her mother's voice that let Julie know this wasn't just a casual comment. "What do you mean, Mom?"

"I'm not sure even your dad knows fully." Hanna twisted the dish towel in her hands. "Julie, I wanted to do things too. Specifically, I wanted to learn to fly. It wasn't just a casual dream. I had pamphlets from a flight school in Calgary. I was going places. Then Gordon came along." Mom's smile was tender. "I chose him instead. I don't think it ever occurred to me that I might have been able to have both. In the circle I grew up in, young wives did traditional things."

"Mom!" Julie felt like blinders had suddenly fallen off her eyes. "Dad tied you down the way Kurt wanted to tie me."

Hanna shook her head. "No, Julie, he didn't. *I* chose, and I've never been sorry. Your father has never tried to limit me. I made the choices. He's let me keep my animals and given me full partnership in the ranch. Maybe I shouldn't have told you."

Julie hugged her mother. "I'm so glad you did. And you're right. Dad isn't like Kurt. But then you're not completely like me, either. I'm glad it worked out for you." Julie laughed. "Otherwise I wouldn't be here, would I? I'm going to ride down to my bouldering rocks by Bent Creek. Do you want to come?"

Hanna laughed. "Thanks for the offer, but I don't think rock climbing is quite my thing. Go have fun."

Julie kicked Denver into a canter. Hearing that Kurt was dating another woman hadn't bothered her. It was the fear of being alone for the rest of her life that hurt.

The traumatic breakup had happened almost two years ago now. Since then Julie had thrown herself into becoming a mountain guide. Her work with Big Foot had become central to her—she pressed her lips together—and now David Hales might take that away.

She leaned over Denver's neck, driving the horse into a faster gallop as though she could run from trouble. The horse's mane whipped her face, and she could feel him take deep gulps of air as he began to tire. Julie sighed and pulled him to a walk. He danced, excited by the run, but panting hard all the same.

"Hey guy, take it easy. I shouldn't take my problems out on you."

The horse tossed his head but steadied as they started downhill. A few minutes later, the horse walked along a small creek. On the far side, the bank rose up into a hillside that steepened into cliffs. Julie dismounted and tied Denver to a poplar tree. She wasn't dressed in climbing gear, but she'd bouldered along this stretch of Bent Creek all her life. A few minutes later, panting with exertion, she was at the top of a short pitch.

She stretched and headed for her thinking rock. The boulder was rounded and sunk into a hollow. Her dad probably knew it was there since he knew all this land intimately, but Julie had never shared it with anyone. It was her own private place, the place where she went to think things through, something she needed to do badly.

Hollywood showed women as strong people, risk takers, and they got lots of male attention. Julie shook her head. They were almost never Christians, and very few of them had stable relationships. It wasn't that Julie lacked male attention. She could think of at least three men who'd definitely made moves on her in the last few months, but she was interested in nothing but a Christian relationship. Even in high school she'd been one to compete with the boys rather than flirt. Most of them treated her as a pal, not as a potential girlfriend.

The image of David Hales came into her mind. Julie shook her head wildly, jumped up, and ran back to the top of the bank. Instead of taking an easy way down, she slid her legs over the cliff. Feeling for holds, she began to climb down. Down climbing was more difficult and dangerous than going up. Julie concentrated hard on balance and rhythm. In a few minutes she was at the foot of the cliff. She grinned. It felt so good to take a risk, challenge herself and succeed. God had made her to live like that. It was so obvious and just felt right. David Hales was a Christian. His expectations couldn't be that different from Kurt's. She'd been burned once. She wasn't going to go through that kind of torture again.

Julie shook out her hands to loosen the muscles in her forearms, pulled off her boots, and started up a more difficult climb. It wasn't smart to boulder alone. She could fall and lie injured for a long time, but at the moment, Julie didn't care. She jammed her hand into a crack, gripped a tiny ledge with her toes, and began to climb. Her whole being felt transformed. Moving with balance, skill, and grace, she searched out holds and danced up the rock.

Six

"SHERYL, I WANT TO DOUBLE-CHECK MY TWO BOOKINGS for this week." Julie had called Big Foot as soon as the office opened.

"I don't think you're booked, Julie."

"Don't say that, please. I know we had some rock climbers booked."

"I'll check. Just a second." There were clicking noises. Sheryl was on the computer. "No, I'm sorry, Julie. Brent is taking some guys out on Tuesday and Wednesday, and—"

"And what? Brent has given my climbers to David Hales? Sheryl, that's not fair, and you know it."

"I don't tell Brent what to do. He does whatever he pleases. You know that." Sheryl's words had a bitter edge to them.

"You're right. Sorry for getting on your case. It's just such a pain. I really do need work. Tell Brent I called, will you?"

"Sure, Julie. Maybe next week will be better."

Julie spent the morning working on her résumé.

She sent it to every outfitter she could think of and called several for whom she'd worked occasionally. Most weren't around. Those she got in touch with were sympathetic but had nothing for her. If she were independently wealthy, maybe she could afford to hang around and hope for work. If things kept up like this, she'd either have to ask her folks for help or look for any job she could find. Laurel had already paid for more than her share of groceries this month.

Julie tried two more places, then slammed down the phone. If she had thought she'd end up doing something other than climbing, she would have stayed in college. There would be no point in taking the rock-guide test this fall if she wasn't ready for it. To be ready, Julie needed to keep guiding and work with experienced guides. She yanked her climbing shoes out of her backpack and stomped out of the house. The tires squealed as she headed for the Banff golf course to do some bouldering.

Late Monday night Brent called. "Want some work?"

"What do you think?"

"Julie, I know I promised you work, but what am I supposed to do? David Hales came all the way from England because of a comment I made. Besides, he's a—"

"Better climber than me. I know. So what happened to him that you've all of a sudden got work for me?"

"Nothing. He's doing great. He keeps asking about you." Brent laughed. "I told him to forget it. You already hate him."

"Brent!"

"Oh, you don't hate him? I'll have to let him know." He paused a moment. "You know, David Hales is one weird duck. He treats people like long-lost brothers or something. He was worrying about Tommy Oshikawa being upset. Then he tried to get me thinking about God of all things. Yesterday I came in to find him and Sheryl in deep conversation. I wouldn't worry too much about the fact that he keeps asking about you. He probably just wants to make you a better person or something."

Julie shut her eyes. "You said you have work for me?"

"Right. Twelve kids from the Southern Alberta Institute of Technology booked. I want you and David to go out early and set up the ropes at Wasooch. Tommy will bring the climbers out to you. I'll be gone for a couple of days taking two people on an Alpine climb."

"Okay, I'll be there."

"Thanks, Jule, I knew I could count on you."

The phone clicked as Brent hung up. Julie juggled the receiver in her hand. Maybe she'd misunderstood the kind of interest David was showing when he'd asked her out the other evening. He'd been talking to Sheryl, too. Julie suddenly felt very tired.

"Rope!" David flung the coiled climbing rope far out into the air. It soared in a graceful arc, unwinding as it flew. It was one of those rare days in the mountains with virtually no wind. Sound carried in the quiet air. The clicking fall of a tiny pebble knocked loose by the rope stood out as if it had been framed in silence. Julie could hear David clearly even though he hadn't raised his voice. David had just finished anchoring the first of three ropes. He'd thrown it so far out that it tangled in the top of one of the poplars at the foot of the cliff. Julie watched as he patiently recoiled the rope and tried again.

"Would you put me on belay?"

Julie hadn't expected that, but she complied quickly, setting up the rope so she could prevent him from falling. Maybe David didn't know he was taking jobs she needed. He didn't know that she'd misunderstood his interest in her, either. Still, when she'd left for work that morning she'd felt angry and humiliated. She slipped the rope through her ATC and tied herself into an anchor.

"Belay is on!" Julie took up the slack in the rope.

David started to down climb doing beautiful gymnastic moves, clowning as he tied himself into impossible positions. Julie laughed in spite of herself. Along with the clowning, he was stretching hard and using different sets of muscles. Having tied himself into a pretzel, he grinned at her upside down. "You like my warm-up?"

"You're crazy. Why are you in such a good mood?"

David shrugged, unwound himself, and landed lightly beside her. His eyes were intense as he looked at her, as if he were asking a question. Julie stepped back. Her hands shook. Did he look at everyone like that?

"We'll set up the other rope over there." Julie wanted him to look somewhere else, anywhere but at her. "See, there are three or four routes that come off the same anchor. That way if any of them are decent climbers there are some moderate 5.9s and 5.10s, as well as the easy 5.7s."

"Sounds like a good idea. Why don't you lead this time?"

Julie nodded and started up, moving easily. These were easy routes. At the top, when she pitched the second half of the rope down, it fell clear, the last couple of coils landing neatly at David's feet.

"Good throw, Julie."

Beating David at anything, no matter how trivial, felt good. She looked down and gave him a wicked grin. "It just takes skill."

With his most British, highbrow accent, David stated, "Oh, thanks. Perhaps the hooking of trees is a special skill in itself. Perhaps I was just practicing the art of rope throwing."

"I stand corrected, your grace." Julie bowed deeply and giggled. "It's your turn to put me on belay." Flexibility was one thing she could handle. She left one foot where it was and climbed down until she was in a hyperextended splits.

"Oooh, ouch!" David mimed terrible agony.

Julie laughed. Her bottom foot was solid on a decent-sized ledge. Bending over backward she put both hands on the ledge, then stepped out in a walkover. David cheered. They were both laughing, but the play had a competitive edge to it.

As Julie straightened up, she heard an approaching sound. It was the van engine. The parking lot was almost half a mile away, but in the still air the sound carried easily. "I think they're here." Julie motioned for David to let her down. Quickly they sorted gear, laying out the harnesses. David's hand bumped hers as they both reached for the same climbing helmet. As if jolted by an electric shock, both of them jerked back.

"Sorry." David bowed. "Your helmet, ma'am."

She could hear voices approaching and the crunching of boots on the rocks of the dry creek. "Okay, I'll lay out the rest of the gear. You go welcome the troops."

"Right." David ambled off. In a few minutes he was back with the climbers and Tommy.

"I should introduce everyone." David smiled at the climbers. "You all told me your names, but they've fled from my head. Tommy, can you help me out?"

Tommy shook his head. Julie glanced at him, then did a double take. Tommy's eyes were red rimmed and shadowed, his features drawn with exhaustion. Definitely not the same kid who had talked so happily the day they met.

Everyone was looking at her expectantly. "Did I miss something?"

"I just said we'd all introduce ourselves and say how much climbing we've done, starting with you." David smiled, his eyes conveying kindness and reassurance.

She blinked and tried to collect her scattered thoughts. "I guess I was kind of up in the air somewhere, but that's normal for most climbers I know." People laughed in a friendly way, making her feel better. "I'm Julie Miller, an assistant rock-climbing guide. I've been climbing since I could walk—"

"Since you could walk? No way."

Julie laughed. "Yeah, up the back of the couch, up trees, the side of the barn, the windmill by the watering trough, cliffs, anything that I came in contact with. I only discovered rock climbing with ropes when I went to the university, and I've been hooked ever since. I've been working for Big Foot for two years on and off. I'd like to make guiding my life."

The introductions went on around the circle. It turned out most of them had climbed once or twice in climbing gyms. Three had been out on real rock. It wasn't until she and David were busy getting the first climbers tied in that Julie realized Tommy had left without a word. Maybe her first impressions of Tommy as a friendly, outgoing guy had been wrong. She shrugged. Maybe he'd just been partying and was hungover.

She moved into the rhythm of a long day guiding. David was busy on the other rope with half of the climbers. Even as they worked, Julie found she was far more aware of David than she'd ever been of Brent. Late in the afternoon the climbers left, full of thanks and excited stories about the day.

Julie watched as the van left the parking lot, then began to collect gear. Tommy looked worse now than he had this morning. As if echoing her thoughts, David said, "Did Tommy look upset to you?"

Julie continued coiling one of the ropes. "Yeah, he did, but then I don't know him very well. Maybe he's just tired."

David looked in the direction the van had taken. His brow was wrinkled, his eyes concerned. Watching him, Julie was sure Brent was right. David cared about everyone. She sighed and began to pack the helmets.

"Julie, are you in a rush? Could we spend a bit of time on the rock?"

"This area won't be much of a challenge for you." She kept working without looking up.

"I don't care. It's always fun to try new stone."

Julie put the last helmet in the huge hockey bag of equipment. She did need the workout. Besides, it felt good to be around David Hales. She pulled the zipper shut with a jerk. Erase that thought. He was just a great guy who cared about everyone, and she wasn't interested anyway, not that way.

"Okay, I can stay."

"All right!" David's smile was so pleased that Julie found herself smiling too. "We can use this as a pyramid workout, go up an easier climb three or four times, then one slightly harder a few less times, and so on. Have you done that kind of workout before?"

"No, but it sounds interesting. I'll belay you first."

Julie had to take in rope as fast as she could to keep up with David on the first pitch. He was basically speed climbing, making huge, precise dynamic lunges on the big holds.

"Quickly!" he called as she started to lower him. Julie let the rope run, only slowing when his feet were directly above the ground.

"Great! Thanks! Climbing." David started up again. By the fourth time, he was panting hard, but his moves stayed precise and graceful. He moved sideways so that the rope ended up over on a 5.10 climb. After going twice up that one, he landed beside her. His hair was dark with sweat, and damp curls hugged the back of his neck outlining the handsome set of his head.

"Anything harder?" David leaned down to stretch his legs.

"Sorry."

He grinned at her. "For what? You didn't make this rock. God did, and it's just fine." He stretched each hand, shaking them out. "Climbing?"

"Climb on."

Julie watched him move with amazed admiration. She was going to look like a real rookie after him. Oh, well. So what if he thought she looked like an idiot. She needed a workout. After the last climb, David leaned against the rock panting. "That was great! Give me a second and I'll put you on belay."

Julie nodded and concentrated on stretching out in the few moments she had. Watching David move seemed to have rubbed off a bit because she positively flew up the first pitch. He brought her down so fast it was basically a long fall. She whooped with exhilaration and started back up again. By the third climb she was beginning to slow down.

As David had, she swung the rope over onto the more difficult pitch. Climbing with great focus, she moved upward smoothly enough, though by the second time, her legs were beginning to shudder with fatigue on the smaller footholds. She had to stop to chalk up several times since her hands were slick with sweat. Back on the easier pitch, she made it to the top on sheer willpower. She gasped for breath and grinned from ear to ear. She'd actually made it through the whole workout.

"Excellent!" David brought her to the ground. His smile made his eyes come alive. Julie spun to return his high five, and her legs buckled, the muscles depleted from the climb. David caught her, and she found herself against his chest, her legs wobbling like a puppet's who'd lost his strings. Julie looked deep into David's eyes, and suddenly neither of them was laughing. He had the same questioning look he'd had earlier. His breath was warm on her cheek.

She pushed away and wobbled into a sitting position. "Sorry, my legs have had it."

David was still looking at her in that disturbing way. Julie pulled her helmet off and ran her hand through her hair. Her heart was still beating hard, and it wasn't just from the exertion of the climb. Julie shut her eyes. *God, I don't want this feeling. I don't want to be attracted to this man.*

"Are you okay? You're not hurt, are you?"

Julie laughed. He didn't have a clue. "I'm just fine. That was a great workout. Thanks. I'll use the idea again."

"You know, watching you move, I think you could be a top-notch climber if you chose to."

Julie looked up, startled. "Me? I'm not even solid on the harder 5.11 climbs right now."

"How much opportunity have you had to train lately?"

"Not as much as I'd like. I've already decided I'm going to spend more time at the climbing gyms in Calgary no matter how tired I am in the evenings."

"I could coach you a bit if you want."

Julie frowned and bent to unlace her climbing shoes. She desperately wanted to improve her skills. Training with a man of David's caliber was just what she needed, but given her reactions to him, would spending that much time together be a good idea? She pulled off her left shoe and rubbed her cramped toes. If guiding was what she wanted to do, she'd better take all the opportunities that came her way. She'd just have to keep a grip on her emotions.

"Yes, I'd like that. Thank you."

David's smile was incandescent. "Okay, I'll help you make up a workout schedule and come with you whenever I can. You can help me too. Until I know for sure what God wants me to do, I'd like to stay in condition. I mean, what good is it if I'm supposed to go back and I'm not fit enough to climb a set of stairs?"

Julie laughed. "I don't think there's much danger of that. Meanwhile, would you like me to give you a belay again here?"

"Thanks." David reached out to pull her to her feet. His fingers, warm and powerful, closed around hers, and her heart did a flip. Swallowing hard, she pulled her hand free and walked away, wondering if she'd just made a huge mistake.

It was almost eight by the time they pulled into Canmore. After a long day working hard in the open air, Julie felt like she could eat a horse. Mentally she was going through what there was to eat in the apartment when David said, "Tommy Oshikawa showed me a good pizza place this weekend. I'm starved. How about we stop there?"

Her mouth watered at the thought of pizza, but Julie shook her head. "I can't, David. I'm broke."

"I'll buy. Come on. You must be as hungry as I am. Think of it as a thank-you for helping me get a great workout this afternoon."

Julie wavered. She could almost smell the pizza. "Okay." She smiled. "Thanks, I am starved."

As they ate, David talked about Tommy. Julie watched him thoughtfully. Brent had said he cared about people, tried to take care of them. It sounded like Brent was right. Apparently David had spent quite a bit of time with Tommy over the weekend. Julie took a big bite of pizza. Cheese, tomato, and spicy pepperoni filled her mouth and slid satisfyingly into her stomach. She took another bite and tried to concentrate on what David was saying.

"Julie, it's not easy for him. He told me he feels like his parents aren't living on the same planet. They came to Canada as adults, while he grew up here. He said his dad does everything exactly the way Tommy's older uncle wants. I think they expect complete obedience from Tommy too."

Julie wiped her napkin across her mouth. "He told me they want him to be a lawyer. It didn't sound like he minded much."

"I don't know. I get the feeling there is something really wrong somewhere." David shrugged. "Would you pray for him with me?"

Julie nearly choked on her pizza. "Here? Now?"

David laughed. "Why not? Is there a law against praying in a pizza joint?"

"I guess not." Julie admired David's openness about his faith. It stirred her deep inside. He acted like it was completely normal for Christians to pray at the drop of a hat. Maybe she could learn more from him than better climbing technique.

Julie snuck a glance out of the corner of her eye as David bowed his head and started to pray. "Father, you know Tommy's needs. Please give him peace and a sense of your presence. Guide us and show us how we can help him." Julie didn't find it hard to join in. Christian people talked about praying anytime, but David was the first one she'd met who really practiced it. He tucked into his pizza eagerly as soon as he'd said amen. Julie reached for another piece of pizza.

"Julie, something Brent said the other day has been bothering me. When I asked him, he downplayed it and said you'd still get work, but I need to know. Has my arrival taken work away from you?"

Caught off guard, Julie fumbled the piece of pizza and bumped her glass, sending Coke across the table onto David's lap. He jumped up and tried to stem the tide with his napkin.

"Sorry! Sorry!" Julie flipped her glass upright catching some of it. It'd gone right across the pizza, soaking it and wrecking the meal. She felt like a total klutz. A waitress rushed over and bustled around clearing up the mess. What was with her? She wasn't usually this clumsy. She'd been enjoying David's company way too much. He was a nice man. He seemed to have a special relationship with God, and he really cared about people, but that had nothing to do with her.

Julie picked up her day pack and stood up. "David, I've got to go. I can easily walk home from here if you don't mind taking the truck in tomorrow."

"I'd rather give you a ride."

Julie just shook her head. "See you, and thanks for a great day."

Outside, the crisp evening air stroked her hot cheeks. A huge moon was just sailing over the ridge. It would have been so much simpler if David Hales hadn't turned up at Big Foot. She would have had more work and wouldn't have had to put up with all the tangled confusion the man created inside her. Julie slung her pack over her shoulder and briskly walked away from the pizza place. She'd just have to keep trying to find other guiding work.

Julie shook her head. She didn't even want to think about the alternatives.

Seven

JULIE WALKED INTO THE APARTMENT AND HESITATED. Laurel should have been home, but none of the lights were on. She shrugged and started upstairs. Maybe Laurel had gone to bed early. She did that sometimes if she was going to be up early with the bears. The sound of the front door opening stopped her halfway up the stairs. She turned, then gasped at the sight of Laurel's face. Swollen and red, her eyes were nearly shut. Her fair skin was blotchy with misery, and her dark hair was disheveled.

"Oh, Laurel, what happened?" Julie rushed to put her arm around her friend.

"They shot Samantha. They killed her. It was terrible."

For a wild moment Julie wondered if someone had been murdered; then she remembered. "Samantha—the bear with triplets? Why?"

"Poachers. Her head and feet were hacked off, and the radio collar had been pitched into the bush. I hadn't been able to pick up her radio signal for the last couple of days. I thought maybe she'd moved on because of Sir Walter, the big boar she chased off. Remember him? Anyway, today I saw ravens circling. I knew that meant something was dead, and that would attract bears. Only when I got there, I found it was Samantha herself that was dead. I couldn't believe it when I found her collar smashed and thrown into the bush."

"What about the babies?"

"I saw the reddish one. Just a glimpse as he ran behind a bush. The poor little guy must have been waiting by his dead mother for days. Maybe the others are there too. Tomorrow Fish and Wildlife is going to help me try to catch them in a live trap. They're probably badly dehydrated already. If we don't catch them soon, they'll die. If we do, they'll end up in zoos. Julie, I hate poachers!" Laurel hid her face in her hands. Her shoulders heaved.

Julie rubbed Laurel's back, hoping that was some comfort. A sharp picture came to mind of Samantha sitting in the sunlight nursing her cubs. Julie's eyes stung. Laurel had spent days watching that bear and thought of her as a friend. With her free arm, Julie reached for the box of tissues on the coffee table and handed it to Laurel.

Laurel took one, blew her nose, and looked up. "Sorry. I know Samantha was an animal. It's not like I agree with people who'd rather save the seals than care for humans, but it was such a stupid, greedy waste." She grabbed another tissue and twisted it in her hands. "They just left her cubs to die. God made the animals. He said they were good, then left them in our hands to tend." Laurel's hands shredded the tissue. She looked at Julie with haunted eyes. "We humans are doing a real great job."

Julie continued to rub Laurel's back. She could think of nothing to say. After a minute Laurel lifted her head again. "It's not just that Samantha died, but she was trashed. Whoever killed her didn't see her as a fellow creature before God at all. Julie, they didn't use her hide or meat or anything. You don't kill a healthy, young female unless you've got to cull a population. The bear population here is already stressed. It doesn't need culling."

Laurel jumped up and started to pace back and forth, still talking. Julie got up and went to the kitchen. The whole area was open, so she could still listen to Laurel as she made tea for both of them and a sandwich for Laurel.

"Laurel, have you eaten this afternoon?"

"Huh?" Laurel stopped her pacing and looked at Julie. "I guess not." She followed Julie into the kitchen and sat down. After the first couple of bites of sandwich, Laurel gave a big sigh and seemed to relax. Julie sat sipping her tea, watching her friend and praying.

Laurel finished her cup of tea and gave Julie a wobbly smile. "Thanks. I've been ranting like a crazy person. I'd better get to bed. It's going to be a long day tomorrow."

Julie looked thoughtfully after her friend, then stretched and went up to bed. It had been quite a day.

David Hales walked to work the next morning thinking hard. Fat clouds sailed across the sky. David left his jacket open, enjoying the brisk wind. Julie Miller consumed his thoughts. He could picture her laughing as she clowned around on the rock. He'd liked her intensity in the workout climbs. She'd worked so hard her legs had buckled. The feel of her body against his had left an indelible impression. He kicked a fist-sized rock off the path.

God, what do you want me to do? Julie was becoming more special to him every day. It had felt so right when she'd been in his arms. Then later when he'd suggested that they pray for Tommy Oshikawa, she'd joined in so easily and prayed with obvious sincerity. David frowned and walked faster. Julie hadn't answered his question. *Father, I hope my presence isn't interfering with her summer work.* The way she'd jumped up and left so quickly, though…that told him she was upset, whether she'd admit it or not. He had no desire for his trip to

Canada to do anyone harm, least of all Julie. He kicked at another rock.

Okay, Lord, so where do we go from here?

"Hi, David." Sheryl looked up and smiled as he walked in.

"Hello. You're here early."

She patted her desk as an invitation to come over and talk. David hesitated. She looked a bit too eager. "Come on." Sheryl's wide eyes seemed sincere enough. "I've been thinking about the things you said. You know, that our value is in ourselves and I shouldn't base what I think of myself on whether Brent likes me."

"Our value is in God's love for us."

"Whatever, anyway, I decided I'm done with Brent. I moved out of his place. I thought maybe I could go to church with you."

Alarm bells rang in David's head. The look on Sheryl's face was one of acute interest, but from the way she watched him, David doubted it was interest in church. He held his ground. "Why don't you ask Julie? She could take you."

Sheryl made a face. "I'd rather go with you."

The thing was, Sheryl did need to find God. He'd have to pray about this. He wasn't sure of the right way to deal with it. Fishing in his pocket, he pulled out the battered little New Testament that always lived there.

"Um, look, Sheryl, why don't you read the Gospel of John in here and tell me what you think of it? Or maybe talk to Julie." He stuck it on her desk, avoiding her hand as she reached for his. "I'll come back when Brent gets here."

When he was a block away from the Big Foot office he stopped. He and Brent were taking a large group on a one-day climb, and Brent had offered to send Tommy to pick him up, but he'd said he'd rather walk. They were supposed to meet at seven. A spatter of rain stung him across the cheek. *This is stupid. It's not worth getting soaked.* As he walked back toward the office, he saw Brent's truck approaching and sighed with relief. There had to have been a better way to handle Sheryl's interest than leaving the office, but at that moment he couldn't think what it would have been. He followed Brent into the building.

Sheryl gave him a pouty look, then turned to Brent. "The people booked with you just called and canceled because of the weather. They wanted to see if they could rebook later."

Brent swore. "Why do they have to be such wimps?"

"I wouldn't want to hike in this." Sheryl sat staring at Brent intently.

"Like I said, wimps. See if there's a time later, then." He headed for his office.

David followed. "Brent, if you have time, there is

something I'd like to talk to you about." Brent beckoned, then shut the office door behind them both. He looked at David inquiringly. "Look." David leaned back against the door. "I don't want to cause Julie Miller to lose work this summer. Please answer me honestly. Is my presence at Big Foot doing that?"

Brent moved a stack of stuff on his desk from one place to another. "Honestly? I suppose so. I've used you when I would have used her." Brent jerked his chair out and sat down. "But so what? She's got her Association of Canadian Mountain Guides qualification for backpacking and has almost finished the one for rock climbing. She can book her own clients."

"So I *have* done her harm. Is there anything that can be done to help her find work?"

"You could leave."

"I've thought of that."

Brent stood up again. "Don't be silly. You can't go. I've booked a couple of groups on the basis of your name. Look, if it's such a big deal to you, I'll try to find her work, call some people."

David smiled, relieved. "I'd appreciate that." *Please help it work out, Lord.*

David was walking back toward his apartment when Tommy pulled up alongside in Big Foot's van. "Hey, man, Brent is sending me into Calgary to pick up some stuff. Do you want to come?" David hesitated. He'd planned to call Julie and see if they could spend some time together. Tommy kept talking. "I've got to go to Mountain Equipment Coop. It's a huge outdoor-equipment store. You'd like it." The boy's eyes were pleading. It was clear that there was more behind the invitation than a casual desire for company.

"Okay, sure." David opened the van door and got in. He studied Tommy and decided the boy looked even more haggard than he had the other day, if that was possible. Now that David was in the van, Tommy simply drove and said nothing. Calgary was a sprawling city full of glittering new buildings. David followed a distracted Tommy through a huge grocery store, then to the outdoor-equipment place. David poked around there but found very little that was new to him. As he helped the still-silent Tommy load gear, David wished he'd stayed in Canmore. It wasn't until they turned up a wealthy residential street that he got some inkling of why Tommy wanted him along.

"I've got to stop at home for some stuff. I want you to come in with me, okay?"

"Sure, I'd like to meet your folks."

Tommy looked at David as if he'd said something remarkable. The boy's knuckles were white as he gripped the wheel. He turned into a cul-de-sac, and

David saw him relax. When they pulled up in front of a big white stucco house, David started to get out.

"No, it's okay. Nobody's home." Tommy looked happier than he had all day. "I've got a key. I'll be right back." True to his word, Tommy was back in the car in seconds. The tires squealed as they left the driveway. Just as they left the cul-de-sac, a black Mercedes turned to come in. Tommy swerved, almost running up onto the sidewalk, and stepped on the gas.

"Careful, man!" David clutched the door. "I'd rather get back to Canmore in one piece."

"What?" Tommy slowed down the van and drove sanely enough, but he kept looking into his rearview mirror.

"Was that your father in the black Mercedes?"

"No." Tommy opened his mouth, then closed it again and shook his head. They drove in silence the whole way back to Canmore. They pulled up in front of David's place. Tommy sat like a statue. David looked at him thoughtfully, shrugged, and got out of the vehicle. He turned to lean in the open window. "Good-bye."

"Wait! I want to ask you something. How important do you think it is for someone like me to do what his family wants?"

"The Bible says we're to honor our parents."

Tommy hit the wheel as if he'd heard news he didn't like and pulled away, the tires squealing again. David watched wondering if he'd said the right thing. Tommy had left without giving him time to add that honoring one's parents didn't include doing wrong just because they told you to, or that he wasn't sure the biblical injunction for children to obey their parents included adult children. For some reason, that really bothered him. He tried to shrug off the feeling. Maybe he was overreacting and Tommy was just a typical kid having trouble making the break from home.

Inside his apartment, David tried to call Julie, but no one answered. He hung up with a snort. The day seemed a total loss. He sat back in his chair, struggling with feelings of frustration. With a muttered exclamation, he finally jumped up and headed for the door. A few minutes later he was walking downtown toward a bike shop. Tired of being dependent on others for transportation, he'd decided if he couldn't get a car, at least he might be able to find a decent bike.

Nothing had worked out the way he'd thought or hoped it would. Maybe it was a good thing he hadn't gotten ahold of Julie. That probably would've gone wrong too.

David sighed and slowed his pace as he silently asked God for the grace to be patient and wait on him.

Eight

HAVING NO WORK, JULIE HAD OFFERED TO GO WITH LAUREL that morning to see if the cubs had been caught in the live trap. "Thanks, Julie, that's sweet of you, but I don't think you'd better. I'm okay now, and you wouldn't enjoy it. If the cubs are in the trap, Fish and Wildlife will take them; then I've got to dissect the sow's carcass."

Julie noticed that her friend didn't refer to the dead bear by name anymore. "Isn't that going to be pretty traumatic? Couldn't someone else do it?"

Laurel lifted her chin. "Alex, my study supervisor, will be there, but the sow was part of my study. I'm not wimping out. You're right; it will be hard. Not to mention pretty nasty." She managed a weak, wry grin. "It's been three days and she stinketh, so there's no need for you to be there."

Julie wrinkled her nose at the thought. "Are you sure? I'll come if you want."

Laurel laughed. "You look so eager. Just pray for me, and don't make much supper."

After Laurel left, Julie got out her information

about the rock-guide certification test in August. She looked at it blankly, shoved it back into the file, and paced the room. It would be so humiliating to fail. She ran downstairs and looked at the phone—then shook her head, frustrated. She'd already called everyone she knew in the business, and that had done no good.

She bit her lip and glanced around the room, her gaze finally coming to rest on the newspaper. She could place an ad for hiking-guide work. That would be a lot better than nothing. Swallowing hard, she sat down to try to compose an ad. She'd just thrown her second attempt into the garbage when the phone rang.

"Is Julie Miller there?" The voice was male with a slight German accent.

"Speaking."

"This is Rolf Setzler. Brent Wilson tells me you're looking for work. I could use a hiking guide week after next. I'm double booked. Do you want the work? If you do well, I'll have several jobs for you over the summer."

"I'd love the work." She knew Rolf slightly as one of the European guides who worked out of Canmore. In a few minutes she had the details she needed. As soon as Rolf was off the phone, Julie impulsively dialed Big Foot. "Hi, Sheryl. Tell Brent thanks for me, would you?"

"He's here. You can tell him yourself."

Julie raised her eyebrows. Sheryl sounded even more hostile than usual. The line clicked as Sheryl transferred her to Brent's office.

"Brent, thanks for getting me work! That was so nice of you."

Brent snorted. "Don't thank me. David was going to quit unless I made sure you had work."

"What?"

Brent laughed. "Maybe you'd better watch out for him. He convinced Sheryl to move out of my place— but then, I can't complain too much. It seems it was the best thing for both of us. Yes sir, he's quite the man."

Slowly Julie hung up the phone. Brent had said earlier that David had been talking to Sheryl. Now Sheryl had moved out of Brent's place. That couldn't be a bad thing, but...Julie frowned. Why did David care one way or the other what Brent and Sheryl did? Unless... David couldn't be interested in Sheryl, could he? She wasn't even a Christian. Julie shook her head and went into the kitchen. It was none of her business who the indomitable David Hales was interested in, or even if he wanted to be a monk! She grimaced, irritated with herself. All it took was Brent mentioning the man and there she went, reacting way too strongly. Maybe she shouldn't train with David after all. Julie picked up a dishcloth, then hurled it back into the sink.

The sight of Laurel's coffee cup on the counter

made Julie feel even worse. Here she was thinking about herself when Laurel was having what was certainly a painful day. Julie sighed and started cleaning the kitchen and silently prayed for her friend. Afterward, she sat down in the living room and looked through the rock-guide certification information. Julie lifted her head and stared out the window, fighting against the tears that suddenly choked her throat. *Stop feeling sorry for yourself!* But the scolding didn't help. All she could think of was how far away she was from her dream and how unlikely it seemed that she would ever reach it.

But if she was going to live for God and these were the skills with which he'd blessed her, there had to be some way she could use them for his glory.

Later that evening Laurel came home. "Well, we caught the cubs, all three of them." Weariness punctuated her every move. "They were terrified, hiding in the corner of the live trap, snarling. Two of them ate the bear pabulum we made. I don't know if the third one is going to make it." Laurel dropped her backpack and slumped against the door. "Alex and I did a necropsy on the sow."

"A nec-necro, what?"

"We opened her up to see exactly how she died."

"Oh, Laurel, I'm so sorry you had to do that. It must have been awful."

118

Laurel closed her eyes for a moment, as though trying to hold back the tears. "The poacher had taken out her gallbladder. The slice went to the exact location. In and out, slick as a surgeon. Before I tell you anything else, I'm going to take a long, hot shower."

As Julie watched Laurel retreat upstairs, a knock sounded at the door, making her jump. Her mind still on Laurel, she went to answer it. At the sight of David standing there, her heart leaped like an undisciplined colt.

"Hey, there. I was out exploring the town and thought I'd stop by to see if you'd like to go climbing this evening."

"I'd better not, but thanks for asking. Laurel had a rotten day, and I want to stay around for her. One of her favorite study bears got killed by poachers."

"By poachers?" The sadness on his face touched Julie deeply. "Laurel said something about poachers when I came to your place before. Are they getting worse?"

"I don't know. I hope not."

"Give Laurel my sympathy. The way she cares about those bears, she must feel the same way I did when my dog died."

"You're right. It's not fun. I'll tell her you sympathize. Oh, and thanks for talking to Brent. He found me work with one of the other outfitters."

"Hey, that's great, Julie. Since you can't come tonight,

how about if we go work out tomorrow evening?"

There on the coffee table lay the material from the Association of Mountain Guides that she'd thumbed through earlier. In order to get her rock-guide certification, she was going to have to demonstrate ability at a 5.11 level. She needed to look smooth and competent and be perfect with her rescue skills. She wasn't going to accomplish that by just sitting here and staring at the material. Training with David was probably her best chance. Surely she had enough discipline to be around the man for several hours without losing control of her emotions.

"Okay, if things work out I'd like that."

"Good." One word, but David's deep tone was full of pleasure...and the smile he gave reminded her of her father after he'd polished off a Thanksgiving meal, homemade pie and all—pure satisfaction and male triumph. It was that I-knew-I-could-do-it, conquering-hero kind of look.

"I'll see you then, Lord willing." David smiled again and headed for the door. As it closed behind him, Julie sank onto the couch, doing her best to get her breathing back under control. *Oh, Lord, please don't let me make a fool of myself. David was just being nice. Like he is to everyone. I'm nothing more than a friend to him.*

But even as she thought it, Julie knew something deep inside her hoped she was wrong.

Julie was glad she'd stayed with Laurel because her friend talked and talked, pouring out her frustration. When Laurel started in on the proper biblical view of animals again, Julie was a little lost but still interested.

Laurel grabbed her Bible and flipped it open. "Look! In Revelation chapter 5 it isn't just people who praise the Lamb of God for redemption. It's all creation. All the creatures praise Christ. See?"

Julie met her friend's impassioned gaze. "Do you think there will be animals in heaven, then?"

"Well, it says the lion will lie down with the lamb, doesn't it? Wouldn't that be hard with no lions or lambs?"

"I guess." Julie frowned. *Couldn't that verse be symbolic?*

Laurel was still talking. "It sounds like there'll be animals on the new earth, but I don't know if it's the same ones from now in new bodies, like we'll have, or new animals. Anyway, it says that creation won't be subject to death anymore. I don't even like it when the bears make a kill, especially when they get a fawn. Everything here runs on death, and I'm sick of it! I almost wish I hadn't decided to study animals."

"Laurel! I can't imagine you staying away from animals."

"I know, but I hate death!" She sighed. "I've been talking your ear off again."

"Don't worry about that. I like it when you share your thoughts. You have neat ideas." She shook her head with a laugh. *"Deep* ideas. You leave me in the dust sometimes. You ought to write them down, you know?"

"I don't usually think about it much unless something makes me mad. Oh! Wait'll you hear what they're doing to catch the poachers!" As Laurel went on, Julie settled back against the couch cushion with a sigh.

Laurel was hardly a conventional woman, yet Ian seemed to find her acceptable without trying to turn her into someone else. Still, even with her animals, Laurel was a nurturer. She liked to bake and wouldn't try rock climbing when Julie had invited her. Julie studied her friend closely and found her throat tightening up when she realized Kurt wouldn't have rejected Laurel. He would have found her different but still acceptable. Laurel might be an unconventional Christian woman, but it was clear she would be a good wife because she was motherly and gentle by nature.

Julie sighed. She didn't have a chance. She could no more be the kind of woman Laurel was than a fish could hop like a rabbit.

For the next month, Julie lived in an odd kind of limbo. She worked for Rolf Setzler most of the time, and that kept her reasonably busy. But the times that she really looked forward to were the evenings when she trained with David. Those times were also her undoing—or they would have been if she hadn't worked as hard as she could to keep herself disconnected from her feelings about the man.

Her climbing skills were improving, no doubt about it. Unfortunately her attraction for David Hales was increasing at about the same rate. It grew week by week. He was careful around her, gentle, a great listener. He had tried several times at the beginning of the month to ask her out to meals, but when she kept refusing, he stopped. Sometimes she caught him looking at her with a kind of longing in his eyes.

During their workouts, they talked endlessly. David told her about his parents. His dad worked with the Capernwray Bible Centers. "I've got one older sister. Since I'm the only boy, I think Mum and Dad kind of wanted me to follow Dad's example." As they sat catching their breath, David looked at his callused and scarred hands ruefully. "Not exactly the hands of an academic, are they?"

Julie wanted to touch those long-fingered, powerful hands and let him know they were far stronger and somehow more articulate than the hands of any academic. Instead she looked away. "So, are they still on your case?"

"Not really. I got them to read Eric Liddel's biography.

You know, the book they used as the basis for *Chariots of Fire*? He explained so well how he felt God's pleasure when he ran. I feel that when I climb."

Julie looked up. "I know exactly what you mean! It's like God is there, right with me."

David grinned, and their eyes met and locked. There was no need for words, no need for explanations. There was only a deep, almost primal understanding. Julie felt like time had come to a screaming halt...as though everything and everyone around them faded away and they were the only two people left in existence. With an effort, she tore her gaze away, forcing her breathing and her pulse rate to return to some semblance of normalcy.

Shake if off, Julie. Get a grip, for crying out loud!

"So the book really helped, huh?" Relief swept over her at how normal her voice sounded.

"It sure did."

She shrugged and looked at him. The intensity in his eyes almost threw her, but she forced herself to go on without missing a beat. "My folks aren't exactly great readers, but maybe the movie would help."

David laughed. "Dad pointed out that Eric Liddel became a missionary when he grew up. I think he's still waiting for me to do the same."

"What, be a missionary or grow up?"

"Both. Actually, I do want to find a way to use

climbing somehow to draw people to God. Like I said the first day we met, I don't want it to be a narcissistic idol for me. The whole climbing circuit didn't feel right. Sure, I like people and I loved the attention, but...I don't know. I'd like to use the skill some way for God."

Another thing we agree on. Julie sighed as David stood and she followed suit. It would be nice, just once, if David Hales didn't seem so very perfect for her.

That night back at the apartment, Julie cried herself to sleep. She was still convinced she could never marry. Because of who she was and what she knew God wanted her to do, she felt marriage just wasn't in her future. David Hales was as unreachable as the moon.

On a Sunday evening toward the end of the month, Laurel and Julie were both in the kitchen. Julie was at the table working on a list of supplies she needed for an upcoming three-day backpacking trip she would be leading for Rolf Setzler. Laurel was in a baking mood. She had coffee cake in the oven and had started on a batch of muffins. Julie heard her crack an egg against the side of the mixing bowl. "You're being silly about David Hales. You know that, don't you?"

Julie's pen stopped moving, but she didn't look up. "What do you mean?"

"It's like some game of musical chairs every Sunday. He tries to sit by you, but you dodge him and move so you're on the other side of me." The timer bell for the oven went off, and Laurel bent to get the coffee cake out. "What's the matter with you? I know you like him. You're always all bubbly and happy when you go to work out with him."

"You're imagining things. He's as nice to you as he is to me." Julie drew rapid squiggles all down the side of the paper in front of her. "He's nice to everyone. He even got us to invite Sheryl to church."

Laurel laughed. "She came once and left in a huff when David actually got up and moved to sit beside you. Look, I know you're lonely, and David is a super Christian man. He loves climbing and so do you. Forgive me for being dense, but what's the problem?"

"It's just that I'm not convinced he's interested in me that way. Like I said, he cares about people." Her quick retort hung there in the air. Julie glanced at Laurel, whose raised brows told her she wasn't buying it. Julie slapped down her pen. "All right, fine! That's not true. It's just that I don't feel like our relationship can ever go anywhere."

"Because he's British?"

Julie shook her head impatiently. Laurel would

never understand. She would never see how different she and Julie were...how unsuited Julie was for a man like David...for *any* man. She swallowed hard and looked at Laurel, who was watching her with a tender, almost motherly look. Julie felt trapped and exposed.

The doorbell rang, and Julie jumped up and ran to answer it. *Saved by the bell.* The thought made her smile as she pulled the door open.

It took her a moment to recognize the young man standing there.

"Tommy! I haven't seen you in ages." He was noticeably thinner, and there were dark circles under his eyes.

Tommy sniffed the air. "Nope, you've been working for the opposition. Mmm! It smells good in here."

Julie laughed. "You must have radar. Both times you've turned up here Laurel has been baking."

Tommy grinned. "Maybe it's just an excellent sense of timing."

"Ask him in," Laurel called from the kitchen.

He waggled his eyebrows. "You don't have to twist my arm, not with a smell like that luring me. Before I forget, I'm supposed to ask you if you can come in tomorrow. There are French climbers booked, and when I went to pick them up at the airport just now, guess what? They'd brought friends. There were twice as many as Brent expected. I called him, and he said I should ask you to come in. I was in the van, so I just stopped here on my way home."

"Okay. I'm not booked."

"Good, that'll make Brent happy. David too." He gave her a teasing grin.

Julie ignored that. "Come on into the kitchen. I'll get you a piece of coffee cake."

Tommy followed her. "You know what? Two of those climbers know David really well. Jacques and Nicole. They're the ones that decided to come at the last minute. David doesn't even know they're here."

Laurel put pieces of cake on the table. "That should be fun for David."

Tommy nodded and dug into the coffee cake. Julie took a bite of the warm, fragrant treat. David had mentioned several times that he was still worried about Tommy. The boy seemed thinner, but he looked happy enough at the moment.

"So have you done any mountaineering yet?" Julie sipped her milk.

"Only day climbs. I'm not sure I'm cut out for that."

"I know what you mean," Laurel said. "I ended up hiking over a ridge following Sir Walter yesterday. I thought I was going to die, and I was just puttering along. Remember him, Julie? You saw him when you came with me."

"I can still see Samantha putting her babies up a tree and facing that big bear." Julie stuck her hand over her mouth. Laurel had never referred to Samantha by name since the day she had found her dead. "Sorry, Laurel."

Tommy looked back and forth from Julie to Laurel. "So who's Samantha? Did the big bear attack her?"

There was a small uneasy silence; then Laurel shrugged. "You can answer him, Julie. I'm not made of porcelain. Besides, that reminds me, Fish and Wildlife asked me to send them the pictures I took. I'd better go get them before I forget." She jumped up and left the table.

Julie turned to Tommy. "Samantha wasn't a person that a bear attacked. She was a mother bear. Laurel had been studying her and her cubs; then she found Samantha dead. Poachers had killed her. Fish and Wildlife helped Laurel catch the cubs, but they won't be—"

Tommy had gone white and slowly pushed his chair away from the table.

"Tommy? Are you—"

Just then Laurel walked back in carrying a folder. "Fish and Wildlife have found a couple of other bear carcasses, one just outside the park and the other farther south. They're trying to figure out if it's the same operators. They wanted to see how the butchering was done. They figure if they've seen three, there are probably many others they've missed."

Tommy stood up. "Uh, I'd better be going."

"You haven't even finished your cake. Sit down. You can't go yet." Laurel dropped the folder onto the table and sorted through the contents. Preoccupied with what she was doing, she didn't look at Tommy, but Julie did. She watched him as he fidgeted and stared at the floor, then looked around the room. There was a picture of another sow with twin cubs on a calendar on the wall. His eyes had locked onto that picture, and he was sweating. Was he sick?

Laurel suddenly stopped sorting. "Ugh, there it is. I should have put it in as a sort of final episode as an end to the record. I didn't even want to touch it. It still makes me sick." She flipped the picture onto the table. "Fish and Wildlife can have it. I don't want it."

The photo spun on the smooth surface of the table and ended up in front of Tommy. He took one look at the jawless and pawless two-days-dead bear carcass and scrambled back, almost knocking over the chair. He all but ran for the door. With his hand on the knob, he turned. "Uh, thanks for the cake. It was great. I've gotta go."

The door slammed behind him, leaving a startled silence. "What was with him?" Laurel tucked Tommy's chair under the table.

"I don't know. When you mentioned the dead bear, I thought he was going to be sick; then he positively ran away from the picture." Julie glanced at it. The photograph was gross, but she wouldn't have thought it would make a kid like Tommy run from the room.

"I know how he feels. This is the first time I've looked at it since I picked it up from the developers." She reached for the photo and stuck it into an envelope. "That was one of the worst days of my life. I shouldn't have just dumped it in front of him. He seems like a really nice person."

Julie nodded absentmindedly. He did seem like a nice guy, but the more she saw of Tommy Oshikawa, the more she was sure David was right. Tommy was in some sort of trouble. It must be something that scraped his nerves raw—why else would he react so strangely to the photo? Julie reached out to clear the plates from the table with a sigh. Whatever was troubling Tommy, he'd done her a favor. His arrival had distracted Laurel from grilling her about David. And anything that took Laurel's mind—and Julie's traitorous heart—off of David Hales was a blessing.

Nine

≈ ≈

THE NEXT MORNING DAVID WAS RUNNING LATE AS HE biked across town toward the Big Foot office. For the last month he'd been extra careful never to go into the office when Sheryl was there alone. Brent had noticed and thought the situation was hysterically funny. David, on the other hand, was not amused.

He'd done his best to discourage Sheryl's interest in him. He'd even gone so far as to go out of his way to avoid sitting by her at church. But it hadn't seemed to help much. Sheryl still was more interested in chasing him than in pursuing God.

Then there was Julie.

Julie he'd *like* to sit next to at church, but she treated him like he had some dreaded disease. He was half tempted to ask her exactly what it was about him that she found so repulsive—but then, he'd have to catch her first. The woman jumped and all but ran from the room—or the pew, or *whatever*—when he came around.

Why do I always get attention from the wrong women?

He shook his head. *Lord, give me a break here, will you? She's driving me nuts. I can't get this woman off my mind.*

Brent had called last night and said he was going to ask Julie to help David out with the French climbers. David smiled and picked up his pace. At least he would be with her today. Meeting Julie might be the best thing that had come out of his trip to Canada…if he could only get her to *talk* to him!

Jesus, I can't explain it. She just… gets to me somehow. Working out with her was just plain fun, but being with her had come to mean a lot more to him than just a pleasant time. Julie Miller just might be the person with whom he wanted to spend the rest of his life. They shared so many values and passions. At least, he thought they did. And if he was right, she would fit in so well with his tentative ideas concerning how he could use his climbing skills to honor God. So why couldn't he get her to stay in the same room with him without looking like she was going to bolt? He shook his head again, his hands tightening on the handlebars of his bike, fighting the frustration that wanted to build inside him. *Patience, Hales. Give it time.*

If only he thought time would make a difference.

I've got my doubts, God. Big ones. But doubts didn't seem to temper the longing growing deep within him…the hope that wherever God led him, he and Julie would be together.

There had been those few times when she'd seemed to relax. At those times, he was sure she liked to be with him. And there was the way her eyes sparkled when they talked…. A couple of days ago, he'd been spotting her when she was bouldering. She'd slipped and fallen into his arms. The connection had shot through him like an electric current. She'd stayed there for a second, her slight body beneath his hands, eyes wide and dilated. Then she'd jumped back and practically scrambled for safety.

He'd let her go, though it was the last thing he'd wanted to do. Every instinct screamed to tighten his grip, to hold her until she stopped fighting him, to lower his head and—

A blaring car horn brought David back to the immediate, and he looked up in time to see a car heading for him. Clenching his teeth, he pedaled furiously and swerved, barely avoiding being turned into a grease spot on the road. He pulled over to the curb to catch his breath and slow his pulse. Glancing back, he saw that he'd been so deep in thought about Julie that he'd run a stop sign.

"Brilliant, Hales. Just brilliant."

He put the bike in motion again, schooling his thoughts to stick to matters at hand. The situation with Julie was simple. He just had to give her time to be comfortable with him as a friend. He would wait and pray. In the meantime... well, in the meantime, it made him happy just to be around her.

"David!" A man's voice with a strong French accent greeted him as he walked into the office.

"Jacques! Nicole!" David greeted his friends from his climbing days in Europe with startled recognition. Jacques grabbed him by the shoulders in an affectionate embrace. "What are you doing here?" David switched to fluent French. *"Que faites-vous ici?"*

"Coming to climb with you." Jacques grinned. "I heard that Georges and Gilbert were coming here, and Nicole and I decided we must come too. We have missed you at the competitions. Franz has been winning everything with you gone."

As soon as Jacques let him go, Nicole embraced him warmly, kissing both his cheeks. "You must come back. With you gone, there is no one who tends to our souls."

David laughed and stepped back. "You never listened to a thing I said."

"True. But still I miss my vicar." She tossed her head. Talking at once, she and Jacques filled David in on the news of climbers he knew. Georges and Gilbert walked up and joined in. David smiled. It felt good to be with his friends again, and yet... for all that he'd missed them, he didn't feel that he *belonged* with them anymore. His goals were different now.

Over Nicole's head David saw Julie come through the door. She hesitated as she took in the roomful of noisy French conversation. Quickly David introduced her, but she still seemed ill at ease. Though David stayed with English, the others soon switched back, and it was obvious that Julie didn't know French.

David felt bad for her, but he couldn't do much about including her with Jacques, Nicole, and the others so eager to speak in their native tongue. They were good friends, and they had come halfway around the world to see him. He relaxed a little when he saw Georges walk over and begin to talk to Julie in English.

Nicole drew his attention when she put her hand on his arm, talking away about a climb she and Jacques had just accomplished. David turned to focus on her. *Give it a rest, Hales! Julie can take care of herself. Stop worrying about her.*

It was just too bad he couldn't seem to take his own advice.

Julie stood by the office door watching the others. She couldn't understand what they were saying, but the woman who'd been introduced as Nicole had her hand on David's arm. Blond and very pretty, she gestured extravagantly with her other hand as she talked. He was smiling straight into the woman's eyes. David really did have one of the nicest smiles Julie had ever seen....

One of the men had come over and was trying to talk to her in slightly stilted English, and Julie tore her attention away from David to smile at him and try to listen. At least he could do a lot better in her language than she could in his.

That bright, windy day was a long one for Julie. Most of the conversation was in French. Everyone but her seemed to be at home in two languages, probably more. Canada was supposed to be bilingual in French and English, but her dad, like most western ranchers, didn't think much of the way Quebec tried to push the country of Canada around. French wasn't even offered at the rural high school she'd attended, and she'd avoided it in college. When she realized what an asset knowing more than one language was for a guide, she'd tried to take German by correspondence, though without much success.

Not only were David and the others more sophisticated with languages, they were also very sophisticated climbers. Julie felt like a poor country cousin. She'd never been out of North America, and these people were citizens of the globe. David fit right in. She did not.

Late in the day, Julie heaved a sigh of relief. They

were almost ready to leave. She'd be free soon....

From what? an inner voice prodded.

She frowned. From feeling like a fifth wheel. From feeling stupid. From watching David and Nicole laugh and climb together like they were a perfectly matched set!

"Julie?"

She turned, startled. Nicole stood there, looking beautiful and sophisticated, a warm smile on her face. "We have asked David to come and eat dinner with us in Calgary and would like you to come too."

Great. Just what she needed. *More* time to watch David and Nicole together.

"I don't want to intrude. You all knew each other climbing in Europe."

"Oh no." Nicole waved her hand, shooing off Julie's excuse as if it were a pesky fly. "David did not know Georges or Gilbert very well before. You would not intrude at all, eh? I have enjoyed getting to know you a little."

Someone called Nicole's name, distracting her and saving Julie from having to answer right away. Brent liked it when his guides spent time socializing with the clients. If she didn't go with them, he'd be on her case, and David would wonder why she wouldn't come. Julie sighed. It seemed she had no choice.

Tommy turned up at the end of the day with the

van. Julie and David were loading ropes and gear into the back when Tommy came up to them. "David, are you free tonight? I really could use some company."

"I'm busy, Tommy, but you're welcome to come with us. Nicole, Jacques, and the other climbers have asked us to come eat with them. You have to drive us into Calgary anyway. If you're too broke, I'll pay for the meal."

Julie watched Tommy hunch his shoulders. "Thanks, but I can't. See, my uncle is supposed to meet me at the Palliser Hotel, and I..."

To her ear, it sounded as if Tommy was almost afraid of his uncle. Well, an evening with Tommy's scary uncle sounded better than hours of feeling like an unsophisticated bumpkin. She put a climbing rope into the back of the van. "I can come with you if my company will do."

Tommy brightened instantly. "That would be great!"

David looked at her, about to say something; then he clamped his mouth shut. In Calgary, when she didn't get out at the restaurant with David and the others, there was a chorus of disappointment. Julie made her excuses, saying maybe later in the evening she'd catch up with them. Everyone waved as they pulled away, and Julie let out a huff of relief. She turned and smiled at Tommy.

"It's you and me, pal." And that suited her just fine.

At the Palliser Hotel, Tommy and Julie sat in the lobby waiting. Tommy fidgeted constantly as he watched the door.

"You're not looking forward to this, are you?"

"No." He made a wry face. "I've never been very comfortable with my uncle. Most of the time he lives in Japan. He is very traditional. He's really my father's uncle, and he runs the family."

"He runs the family business?"

"That too."

Julie laughed. "We used to have a neighbor kind of like that."

"I doubt it. Honoring your elders and family solidarity are longtime Japanese traditions. Even my dad thinks the way North Americans are into individual rights is disgusting."

"And you?"

Tommy frowned. "I don't know. Sometimes I think my dad and uncles are right, that it's just plain selfish and decadent to put your individual interests first. Other times I feel so pressured that—" Tommy stopped midword and jumped to his feet. Julie looked up to see a compact, well-dressed man striding toward them. Tommy's uncle. It had to be.

He held his head at an arrogant angle, and his eyes were direct and hard. Stopping squarely in front of

Tommy, he gave a very small bow. Tommy bowed more deeply and indicated Julie.

"Uncle Atsuko, this is Julie Miller. Julie, this is Mr. Atsuko Oshikawa. Uncle, Julie is with us tonight because my job requires me to make sure she returns safely to Canmore. I have invited her to eat with us."

Uncle Atsuko gave Tommy a look that would have melted steel, then turned his eyes on Julie. For a second she thought he was going to order her away. She could see now why Tommy had wanted company. The man seemed incredibly overbearing. *You've only just met the man and yet you've passed judgment on him?* Julie's conscience reprimanded, and she felt her face flush. Maybe she misunderstood. She bowed timidly, hoping an attempt at Japanese manners might ease things. Atsuko Oshikawa looked past her as if she weren't there. At the table he continued to ignore her, talking to Tommy in harsh-sounding Japanese. Julie sighed. It seemed to be her day to feel ignorant.

Mr. Oshikawa ordered without questioning either of them. Taking the menu from the waitress, he jabbed a finger at a meal and ordered three. The conversation between Tommy and his uncle had heated up. It didn't seem like she was much help to Tommy after all.

The food arrived, and Julie dug in hungrily. At least she was going to get a good meal out of the evening. She noted that Tommy had stubbornly said the same phrase several times, and each time his uncle's response got louder. The last time the older man leaped to his feet and made some sort of pronouncement. He stood there straight as a ramrod, glaring at Tommy until the boy slowly lowered his head in acquiescence.

Mr. Oshikawa sat down and ate rapidly and neatly. Tommy tried to say something to Julie, but his uncle cut him off. Tommy said a quick impatient phrase, and for the first time his uncle really looked at her. There was a moment of silence; then the older man said, "Tomosuke tells me that it is his job to be polite to you. Please forgive his rudeness in bringing you to this meeting."

Julie blinked. It took her a second to realize that "Tomosuke" must be Tommy's Japanese name; then she just managed to stop herself from blurting, "Tommy's rudeness?" Luckily the man didn't seem to expect an answer. A few minutes later, he got up abruptly, paid the bill, and left.

Tommy slowly let out his breath. "He's not actually such a bad guy. I mean, he really does want the best for our family. He was right. I shouldn't have asked you to come. He said it was inappropriate for me to have brought a woman to our meeting."

"Is he still living in the Stone Age?"

"No. It's just another way of looking at things. In Japan, generally men are friends with men, and women

142

with women. Each stays in their own sphere."

"So he wasn't trying to be rude." Julie looked after the man, leaning back in her chair. "It's hard for me to understand even a little bit how different the world must look through your uncle's eyes. No wonder David said it's hard for you to live in two worlds." She studied him for a moment. "So what was the argument about, or don't you want to tell me?"

Tommy shook his head. "You said your parents didn't want you to be a guide. How did you get them to let you do what you wanted?"

"They didn't really try to make me change my mind. They don't try to control my interests—or my life."

"I thought maybe you would know a different way of doing things." Tommy had slid way down in his chair.

"What do you mean?"

"My family expects to run me like a puppet, even when I *hate* what they have me do." He spoke so vehemently that he literally bounced in his chair. "The thing is, I don't like the way a lot of my friends have it, either. They don't really have family at all, just one or two parents who don't care what they do. I used to be jealous, but so many of them are kind of lost, rootless. You seem different."

Lord, help me to get this right. "What is your family like?"

143

Tommy crossed his arms tightly, and Julie could swear he shivered. "It's huge, and everyone is supposed to work together for family wealth and prestige. It's really political. The pressure makes me want to scream." He gave a little snort of laughter. "At least I'm not rootless. Don't you have powerful uncles, grandparents?"

"It's not like that." Julie paused, trying to find the right words. "I am different than a lot of people because I do have a big family to work for and answer to, but it's not a family based on human descent. It's God's family— the church. Dad and Mom and I all agree. Our real family isn't only blood relatives like yours. We're all part of the group of people that have given their lives to God through Christ. As an adult, I don't answer to my parents so much as we all answer to Christ."

"Do your parents actually do that? Leave you to make your own choices as long as you follow your God or whatever?"

Julie laughed. "No, but I think they try. I mean they are my parents, after all. They raised me with boundaries and all. I knew what lines I could and couldn't cross. And I knew they did what they did for my own good. I mean, I had to learn what was right and wrong. Now that I'm an adult, they try to be more hands-off. They still give me advice, and I can tell with Mom especially that she really wants to tell me what to choose sometimes. Neither of them liked it when I left college to train to be a guide, but they supported me anyway. They just want me to follow God and be happy."

And, of course, to get married and give them grandchildren. Her throat closed on that thought, but she swallowed hard and continued. "Even if my parents hated what I was doing, if I was sure I was following God, if I prayed and read the Bible and talked it over with people I knew who listened to God and followed him, I wouldn't stop. My folks might be mad at me, but I believe God would work in that situation and bring us to peace. As long as I was honoring him—and them— as best I could. And I would still be part of the family of God, so I wouldn't be alone."

Tommy shook his head. "I don't get it. David talked to me about the family of God thing, and I didn't get it then either, but I still think you've had it good." He banged the table with his fist and stood up. "We'd better go or we're going to be late picking up David and the others, and I've had enough yelling to last me awhile."

Over the next week, the conversation she'd had with Tommy kept replaying through Julie's head. She prayed for him often, aware each time that David was praying for him too. Very early on Friday morning, Julie was reading her Bible and found herself thinking about that conversation again. She looked out the window at high clouds flushed with the sunrise. Actually, talking to Tommy had been a good reminder. No matter what happened, she wasn't really alone. She still had a family—the family of God. Friends who cared about her and prayed for her...friends like David, whose eyes lit up whenever they saw her....

Julie slammed her Bible shut and reached for her jogging clothes, but David's image wouldn't leave her alone. She'd worked out with him twice that week. The shape of his strong hands, the way his hair curled on the nape of his neck, and especially the direct kindness in his eyes—these things were like a hook that had caught somewhere deep inside her. They tugged relentlessly, hurting her heart and spirit in ways she just didn't understand. Well—she jerked on her jogging shoes, pulling angrily at the shoestrings—according to what she'd told Tommy, she and David were sister and brother. She'd just have to keep it that way—or risk an even deeper hurt when he finally turned away from her. Like Kurt had.

On the way back from her jog, she detoured to stop by the Big Foot office. Rolf hadn't had any work for her that day, and no hikers had called. Usually Sheryl called if Big Foot unexpectedly got any work for her, but it wouldn't hurt to stop by and ask. It was still early. David might be there just starting the day. Julie found herself going faster, then deliberately slowed down. The morning wind lifted her hair. She relaxed and turned her face into it. It seemed like a touch from God's hand. How could anyone miss God's love exhibited in nature?

As she neared the office, she saw David's bike out front. She hesitated and started to turn away. Stomping her foot, she turned back again. This was stupid! She could hold her composure while training with him. It was silly to miss the chance of a day's work, however slight, just because the man was in the office. Julie lifted her chin and marched through the door.

"I'd show you around Calgary." The low, purring voice was Sheryl's. She was leaning across her desk toward David. Brent stood to the side, a wry smile on his face.

David looked up at the sound of the front door, and his face lit up with a welcoming smile. "Julie!"

"Hi, David. Sheryl. Brent. I came in on the off chance you might have some work. I don't have anything booked for the next couple of days."

"We don't have anything."

Julie wondered if she was imagining the cold hostility in Sheryl's manner.

Brent nodded. "I told David to take some time off and look around Alberta. Sheryl was just offering to show him Calgary." There was laughter in his voice, and

Julie gave him a puzzled look.

David stepped away from Sheryl's desk. "What I'd really like to see is some of the whole western scene. Cowboys, ranches, rodeos, and all that. All the tourist information is full of it."

Brent grinned broadly. "Well, then, isn't it lucky for you that our sweet little Julie is the proverbial ranch woman?"

Julie was stunned at the venom in the look Sheryl shot Brent, but before she could say anything, David gave her a grin.

"Ranch woman, eh?"

Brent was on a roll. "Oh, yeah! She grew up on a ranch." He slapped his palm to his forehead. "Hey, here's an idea. Julie, you and David both aren't working today. Take David to see your folks' place. You told me before that you could take clients on rides there if I needed you to. So why not show David the sights?"

David shook his head. Ignoring the others, he looked straight at her. "Sorry, Julie. I had no intention of putting you on the spot like this."

Julie swallowed hard. Everyone was looking at her. She tried to think of an excuse, but David's eyes seemed to block rational thought. Besides, it would be fun to show him her home. Just a brother, a good brother—that's how she needed to think of him. She lifted her chin. "It's no problem. I'll call Mom and Dad and see if it's okay, but I'm sure you'll be welcome. I could come by your place and pick you up in an hour."

"Are you sure?" David's intent gaze didn't falter, and Julie hesitated. Was that a challenge she saw reflected there?

"Of course she's sure." Brent was playing the jolly organizer to the hilt. "She wouldn't have said so if she wasn't. Now get going, you two. And don't do anything I wouldn't do out there—" he took their hands in his and led them to the door—"all alone—" he shoved the door open with his foot—"just the two of you."

Julie opened her mouth to tell Brent what he could do with his comments, but he cut her off by shoving the two of them out the door. Taken by surprise, Julie stumbled and fell against David, whose arms came around her protectively.

Brent beamed at them from the doorway. "There, now, don't they make a cute couple?" He directed the question at Sheryl, whose only response was to glare at them all from her desk.

If looks could kill, Julie knew she'd be six feet underground. *Come to think of it,* she thought as she stepped back out of David's arms, dismayed at her reluctance to do so, *that might make life a whole lot simpler!*

As Julie walked in the front door, Laurel looked up from her computer. "I thought you were going to pick up some milk on your way back from your run this morning."

Julie stopped dead. "Milk!" She'd completely forgotten. "I'm sorry."

Laurel laughed. "What happened to give you that glassy-eyed look?"

"I just invited David Hales to come out to Mom and Dad's place for the day."

"What?"

Julie circled her friend. "Don't you start getting ideas. I was railroaded into it. It would have looked really stupid and rude if I hadn't invited him."

"David railroaded you?"

"No, Brent did. Excuse me, I've got to call Mom." Julie went to her room and flopped onto her bed, reaching for the phone on the nightstand. Listening to the phone ring, Julie could clearly picture her parents' house. When her mom answered the phone, Julie felt a joyful lift.

"Mom, did I tell you about David Hales, the British guy that's working for Big Foot now? Anyway, he'd like to see a ranch, and both of us are free today. Would it be okay if I brought him home? We'd get there just after lunch, probably go for a ride and stay for supper."

"Of course, Julie. You know you're always welcome to bring friends home—anytime."

Julie hung up the receiver with a smile on her face.

Tommy had been right. As far as family went, she was lucky. When it came down to it, did anything feel as good as home and family?

Not much, her thoughts agreed. *Except, of course, for being in David's arms, safe, protected, held close to that broad, solid chest—*

"Arrrggghhh!" Julie grabbed her pillow and pulled it over her face. "I give up!"

But even as she said it, she knew it wasn't so. She wouldn't—*couldn't*—let down her guard with David. No matter how appealing the idea—or the man—happened to be.

Make me strong, Lord, for both our sakes. Please?

Silence was her only answer.

Ten

HE WAS NERVOUS. HE COULD HARDLY BELIEVE IT, BUT HE was nervous! The last time he'd felt this way had been at his first major climb. His stomach was clenched into knots, his hands were clammy, and he could feel the sweat on his brow.

This is just a visit to a ranch, for Pete's sake. It's not like she's invited me home to meet her parents!

But she had, hadn't she? It was her parents' ranch, after all....

"Ahh!" He threw the pen across the room and stood, pacing from one end to the other. What he needed to do was stop thinking about this—about her—so much. What he needed to do was focus on his life and where it was going, with or without a certain woman...with eyes that seemed to look right through him and hair the color of polished walnut and skin that smelled like a spring day after a rain....

"Stop it!" He threw himself into a chair, covering his head with his arms. Arms that had held her less than

152

an hour ago. The contact had been brief, but it had taken all his control to let her go.

Julie hadn't said a lot since she picked him up, but David didn't mind. After the battle he'd just gone through with his emotions, the silence was a relief. Besides, Julie seemed happy enough, just thoughtful. David studied her surreptitiously. He liked being near Julie, watching her drive. He even liked her untidy little car. David shook his head. A man had to have it bad when his affection spilled over onto a woman's vehicle.

Deliberately he took his attention off Julie and focused on the scenery. It wasn't hard to do. He'd never been in a place quite like this. The rolling landscape gave the impression of limitless space. Toward the west, the hills folded into higher ridges, then into jagged peaks, but here the shape of the land resembled gigantic, rounded ocean swells.

"We're almost there." Julie turned onto a gravel road. "This is Dad's land on the north side of the road. See the cattle on that ridge? They're ours."

David looked, then blinked. "Those tiny dots are cattle? How far away is that ridge?"

"A couple of miles."

"All your dad's land?"

"No, some of it is lease land owned by the government,

but our family has held the lease for three generations now, so it feels like ours."

The wide valley was furred with tufted grass that flowed up the hills into the dark stubble of evergreens. Lighter aspens filled some hollows. David could see that at the bottom of the valley lined by silver willow brush a bright stream sparkled. "That looks like a perfect trout stream."

Julie gave him a quick look. "Yeah, fishermen come into our pastures sometimes. There's some pretty good native cutthroat trout. Do you fish?"

"Dad tried to teach me to fly-fish, but it never really took. He would love this place. Did you have any idea how lucky you were to grow up here?"

Julie slowed the car and turned onto a smaller road. "No, not really. I think every kid thinks the way they grow up is normal. It wasn't until I left and tried to live in the city that I knew. It's hard to imagine growing up in suffocating apartment blocks the way so many kids do. Just living in the dorm on campus nearly drove me nuts."

David laughed. "Wild woman of the hills, are you?"

Julie gave him an intent glance, then turned her face away as if he'd said something hurtful. David thought it over but could find nothing offensive in his comment. They rode in silence for some moments; then Julie pointed. "See the buildings there, down past the ridge? That's the main yard."

It still looked to be a quarter of a mile away when Julie suddenly slowed. There was a group of glossy-coated horses not far from one side of the road. She rolled down her window. Looking at the animals, she yelled what sounded like, "Caa-boe-ee!" in a rising intonation.

The horses threw up their heads and watched with pricked ears. "Caa-boe-ee!"

Trotting, then breaking into a full gallop, they raced the car toward the ranch buildings. Julie laughed, clearly delighted. "That'll save us a long walk. I don't think I'll ever get tired of watching the horses come in."

He could see why. The animals were beautiful. Their tails were flying high, and they bucked and kicked as they ran. "Um, Julie, I haven't ridden much—well, not at all actually."

Julie threw him a wicked grin, and David suddenly wondered exactly what she had in mind. "What are you going to do? Put me on some bronc for a truly western experience?"

"Who, me?" Julie's eyes twinkled. "See that buckskin on the left? He's Denver, Dad's old roping horse. You can ride him."

"Buckskin?"

"Yeah, the tan horse with a black mane and tail. See, the one that just kicked out? He's real gentle."

"Kicking like that, he really looks it." He glanced at Julie. Was she serious?

155

Julie laughed. "No, really, he is gentle. You'll see."

"I bet." David leaned back, smiling. He wouldn't mind if the horse was a little spirited. He liked a challenge. *As evidenced by your choice in women, eh?* The thought spurred a snort of laughter, which he quickly curtailed at Julie's curious look. Before she could ask him what was up, he nodded at the horses. "What was that you yelled to call the horses?"

"Come boy." Julie laughed. "It doesn't sound much like it anymore does it? That's how Grandpa used to call horses, and everybody has since. I guess we've only kept the parts that are easy to yell."

"I'll have to practice."

They were pulling into the farmyard. Compared to farms he'd been to at home, this place looked new, wild, and vastly oversized. Julie jumped out of the car. "I'd better give the horses some oats first since I called them in." David got out of the car and watched her duck into a shed, then emerge carrying two big plastic pails filled to the brim with oats. She only came up to his collarbone in height, but she carried those pails easily and went in among the milling horses with complete confidence.

"Hey, who are you?"

David turned to find himself looking at a towheaded boy who seemed to be about five or six years old.

"David Hales. I came with Julie." He put out his hand. After a moment of hesitation, the boy stood up very straight and shook David's hand.

"I'm Nathan Miller. I guess you're okay if you came with Julie." He ran off, almost colliding with an older woman.

"I see you've met Nathan." The woman dusted off her hands on her pants. "I'm Hanna Miller, Julie's mom."

David shook her firm, work-hardened hand. Hanna Miller was a slender, tall woman with a lived-in face. His strongest impression of her was one of serenity.

"Julie told us she wanted to take you riding."

"That's right. It's kind of you to let me come on such short notice."

"Julie is always welcome to bring friends." Hanna looked at him with obvious curiosity. He found himself standing straighter, hoping her first impression of him would be as positive as his of her. "She said you were from Britain?"

David smiled. Julie had remembered not to say England. "That's right. Scotland, actually. I came here to see another continent and to do some thinking."

Just then Julie joined them. Dropping the buckets with a clatter, she gave her mother a hug. "Mom, this is David Hales, but I bet you've already introduced your-self." She turned to David. "Mom never stays strangers with anyone for long, but you probably already figured that out. She is the most amazing woman. Mom does all the financial work for the ranch and puts up a huge garden each year." Julie gave her mother a smile, but—David noted, a bit surprised—it seemed more forced than affectionate. "All that in addition to being the most perfect, gentle, and caring wife and mother alive."

Was he imagining it, or was Julie's tone almost bitter? Apparently he was right because Hanna reacted to it as well. "Julie, that's silly. I'm a perfectly ordinary human being."

"Ha! David isn't ordinary, either. He's one of the top sport climbers in Europe. He's a strong Christian and as kind as they come—" Julie stopped, then shook her head. "Excuse me, I'm going to get the halters."

David watched her walk away. Her description of him had held the same bitter edge as her description of her mother. *Lord, what is going on in that beautiful head?*

"Have you ridden much before?" Hanna's question broke the awkward silence.

"No." He had to make an effort to take his attention off Julie. "Not at all actually, so this should be interesting to say the least."

"Treat the horse the way you'd treat a three-year-old child, with calm authority, and you'll be just fine." Hanna had a very nice smile. The old saying that one should look at a woman's mother to know what she'll be like came back to David. If Julie was going to be like this lovely woman, whoever spent his life with Julie would be a lucky man.

Julie came back carrying what looked like a tangle of rope. She held out part of it to him. "Here, this is Denver's halter. Mom, we'll be back early enough so that I can help you with supper. Come on, David." Julie opened the gate into the corral. As soon as he was inside she pulled it shut again.

Nathan ran up and wiggled through the fence. "Who you going to ride, Julie?"

She smiled at him. "You figure I can take Dot?"

Nathan hopped from one foot to the other. "Can I catch her for you? Please? Please?"

"Maybe you'd better help David. He can climb sheer cliffs, but he's never ridden a horse before. I figured he could ride Denver."

Nathan turned wide eyes on David. "You really never rode a horse before? I have! Lots of times. Come on. I'll help you."

A small hand grabbed his and towed him eagerly in the direction of the buckskin horse. Denver moved off a few steps, then turned to face them. David paused, very aware of the creature that was looking back at him through big, dark eyes.

"Come on!" Nathan tugged on David's hand. "Denver won't put his head down for me, so you've got to put the halter on him. See, you just put that strap part over his nose and do the other part up around his neck. Not that way!"

The horse's mane was unexpectedly rough and warm under David's hand as he tried again. "Like this?"

Nathan nodded, then again began hopping from one foot to the other. He suddenly ran for the fence, slid through, and disappeared in the direction of the house. When David turned, Julie met his eyes, laughing.

"Nature calls?" David raised an eyebrow.

"Looks like it."

"He's cute. Is he your little brother?"

"My cousin, but he'll be out here all summer. You've got the halter twisted." She led her horse over, and with a few deft movements, straightened Denver's halter. They were standing very close together. Suddenly David was aware of nothing except Julie's closeness. She looked up at him. He reached out and gently stroked the smooth line of her cheek.

Julie's eyes closed, and for a second she let her head rest against his hand. Then her eyes snapped open, and she jerked back. "Come on, we'd better get the horses saddled." Her voice was unsteady.

David took a deep breath and tried to steady himself. Her skin had felt cool and smooth—and he *knew* she had been as affected by the contact as he. He clenched his teeth. *Lord, I know I'm supposed to give this woman time, but even you have to admit she's straining my good intentions!* He drew in a deep, calming breath. Giving her time was one thing, but his temporary work visa would run out at the beginning of September, which didn't leave a lot of time for...for...well, much of *anything*.

She walked away quickly, leading her mare. The colt danced alongside his mother. David shook his head and followed Julie out of the corral.

"Tie up your horse right here." She indicated the spot next to her mare on a hitching rail. She wouldn't meet his eyes.

The colt pushed in between Julie and the mare. He planted himself in front of Julie, ears flat back against his skull. Julie laughed and swatted his behind.

"You think that Dot belongs to you. Well, I'm going to ride her whether you like it or not, so you might as well get used to the idea."

"He's coming with us?" David tied Denver where Julie had indicated.

"Sure, Dash is more than a month old. It'll be good for him to tag along with his mother. We won't be near traffic or anything. Look, I'll saddle my mare first so you can watch and see how it's done."

The whole time Julie was saddling her mare, the colt kept trying to interfere. Watching her deal with the colt made David smile.

"This is one thing you certainly do better than me."

She gave him a quick smile that was like a flash of sunlight. "About time, isn't it? You've been showing me up for months."

161

He protested, but she only laughed and came to help him saddle his horse. Julie seemed so relaxed with him now. As long as he kept things platonic, she was willing to be good friends, but that wasn't all he wanted. She had responded to him for a moment, so she obviously wasn't indifferent. Well, there was only one way to find out what was going on.

"Julie—"

"Come on, David, let's go." She swung onto her horse.

He stared up at her, fighting the urge to reach up and pull her back down, into his arms, where he could hold her still while he demanded some answers. Of course she'd respond to that.... *Yeah, probably by smacking me right between the eyes.* He sighed and turned to his horse. He might as well just enjoy being with Julie and trying something new. He clambered onto Denver's wide back. It was an odd feeling, sitting on top of the beast. As they headed out into the open country, Julie told him how to direct the horse. Both of them laughed when he overdid his command for a turn and Denver spun so quickly he almost left David behind. They started up a long hill. Little Dash lived up to his name with spurts of speed as he circled the two older horses.

"You know, you're catching on quickly." Julie took her mare out in a wide circle, trotting. The colt pranced alongside with his tail in the air. As Julie came back toward David, she dug her heels into her mare's side, and the horse burst into a gallop. "Kick him in the ribs, and hang on!"

Without giving himself time to think, he did it and grabbed onto the saddle horn as Denver accelerated with powerful lunges. Catching his balance and the horse's rhythm, David whooped with excitement as Denver passed Julie's mare. Laughing, David looked back and caught Julie's exultant grin. She yelled and leaned forward. For a few seconds, the horses raced side by side.

"Okay," she called over the sound of pounding hooves, "slow down. Sit up and pull back on the reins, firm but eas—"

The horse literally sat down and slid. David lost one stirrup and ended up with his face in the mane. Julie, slowing down more gradually, looked back and laughed. "Never do anything by halves, do you?"

Denver stood stock-still with his ears back. He turned his head and gave David a look. "I don't think the horse thinks much of my riding ability."

"He'll survive."

"How long have you known how to ride, Julie? You seem so completely at home on a horse."

Julie gave him a startled look. "I've never thought of myself as a horse kind of person. Not like my brother, Ben. But I can't remember when I didn't know how to ride. One of my first memories is sitting in front of Dad on Twister. I felt so high up and important. You know, Tommy said I was lucky to have the family I've got. He was right."

"Tommy was talking to you about family?"

Julie nodded. The horses were walking quietly side by side now. "I think his uncle wants him to do something Tommy doesn't like."

"I wondered, but then I thought maybe he's just having trouble figuring out who he is with the two cultures."

"I think it's something else, too. He said you'd told him about being part of the family of God and that he didn't understand when you talked about it, either. We'll have to keep praying for him."

Her fine-featured face was intent with concern for Tommy. A feeling of something close to jealousy welled up in David. He wanted Julie to care about him that way—no, that wasn't quite true. What he wanted was for Julie to belong with him, be connected to him, emotionally and spiritually. He swallowed hard against the emotions churning through him. He'd never felt this way before, never known the intensity of longing for one woman, wanting her to look at him—only him—with eyes filled with love....

Jesus, help me.

"For I know the plans I have for you—" the verse rang

strong and true in his mind, his heart——"*plans to give you hope and a future.*"

He closed his eyes for a moment, then nodded. It was in God's hands.

"David?"

His eyes opened to find Julie watching him, uncertainty etched on her features.

"Are you okay?"

He smiled. "Yeah. I'm fine." He looked around them and felt his smile widen. "Who wouldn't be on a day like this?" He might not know the answers to his dilemma with Julie, but he was certain how to handle Tommy's situation. "How would you feel about praying for Tommy?"

Those beautiful brows arched, and her mouth tilted in a smile. "Now? Here?"

"Now. Here."

"So long as we can pray with our eyes open." Julie's smile widened. "Both Denver and Dot are gentle, but I'd rather not ride with my eyes closed."

She was right. Just as they finished, a couple of grouse flew up almost under the horses' feet. Both the colt and mare shied, making even the calm Denver jump. Julie rode it out easily, but David found himself off balance and grabbing the saddle horn. Once again, Denver stopped and gave David a disgusted look. Julie laughed. "Come on, I want to show you where I started climbing."

A few minutes later, they tied their horses. Immediately the colt pushed in and began to suckle, his fuzzy tail twitching. David watched Julie scratch the little horse's back. The tenderness in her expression moved him deeply. She looked up, caught him watching, and blushed.

The words came out before he could stop them. "Julie, have I hurt you in some way?"

"No! It's not you, David." Her answer was so vehement it made the colt jump. "Just don't expect too much of me, please?" The near desperation in her eyes as she turned away pierced his heart.

Jesus . . . Jesus . . .

It was all he could think to pray. Thankfully, he knew it was enough.

Julie led the way downhill and across a little creek to a granite outcrop. Slipping out of her boots, she climbed barefoot, moving fluidly up the rock. David couldn't remember her sequence of moves at all. He'd been too distracted by watching her move to remember where she'd put her hands and feet. Still, she was beckoning. Quickly he pulled off his shoes and followed.

"Hey, that's a completely different way." She studied the path he'd climbed. "I'm going to try it."

This time he managed to pay attention to her climbing technique as she moved down the face and then up again. She was grinning as she came up to him.

"I like it! That's a great route."

"You climbed that beautifully, Julie. You're not going to have any trouble with any 5.11 for your guiding test."

"You think so?"

"I know so."

Her eyes studied his for a second; then she slid back over the edge. "Come on, I'll show you a different place."

David shook his head. *She's like a shy wild creature. God, keep me faithful to your timing, your ways.* They spent the rest of the afternoon bouldering on the rock face, and when it got hot, splashing in the creek.

As they rode into the yard, the first thing David saw was a huge, slanted trailerlike thing loaded with bales of hay. A solid man who looked to be in his fifties was unloading the bales one at a time. Nathan trotted at his side. Julie stopped her horse beside them. "Dad, this is David Hales. David, Gordon Miller, my father."

Julie's father looked at David with obvious interest and nodded. "Good to meet you."

"Dad, what on earth are you doing? Why are you unloading by hand?"

"The unloading thing broke!" Nathan's high voice cut in. "It screeched like a dinosaur and smoke came out. We're going to fix it, though."

"I guess that about explains it." Gordon chuckled. He knuckled the top of Nathan's head.

"Could I be of help?" David dismounted.

"If you're sure you want to. There's a pair of gloves in the tractor, so you don't tear up those tender hands."

"Tender hands? I don't think so. David is a climber, remember?" She dismounted and took Denver's reins. "David, you can stay and help Dad. I'll put the horses away."

"Us guys will take care of it," Nathan called after her, and everyone laughed.

Left with Julie's father, David found himself fighting a sudden case of nerves. He began to help unload bales with a vengeance. Gordon Miller seemed to be watching him, sizing him up. The bales weighed about seventy pounds, but Gordon moved them easily. David had a bit of trouble until he was able to copy Gordon's technique. Sweaty and covered in bits of hay, the two of them moved the last bale into a long hay shed.

"Well, you can work hard in any case." Gordon was breathing hard, but there was a smile on his weathered face.

"He moved bales even faster than you!" Nathan piped. "He's not puffing, either."

Gordon laughed. "I should have known better than to try to keep up with a young buck."

"Do you always work that hard?" David wiped a little sweat from his brow with his sleeve.

"Just when the machinery won't work for me." He

168

leaned against a post of the hay shed. "So, David, tell me about yourself."

As he did so, David could tell Julie's father felt that he and Julie might be interested in each other as more than casual friends. All David could do was answer his questions openly and hope that Gordon Miller was right.

Eleven

~~ ~~

AS JULIE SAT AT THE SUPPER TABLE THAT EVENING AT HER parents' house, she fidgeted in her chair. Her parents were getting along well with David. Too well. Both had speculative gleams in their eyes. Julie wanted to shout at them to stop it, but she remained silent.

Her mother poured Nathan some more milk. "So what have you enjoyed most about Canada, David?"

"It's been interesting to see another continent. I love the open spaces, the scope of the place. But what have I enjoyed most?" He hesitated. "One of the best things about coming here has been meeting Julie."

Julie nearly spilled her drink. Soft soap didn't seem David's style, yet here he was talking as if he were full of blarney. Julie looked up just in time to see a pleased and significant glance pass between her parents.

This was crazy! She had to get them on another subject. "Um, Dad, did you and David get the hay stacker fixed? What was wrong with it anyway?"

"It was a bearing!" Nathan was clearly thrilled. "It was all burned up, really neat! David let me help him get it off the machine." He ducked under his chair and held up a blackened metal object. "See."

"Nathan!" Julie's mom scolded. "You take that outside right this instant."

"Uncle Gordon said I could have it!"

"I didn't say you could bring it in the house." There was laughter in her father's voice. "Do as your aunt says."

Nathan left with a pout, but finally the attention had shifted from her and David. For the rest of the meal, without too much effort, Julie was able to keep the conversation on the ranch operation. After supper, Nathan pulled at David's hand. "Come on, I want to show you some neat stuff."

Julie smiled as she watched them head out. David's dark head was bent low to listen over Nathan's small, blond one. Then she followed her mother into the kitchen to help with the dishes. Mom asked several questions about David that Julie answered monosyllabically. She had never talked with her mother about her relationships or her feelings about her boyfriends. It was just too uncomfortable, especially now. She was fairly sure how her mother would react if Julie told her she simply wasn't cut out for marriage. Better to keep that part of herself hidden, the way an injured dog hides in a corner. Her mother gave Julie an intent look and changed the subject.

Julie heard David and Nathan come back inside

just as she and her mother finished the dishes. Her mom went into the living room and sat down, obviously expecting Julie to follow suit.

Julie followed her into the living room but remained standing. "I hate to break up a pleasant evening, but I need to get back."

"Not yet!" Nathan's face fell. "I didn't show David the cool snakeskin I found."

"Maybe he'll come back another time." Hanna stood up.

David got up quickly, and in minutes he and Julie were on their way back to Canmore. "That was a great day, Julie. Thank you. I like your family."

"You were super with Nathan."

David laughed. "He reminds me a little of my nephew. Thank you for sharing your home." He turned and looked at her, started to say something, then fell silent. She was terrified that David would say something about being more than friends or ask her why she'd said not to expect too much of her. Instead he just concentrated on driving. She was both relieved and disappointed. She looked over and noticed that his hands were clenched into fists so tight that his knuckles were white. He seemed to be praying. The big question was...for what?

Julie and David were supposed to get together on Thursday to train. She was gone until Wednesday working on a three-day hike for Rolf. Several times Wednesday night, Julie almost called David to cancel. It was getting too difficult to be near him. Yet she couldn't stay away. It was as if David Hales were some kind of addiction.

Alone in the apartment Wednesday evening, Julie flopped onto her bed. She stared at the ceiling as if she could find some sort of answer there. It just wasn't fair. "Why did you make me who I am, God? Why couldn't you have made me more like Mom or Laurel or Amber for that matter?" Warm tears tracked back toward her ears. Julie rolled over and pounded the pillow. "If you were going to make me as a risk taker, the kind of woman who did things women don't usually do, why didn't you just make men disappear from my life? Why must I be tortured by David's friendship?!"

Julie felt like a corked bottle full of rage. She reached for the information on the rock-guide test. It started in two days in British Columbia. She'd be there for six days of rigorous examinations, doing everything from rescue scenarios to complicated leading on multi-pitches. She *had* to keep training to be ready for that. She couldn't fail. With tears stinging her eyes and her anger subsiding, she finally asked God for help.

She heard the apartment door slam. "Julie?"

"Up here, Laurel." She wiped at her face hastily to get rid of any traces of tears.

There was a light staccato of feet on the stairs, and Laurel was at her door. "We've got a lead on the poachers. The same truck has been seen in the vicinity of several kills."

"Great!" Julie made an effort to forget her own struggles and focus on what Laurel was saying. "Have they traced the vehicle yet?"

"Not yet. No one got the whole license down, but it's a brown Ford pickup crew-cab."

"Do you know how many brown Ford pickups there are in Alberta? My dad has one. Big Foot has one. There must be hundreds of thousands."

"It's better than nothing, and they do have a partial license-plate number. That narrows it down a little. The RCMP are going to do a computer search. Hey, how was your day with David?"

"Great."

"If it was so great, why do you sound like you just lost your best friend?"

"Maybe I did."

"What?"

"Never mind. It was a stupid thing to say. I just booked my rock-guide test for Friday."

"All right! You'll do well." Laurel sat down on the

chair by Julie's dresser. "Now, back up a minute. Why did you say you lost your best friend?"

Julie looked at Laurel. The woman was a pit bull. Oh, well. She'd been holding things in long enough. Maybe talking about it would give her a better perspective. Julie coughed and looked down, tears welling in her eyes. "I'm mad at God, okay? I haven't told anyone, not even my parents." Julie took a deep, ragged breath. "I told you I was engaged before, right?"

Laurel nodded. "You said you broke it off."

"I couldn't do it." Tight with unshed tears, her voice came out in a squeak. Julie swallowed hard and tried again. "Kurt was a great guy. A super Christian man, but I couldn't stand it. I'll never be able to get married."

"What are you talking about, Julie? You're a great person."

Julie pounded her pillow. "I just couldn't stay in that little house working at the stupid bank. A whole life of being Kurt's good little wife working in that little hardware store was *not* my idea of wedded bliss. He wanted me to quit climbing, quit taking risks, and be there for him all the time. He said any Christian man would expect the same thing. I've thought about that a lot, and I think he was right."

"Julie, that's crazy. He was trying to stop you from being yourself. No man who really loved you would do that. Sounds to me as though Kurt wanted you as sort of a possession. He wanted to make you into some kind of Barbie-doll wife."

Julie took some more deep breaths and managed to get a bit of control. "Kurt is a good person, really. I just couldn't fit in as his ideal wife, no matter how much I wanted to." She took another shaky breath. "I'm not sure I can fit in with anybody. It's not that I don't think wives can do things. Amber is going to marry Ben, and she's a doctor, but... Oh, I don't know! Even in high school and junior high, guys were turned off when I didn't hesitate to do something that they were scared to do or if I would compete with them. And when I beat them, well, I might as well have kissed dating good-bye. Let's face it, my temperament is all wrong for being someone's sweet little wife." She looked up and met Laurel's stunned gaze. "But what I want to know is if God made some people to stay single, why doesn't he take my ache away?"

Julie felt Laurel's arm come around her.

"You told me I was being stupid about David Hales. Laurel, I'm not being stupid. I think with Kurt I was just glad some man was interested in me, like it made me an okay person, normal. With David, it's different. He is so amazing. I don't want to end up hurting him the way I hurt Kurt. David's really great. He's everything a woman could possibly want in a man. He's sure the most dynamic person I've ever met, but it's just going to end up in pain. Why do men and women have to be attracted to each other? Why can't we just be...I don't know, around each other without getting all confused?"

"We should be neutered, like angels?" Laurel gave her a wry smile.

"Yes!"

"Actually, I kind of like men the way they are, and I'd rather not be neutered. Thank you very much."

"It's different for you. You're gentle, motherly, and all that."

Laurel laughed. "I don't know about that. Julie look, God made you who you are on purpose. He didn't make you a misfit. I think you're being way too hard on yourself."

Julie just shook her head.

"I don't know for sure if I'll ever get married either, but that's not all there is to life."

"I know that. Why do you think I'm working so hard on my guiding?" Julie sighed. "God made me what I am. I might as well make the best of it." She stood up abruptly. "Sorry for dumping on you. Promise you'll never tell David what I said."

Laurel hesitated.

"Please! I couldn't stand it if he knew."

"Okay, but I think that David might have some things to say to you if he knew how you were feeling."

Did Laurel really think that marriage was possible

for her? Laurel wasn't stupid. She had listened to Julie's reasons and wasn't convinced. A tiny glimmer of hope fluttered in Julie's soul. She quashed it, though. Hope only made things harder.

"Promise?" Julie put her hands on her hips.

"I promise." Laurel grinned.

"What's so funny?"

"We sound like two junior high kids."

Suddenly seeing things from Laurel's point of view, Julie giggled. "You're right. The trouble is I think I'm more confused now than I ever was in junior high. David Hales puts me off balance. I hate it."

"Hate him?"

"Yes! No, I don't hate David. I just hate what he does to me."

Laurel laughed. "And what is that?"

Julie gave her a loud raspberry and headed for the door. "I'm going to find something to eat. Come on, you must be hungry too."

A few minutes later, both women were sitting at the table in the kitchen eating nachos and salsa.

"Oh!" Laurel said with her mouth full. "I forgot to ask you. The pastor called. He asked me if a couple of us would do something with the teenagers. You know the church is too small to have a youth pastor, so he wanted us to organize some stuff. Seth suggested rafting. He works for a rafting outfit and thought he could get us a deal. He'd need two other adults to go along. Want to do it?"

Julie smiled. "Sounds fun."

"He says he can fit us in a week from Saturday. You'll be back from the test by then. Are you booked that day?"

"It's open so far. I'll book it. It'll be fun to go rafting together." Julie got up and gave Laurel a quick hug. "Thanks for being a friend, even if I act like a hysterical teenager."

"That's okay. You're worth it."

The next evening, Julie trained with something close to fury. David was friendly and supportive, but their conversation stayed strictly on climbing. Fighting tears, Julie pushed herself even harder. Climbing at her limit, she fell off a tiny pinch hold and ripped the little fingernail on her left hand nearly off. Dripping blood, she dodged David's concern.

For a moment, she thought she saw a flash of something in his eyes...anger? Frustration? But it was gone before she could be sure. Instead, he gave a rueful—albeit somewhat forced—laugh. "You're a tough one, aren't you?"

Julie lifted her chin in defiance. "Yes, I am. I'll manage just fine, thank you."

Quick color filled David's face, and his jaw hardened. When he spoke, his tone was controlled. And glacial. "Glad to hear it." She caught her breath, amazed at how much the distant, cold tone hurt. She opened her mouth to apologize, but he cut her off. "Now, if you'll excuse me, I'd better gather our gear."

He turned and walked away with long, determined strides, and Julie swallowed hard against tears that she didn't fully understand.

Drawing a deep breath, she went to find a first-aid kit. What a liar she was! She wasn't a "tough one"—not even close. But she couldn't admit that...not to David. Not to anyone. Better to keep up the front than take a chance on being hurt.

Tears rolled down her cheek as though to mock her. *Don't get hurt, eh? What do you call the way you're feeling now?*

Her left hand quivered with pain as she started to wrap the finger. Suddenly a broad, strong hand came over hers. She looked up to find David watching her, his eyes dark and unreadable.

"Sit down, Julie. I can do this."

His hands were so gentle as they took care of her injury that Julie could hardly bear it. She shut her eyes and clenched her teeth. If he looked up and noticed, hopefully he'd just think her reaction—and her tears—were from physical pain.

"You're going to be taking the rock-guide test with an injured finger."

"Don't you think I can do it?" She fought to keep her voice steady.

"You can do it, all right." Had that been a grudging admiration in his voice? She opened her eyes. David's strong, gentle fingers were just finishing a very competent dressing. He turned to her, his expression somber. "I'm sorry, Julie. I shouldn't have gotten frustrated back there."

She shook her head. "No, it was my fault."

He smiled suddenly, and a gentle laugh escaped him. "You're something else, you know that? As for whether or not I think you can do the test with an injury, well, as far as I'm concerned, you could do just about anything you decided to do, Julie Miller." He looked down at her hand, still held firmly in his. He reached out a finger to touch the back of her hand gently. The contact shot through her like an electrical jolt. He looked up to meet her mesmerized gaze. "I've climbed with hands torn up worse than this. You'll do just fine."

"Thanks," she managed to gasp, grateful her suddenly weak knees were still holding her upright. He let go of her hand then, and she followed him to gather their gear.

It wasn't until they were back in Canmore, outside

of his place, that he dropped the bombshell.

"Oh, Julie, thanks for the wedding invitation."

"What?"

"I got the invitation to your brother's wedding in the mail today."

"You did?" Julie's thoughts whirled, and she spoke them out loud without thinking. "Mom did that! She got them to send you an invitation. She's trying to—" She'd almost blurted out that she thought her mother was trying to pair them up. Why else would Mom have gotten Ben and Amber to send him an invitation? Julie felt her face flush hot with shame. What must David think of her and her family? "David, you don't need to come."

His steady gaze never faltered. "I'd like to come. That is, unless you don't want me to."

What could she say? Julie stammered that he was welcome and watched with a feeling of numb confusion as he walked away from the car. Laurel, her mother, Ben, and Amber—her dad, too, probably. It seemed like everyone who cared about her was pushing her toward David Hales. She gritted her teeth. She'd told Tommy Oshikawa that she'd do only what she thought was right and that she wouldn't be separated from the family of God, but now that whole big family was pushing her. She knew exactly how Tommy must feel.

Well, maybe Tommy couldn't talk back without

getting into big trouble, but she could, and she'd start with her parents. Instead of going back to the apartment, Julie turned and drove southeast, toward home. When she stopped for gas, she telephoned Laurel. "I'm on my way home. I need to get some things straightened out with my parents before I leave for the guide test."

"Oh, okay. I'll be praying for you. I might not see you before you leave."

"Thanks."

It was well after midnight when she got home. Julie had cooled down a lot by then. Her parents wanted only her happiness. Mom didn't know what she was going through. Everyone liked David. It was hard not to. He was a remarkable man.

So remarkable you'll do almost anything to avoid him.

"Shut up," she muttered as she opened the front door and went inside.

The house was dark and quiet. Julie crept up to her old room. Her mom kept her bed made up just in case. She gratefully climbed in between the warm flannel sheets and was asleep in seconds. She didn't wake until midmorning. Glancing out the window, she saw her mother walking toward the chicken house with a slicker pulled around her. The loose wisps of her hair whipped around her face in the wind.

After a quick shower, Julie headed for the kitchen.

Coming back in the door with a basket of eggs, her mother yelped and nearly dropped them. "Gracious, Julie! I didn't know anyone was in the house. What are you doing here?"

"Mom, why did you get Ben and Amber to send David a wedding invitation?"

"Oh, I see." Mom put down the eggs. "Come sit down, Julie."

As soon as they were seated on the old couch, Julie fixed her mother with a look. "Well?"

"You think we're trying to encourage a match between the two of you?"

"What am I supposed to think? What other reason could you have?"

Hanna smiled at her daughter. "Julie, honey, David and your dad were talking while they unloaded that hay. For some reason, Gordon ended up telling David about Ben. I think from what he said, David had asked him whether you had any siblings. After talking about Ben and Amber, it just seemed natural to invite him, so Dad did that. The invitation was just formal notice of what your father had already said."

It made sense. Julie sighed. "I guess I was jumping to conclusions and talking without thinking again. Am I supposed to bring David when I come the day before for the rehearsal?"

"It wouldn't hurt. Ben wants you to bring Richard

too. You know how unreliable Richard's vehicles always are."

Julie laughed. "I do." Richard was a good friend of Ben's who lived in Canmore. He and Julie were both in the wedding party.

Hanna touched Julie's arm. "To be perfectly honest, I was happy to see you enjoying yourself. David seems like a good man, a fun person who loves God, but I won't push you. I'm not going to make the same mistake again that I made with Kurt."

Julie gave her mother a hug. "I'd better get back. I'm leaving for the rock-guide test. It's really tough, more than a week long, and we have to demonstrate competence in every area—from first aid to leading multipitch routes. Pray for me, okay?"

"I've been praying about that for you, Julie. I'm sure you'll do well. Oh! There's something else that I wanted to tell you. I told your father about the talk we had, you know, when I told you I'd wanted to fly. You know what Gordon did? He bought me flying lessons. I'm starting right after Ben's wedding."

Julie laughed and swept her mother into another hug. "That's fantastic! Tell Dad for me that he's a great man."

Mom smiled almost shyly. "It's nothing really. I have a full life here, but you know, I'm really looking forward to it."

The door flew open, and a small blond missile shot into the house. "Aunt Hanna, Julie's car is—" Nathan's eyes got wide at the sight of her. "How come you came home, Julie? Is David here? He was neat."

Julie smiled. "No, David is not here, and I came home to talk to my mother."

"Oh, that's okay, then. Can I have a cookie?" He grabbed one and ran back outside.

"He doesn't sit still for a minute, does he?" Julie laughed.

Hanna laughed too. "You were worse. You still don't sit still." She gave her daughter one last hug. "I'm sure you'll do well on your rock-guide test. Now get going."

Twelve

"JULIE MILLER," THE MC ANNOUNCED. "YES!" JULIE LEAPED high into the air. People cheered and whistled for her as she'd done for them. Quickly she sobered and walked to the front for a handshake. "Congratulations, you're an official rock guide."

After more than a week of testing, days of grueling work and anxiety, she had done it. Finally the relaxed ceremony was over. The people who had passed and the guides who had tested them milled together in an exuberant group. Julie congratulated others, laughing and exchanging high fives. All of them grinned with the joy of having accomplished something very difficult.

Julie hesitated, catching Lisa's eye. One of the women she'd tested with had failed, and now she was crying. Julie swallowed hard, suddenly very aware of those whose names hadn't been called. Almost half the people who had tested with her hadn't passed. She could've easily been in the same boat. Lisa turned away and walked toward the door. Julie hurried after her and caught her arm. "You'll make it next time."

"I don't know, maybe, but thanks for all the times you tried to help. You were awesome. You deserved to pass."

Julie shook her head. Without David's help in preparing, she would have never made it. Over and over the things she'd learned and rehearsed in those hours of training had helped her to excel. *Thank you God!* She hadn't voiced that prayer aloud, but suddenly she remembered David telling her how he'd decided to honor God no matter who he was with. Why not?

"It was only with God's help that I passed, Lisa."

Lisa turned to face her, frowning. "You're crazy. Your passing had a lot more to do with your own effort than any God."

"Oh, I worked hard, but it was still a gift. God gave me the ability, the chance to learn, and…oh, just everything." Julie hesitated, then pulled her New Testament out of her pocket. "This is my most important piece of equipment. It keeps me safer than any anchor I put in a rock face."

Lisa stepped back and looked hard into Julie's eyes. "You actually mean that, don't you? Maybe I ought to check it out. It sure didn't do you any harm."

"Do that. He loves you too." Julie gave her friend a quick hug.

Julie could hardly wait to tell Laurel the great news. "Laurel!" She slammed the apartment door. Only silence answered her. She frowned. Laurel seemed to be gone more and more. Hopefully there wasn't more trouble with poachers. Julie ran for the phone to call her parents. She was about to burst with excitement. She hung up ten minutes later with their happy congratulations echoing in her ears. Mom had been almost as excited as Julie was.

Julie reached for the phone again, then jerked her hand back like she'd been burned. More than anything she wanted to call David, but she just couldn't. Quickly she dialed another number. "Brent, I did it. I'm an official rock guide."

"Oh?"

"Aren't you going to congratulate me?"

"Congratulations."

"What's the matter? You sound like your favorite cat just died."

"Tommy left a message on my answering machine, said he's quitting and leaving Canmore."

"Tommy is quitting? Why?"

"I don't care why. He seemed reliable at first, but lately he's been more and more strung out. I need a driver. He can't do this to me. Do you have the phone number of the place he's staying at in Canmore?"

"No. Don't you? You must have to call him at home sometimes."

"It's somewhere in the office. I went and looked, but I can't figure out Sheryl's system and she's not home. I can't get it from directory assistance, either. It's listed under his roommate's name, and I don't remember what that is. I found his parents' number, though. I was just going to call them to get his number. He should stick around at least until I can find another driver. He can have his nervous breakdown or whatever then. I've got calls to make. Bye."

"Brent, wait!" Julie tried to stop him, but the phone went dead. She stared at the receiver in her hand. If Tommy had left, she didn't think he was going to like it if Brent told his folks, not the way he'd been talking about his extended family. Julie shut her eyes and prayed for Tommy, wherever he was.

When she finished praying, the temptation to call David was even stronger. David would want to know about Tommy. In fact, he probably had Tommy's phone number. Julie jumped up and paced the floor. She wasn't so sure it was a bad thing that Tommy had quit. Brent was hardly a good influence on a young, impressionable boy. But from what Brent said, Tommy had been upset. She bit her lip. What if Tommy was in some kind of trouble? Maybe David could help. There was already a bond between the two of them, and David really cared.

190

Julie clenched her teeth and reached for the phone. So what if she was mixed up about David Hales? Tommy needed help. The phone rang three times. *Come on, David, answer the phone.* She was just about to hang up when there was a clatter and thud on the other end. "Hello?"

Just hearing David's voice sent a wave of happiness through her. In spite of herself, she smiled. "Do you always answer the phone by throwing it on the floor?"

"Julie!" He laughed. "I knew you'd be back today. I was hoping it was you, so I bolted out of the shower and fumbled for the phone. Hey, how did the test go?"

The joy in David's voice made her heart pound. "It went really well. I passed."

"Good! I knew you would. Congratulations!"

"I couldn't have done it without your help. Thanks!"

"You would have found a way."

"Well…that's not the reason I'm calling. I just found out that Tommy quit. Brent is looking for him to try to make him come back to work until he can find another driver. He can't find Tommy's phone number, but I thought maybe you—"

"I don't know that I'd try to talk him into going back to work for Brent."

Julie shut her eyes. It was like she and David thought on the same wavelength. "I know what you

191

mean. That's his choice and no big deal either way. It's just that Brent said Tommy was really upset, and you and Tommy have been talking. I mean, he talked to me a little but probably not as much as with you."

"Right. I'm not going to call him. I'll go over to his place."

"I'll be praying."

It wasn't raining anymore, but there was a sharp, damp wind as David headed out the door. Julie's last words were still in his ears. Knowing that she was praying for him and Tommy gave him a confidence that was very close to elation. They were working together to help Tommy. *God, please open Julie's heart to—*

He stopped suddenly, stunned by what he'd been about to pray. Open Julie's heart...to my love. A rush of emotion swept over him. *God—* He drew in a steadying breath. *Jesus, is this for real? I—I love Julie Miller?*

The answer rang from deep within him, and he couldn't stop the grin that suddenly broke out over his face. "I love Julie Miller." It wasn't a question this time. It was a fact. He was as sure of it as he was of his own existence. He laughed, lifting his face to the overcast sky. "I love Julie Miller!" It was a proclamation, a joyous announcement to anyone who cared to listen.

He nodded, breathing the crisp air deeply, feeling such joy that he could barely contain it. More than anything, David wanted to work as a partner with Julie, not just tonight, but for the rest of his life. And as soon as God opened the door, he planned to tell her so. But for now…

He got on his bike. For now he needed to concentrate on Tommy. And on what God wanted him to do for the troubled young man. Peddling his bicycle in the late summer dusk, David tried to focus his prayers on Tommy Oshikawa. In a few minutes, he was knocking on the door of Tommy's basement suite. Tommy's roommate, Jeremy, came to the door. Jeremy washed dishes at one of the restaurants in town. He had told David he was into mountain bikes and snowboarding, but as far as David could tell, he partied more than he did anything else.

"Is Tommy home?"

Jeremy nodded. "Yeah, he's on the phone."

David walked into a room in complete shambles. A couple of big boxes on the floor were half full. Two suitcases stood by the bedroom door. Tommy was standing rigidly, almost as if he were at attention as he held the phone. Twice he started to speak in Japanese and stopped again, as if he'd been interrupted.

David looked at Jeremy. "Who's moving?"

"Tommy, and good riddance. I was getting pretty

weirded out by how he was acting. I've already found another guy who wants to move in tomorrow."

David knew from his own experience that cheap housing was scarce in Canmore. He wasn't surprised that Jeremy had found another roommate so quickly. Tommy snapped out two sentences, then stood listening, his jaw clenched. David could tell when the other party hung up because Tommy's shoulders suddenly slumped. Moving like a very old man, he hung up the phone and sat on the couch. He didn't seem to see anything that was in the room and gave no indication of recognizing David.

"Julie told me you've quit your job with Big Foot." David sat down beside the boy.

Tommy answered in a monotone. "I have to work until the end of the month. Something else will be arranged by then."

"You told me you were leaving tonight." Jeremy sounded less than pleased. He was standing in the middle of the room with his hands on his skinny hips. He tossed his hair out of his eyes. "Nothing against you, man, but I got somebody coming in here tomorrow."

Slowly Tommy looked up and made an obvious effort to focus on Jeremy. "I told Brent I was quitting today. I *wanted* to go now." The desperation in Tommy's voice made David ache for him. "I wanted to be gone from Canmore, from my parents, from my uncle, from

Canada. But they won't let me go yet. I have to wait."

Jeremy's face wrinkled with exasperation. "Hey, I feel for you. I do, really, but you can't stay here."

Tommy sat immovable with his head hanging.

David cleared his throat. "You can come to my place. It's tiny, but you're welcome to stay. I should be able to fit in a bed for you on the floor."

"Great idea. I'll even take you over there in my car." Jeremy started dumping things into the boxes. Tommy continued to sit like he was made out of wood while David and Jeremy packed around him.

It was the same at David's tiny one-room suite. Jeremy dropped David and Tommy off and shoved Tommy's stuff onto the sidewalk. Tommy walked in empty-handed and sat in the ancient easy chair while David carried in his gear. After the second load, David stopped in front of the seemingly comatose young man.

"Tommy, get it in gear."

The boy looked up at him and blinked. David indicated the door.

"Your stuff is out there, Tommy. And while I don't mind helping, I'm not inclined to carry it all in for you."

A quick flush filled the young man's face, and he jumped to his feet. "I-I'm sorry."

David reached out to put a hand on Tommy's shoulder, giving him a reassuring squeeze. Tommy nodded and together they went to bring in the rest of his things.

As he brought in the final load, David glanced at Tommy, who was now sitting on the bed with a glassy-eyed expression. "Have you talked to Brent? Does he know you'll be working until the end of the month? He'll be looking for another driver."

Tommy's head jerked up. "No! He can't! I have to stay. Where's the phone?" David indicated the phone only feet away on the wall of the tiny kitchen. Tommy's hands shook as he dialed. "Brent? I'm glad I caught you. My uncle told me you'd like me to work for a couple more weeks. I'll work for you until the end of the month, okay?"

Even across the room, David could hear the stream of curses Brent poured into the phone.

"Look, have I ever missed picking someone up or getting them where you wanted? I've done a good job for you." Tommy's voice was so tense it was almost falsetto. "Let me stay until the end of the month." Tommy sighed. "Okay, I'll be there tomorrow morning to pick up the Alpine climbers from the airport." He hung up the phone and returned to slump on the chair.

David realized very quickly that asking Tommy questions was futile. Tommy's mind was off somewhere else entirely. The boy stumbled into bed, rousing long enough to make sure his alarm was set early so he could pick up Big Foot's clients. David had given Tommy the only bed. David lay on the floor in his sleeping bag with his eyes wide open. Tommy's passivity worried David. Was the boy suicidal? How could he watch Tommy all the time? Should he cancel the church rafting trip that he'd told Laurel he'd help out with?

The next morning David woke to hear the shower running. Maybe Tommy would go to work and he could go rafting with Julie. David swung out of bed and put cereal and milk on the table.

Tommy came out of the bathroom with a towel around his middle. "Thanks for helping me last night." He didn't make eye contact, and his voice was flat. David's heart sank. The boy didn't seem much better than yesterday.

David gestured toward the table. "Come have some breakfast."

Tommy simply sat and ate silently, almost mechanically.

David found that his fists were clenched. He unclenched them and sat down. *If God needs me here to help this boy, then I'd better be here.* "Is there anything you want to talk to me about?"

Tommy kept his head down. "Nope, I've got to get to work."

A few minutes later, the door closed behind Tommy. "God, I want to reach him with your love, but thanks for giving me this day with Julie."

Maybe today she'd open her heart to him.

Thirteen

JULIE PARKED HER CAR AND WALKED TOWARD THE CHURCH. Yesterday's rain had washed the sky clear. It was a still morning, promising a perfect day. Laurel had come into the apartment late at night and left early, so Julie didn't get a chance to talk to her. There'd been a note on the kitchen table: "Sorry I can't come rafting after all, but I found someone to sub for me." The smiley face above Laura's signature made Julie uneasy. Laurel wouldn't have called David, would she?

Julie had her answer when she pulled into the church parking lot. There, leaning against the church, was David's bike. Julie spun on her heel to leave. With her hand on her car door she stopped, swallowed hard, and turned back around. They needed two adults to come along, and she had said she'd come. She took a deep breath and walked toward the church building. At least she'd be able to ask David what had happened with Tommy.

Several of the kids greeted her before David saw her. At the sound of her voice, he turned around. He had such a great smile. "You know," David said as she drew near, "we ought to take these kids climbing some Saturday." Her gaze met his, and she paused, startled. There was something...*different* in the way he was looking at her. She couldn't put her finger on it, but for some reason, it made her even more nervous than usual.

"That would be awesome!" Tim Brown, who was twelve, couldn't contain his excitement. Most of the others chimed in, except for Brenda, a very prim sixteen-year-old. "Count me out; rafting is scary enough. The only reason I'm here today is because Chad wanted me to come." She gave one of the older boys a sugary smile that made Julie want to gag.

David laughed. "So if Chad asks you to come climbing, will you?"

"Oh, I don't know. Maybe."

It was amazing the amount of noise twelve teenagers could make in a van. David seemed to be in the center of the action. Secretly watching him in the melee, Julie smiled. He was so great with these kids.

They piled out in the parking lot by old school buses with rafts tied on top. Seth came out to meet them. As he explained the safety rules, there were a few minutes of relative quiet. Julie thought of asking David about Tommy, but David was obviously listening intently to the instructions.

"Okay." Seth closed his notebook. "You've all heard the rules. It's gonna be one wild ride. If anyone doesn't want to go, now is the time to speak. Once you're on the raft, the only way out is through the rapids. Is that clear?"

He got a chorus of answers from the kids and some wisecracks about chickening out.

"Cut it out, guys. Not going along is a choice. No one needs to be ashamed. Everyone on the face of the earth has some things they'd rather not do, and this is supposed to be fun. Last call. Any takers?"

None of the kids backed out. At the end of the talk, yelling kids piled into the bus. Laughing, Julie turned to David. "Have you ever done this before?"

"No. You?"

Julie nodded. "It's fun!"

The look in David's eyes was disturbingly tender. Julie felt herself blush. She tried to focus attention away from herself. "Did you find Tommy?"

"He's at my place. He seemed—" A loud wolf whistle sounded, and Julie looked up to see most of the kids grinning at them out the bus window. "We'll have to talk later." David turned and walked to the bus. "Okay, okay, we're coming."

He took the bus steps in one bound and knuckled Tim on the head. Several kids yelled for him to sit with them. Two girls called out to Julie. Within minutes she had heard all about their most unreasonable social stud-

200

ies teacher. At least that's how those two girls saw things. Julie smiled, remembering feeling exactly the same way.

It seemed to take no time to get to the place where they were to put into the river. David and Seth slid the raft off the top of the bus while Julie got the kids into life jackets. Seth had on a wetsuit and a form-fitting jacket, but she and David wore the same oversized jackets the kids did.

"David, you gotta come up here!" Two of the boys yelled at him to sit in the front of the raft. Julie grinned knowing that the fronts of the two pontoons were the wildest spots to ride. David was about to receive a serious dousing—and Julie was just glad she was there to see it! From the sound of it, quite of few of these kids had been rafting before. They were edgy and excited. David straddled one pontoon. The kids were shying away from the front of the other pontoon so Julie happily took that spot. She loved a wild ride.

"I hope you two are ready for this." Seth moved the raft into the current.

"Here it comes. Here it comes. Here it comes!" Tim Brown chanted.

"Shut up, Tim. I'm scared enough already." Brenda's voice shook. She grabbed at Chad's arm.

"Don't hold onto me. Hold onto the rope like Seth told you!" Chad shied away from her.

"That's right. Everybody hang on." A roar was building ahead of them. Julie could see a haze of spray in the air after the first big hump of water. Seth held the raft sideways in the current, timing it just right so that the front slid smoothly into the vee of water that fed the center of the rapids.

Julie whooped as she and David swung high into the air. The raft pitched up over the first haystack. Knowing what was coming, she clenched her fists on the ropes and held her breath. The front of the raft plunged down, going completely underwater. Ice-cold water slapped Julie from head to foot, and she yelled and looked at David as they came up. Their eyes met, and with identical grins they hit the next haystack. Kids were screaming and laughing behind them. Two more wild bucks; then the raft bounced through milder rapids and out into calm water.

Julie shook the water out of her hair, feeling it come unplastered from her head. It was probably sticking straight up too, but she didn't care. Wet, David's hair curled even tighter. His eyes were snapping with fun.

"Like it, guys?" Seth slapped the raft and was answered with a loud chorus of approval. Only Brenda was silent, clutching the rope with white-knuckled fists.

"Can I get off? Please?" Brenda's voice was so quiet Julie barely heard her, but before she could answer her, Seth did.

"Nope, you got on; you've got to ride it out. Look up. Can you climb those cliffs?" At Brenda's miserable shake of her head, Seth's voice gentled. "You'll be okay. Sit in the bottom, and hold on. I haven't lost anyone yet."

Brenda gulped and nodded, but she still looked terrified. She wasn't even flirting with Chad now, which told Julie just how frightened the girl was. As for Chad, well, he looked a bit worried too. The noise of another rapid began to build ahead of them.

"Brenda, listen." David spoke calmly. "Who made the river?"

"God." Brenda said in a small voice.

"Can he handle it?"

She nodded.

"Ask him for help, then, and remember, he's no small friend. Chad couldn't stop a storm or empower you to walk on water, but Christ did both."

There was a ghost of a smile on Brenda's face. Then she shut her eyes tight, obviously praying. The roar of the rapids was very close. "All right, guys!" Seth worked to get the raft in position. "Let's ride God's roller coaster!"

This time the entry was in a four-foot drop. The raft twisted and bent as it dove over the edge. Julie rode out the wild bounce. This time David yelled with glee, and again their eyes met. Julie couldn't stop the laugh of pure joy—though she didn't know what thrilled her more, the rapids or, for the first time in her life, finding someone who enjoyed the wild side of God's creation as much as she did.

As they piled off the raft at the end of the run, shivering and laughing, Tim pointed to the right. "Hey, what's that?"

"A sweat lodge!" Chad rubbed his hands together. "Warmth! I'm ready."

There was a six-foot-high rounded heap of what seemed to be spruce branches. Wisps of steam smoked up into the blue sky. The man that had driven the bus down had obviously gotten it ready for them. Julie turned to Seth. "I didn't know you guys did this."

Seth shrugged. "It's standard procedure. I've seen rafters come out of the river an interesting purple-blue color on a windy day. Besides, the owner is kind of into native religion, or at least thinks its a drawing card." Seth grimaced. "I didn't tell the bus driver not to make it, so he must have just gone ahead. I hope that's okay."

"As a warm-up, it looks good to me."

David said something about food offered to idols as they ducked through the tiny door.

"So are we going to do native chants or something?" Chad grinned. "They did that the last time I was in a sweat lodge."

"Hey, we're here to honor God, not do pagan rituals." David frowned at Chad.

"But sweat lodges are supposed to be good. You know, they sweat out the bad in you and make you pure. This guy came and told us all about it at school. He called it spirituality."

Julie could see the confusion on Tim's face. "You mean you think this is bad, David?"

David laughed. "Sweating isn't bad, and I love being warm after all that cold water, but I don't think any amount of steaming in the dark is going to make me a better person before God. How about you?"

"No, I guess not."

Another voice said, "It's only Jesus' blood that can really make us clean."

Julie turned to Brenda, surprised at the girl's sudden fervor. Brenda looked almost as surprised as Julie that she'd spoken up, and she glanced at David. When he nodded, she went on.

"I learned something about how strong Jesus is today too. I mean, if I can trust him to take me through that insane river you crazy people dragged me through..."

Everyone laughed. Julie quit shivering and could feel sweat starting to trickle down her back. "I don't know about you guys, but I'm hot enough." She ducked outside and closed her eyes, turning her face so she felt the cool wind sweep across her. It was gentle and exhilarating all at once. She gave a small laugh. That was a feeling she was coming to know well, that off-balance, love-it-hate-it feeling.

That was how she felt every time she was near David.

Her eyes snapped open at the startling thought, and she found herself staring into David's thoughtful eyes. He must have followed her.

"You know it's all the way around the northern half of the globe." David rubbed his arms.

"What is?"

"Sauna, sweat lodge, banya, whatever you want to call it. People do it right across Siberia and into Scandinavia. I didn't know there was a North American tradition as well."

Julie laughed. "Some days I think you sound like a walking encyclopedia." He knew so much and was always interested in things, always learning, nothing like the small-town kids she'd grown up with. "Did I actually hear you say, 'food offered to idols,' when we were going into the sweat lodge, or was that my imagination?"

David grinned, wiping the sweat from his brow. "You heard that, did you? Check out Romans chapter 14."

The kids poured out of the lodge. "Eew, Chad, you're all sweaty." Brenda dodged Chad as he tried to put his arm around her. Chad lunged at her playfully, and she dodged again, but this time she ran into Julie, knocking her off balance.

Before she had the chance to think, strong arms caught her and held her fast. Julie looked up, and David's tender grin took her breath away. He lowered his head slowly, and Julie thought her heart would stop. Was he going to kiss her? Right here?

But his lips stopped next to her ear. "I think you should tell Brenda she doesn't know what she's missing, don't you?" The whispered question sent shivers soaring through Julie. Before she had a chance to pull away, he simply set her back on her feet and stepped back, that infuriating, teasing smile still in place.

Tim and some of the younger kids were racing for the bus, and with a mock bow in her direction, David whooped and went to join them. Back at the church parking lot, kids scattered in all directions.

"Come walk with me so we can talk?" David laid a hand on Julie's shoulder.

She swallowed hard. He probably only wanted to tell her about Tommy, but she found that her heart was pounding. "I want to get home and get changed."

"Okay, I'll come over in half an hour." David got on his bike and pedaled off without giving her a chance to refuse. Forty-five minutes later they were walking along the bank of the Bow River.

"I read Romans 14." Julie clasped her hands in front of her. "You figure the sweat lodge would only be a problem to someone who saw it as a pagan act of worship?"

"Something like that." David stared intently at her as she spoke. His gaze never left her face.

"You were going to tell me about Tommy."

David gave her an odd look, then blinked as if he were snapping out of a trance. He inclined his head. "That was one of the things I wanted to talk to you about." He pulled himself together. "I think Tommy quit because he wanted to run away from his family. They insisted he stay here and finish out the month. Tommy says they'll let him go after that." David kicked a fist-sized rock ahead of him. "Julie, it's almost like they are blackmailing him in some way. The idea that Brent might not keep him on for that long had him close to a panic."

"I don't see why keeping Tommy working for Big Foot should be such a big deal to them."

"Neither do I."

They walked together in silence, river-smoothed pebbles scrunching under their feet. Julie was almost painfully aware of David beside her, as though she were standing too close to a fire after being sunburned. Her every nerve ending seemed to be alive and sensitized to his warmth, his easy stride, his very presence.

"You know, today confirmed something for me that I've been thinking about over the last month." David flipped another pebble into the air with his toe. "I told you I came to Canada to think about what God wants for me?"

Julie nodded. "Because you were afraid climbing was becoming an idol."

"That's right. I've been thinking about a way to use climbing in God's service." He gave her a quick glance, then looked away again. "I think I'd like to run an operation kind of like Big Foot but have it focused totally on Christ and advertised that way. I mean, even today we saw how the power of God's creation affected Brenda, how it made her feel small and afraid. And then how it turned her awareness to the One who created it, the One who was there to protect and help her." The passion in his voice stirred Julie's heart and spirit.

"It was great to see how nature helped Brenda realize something of God's greatness." His smile broadened at her words, and she found herself smiling in response. "I really liked what you said to her in the raft to calm her down. That had a lot to do with it."

David shrugged his shoulders and gave a half smile. "I could say what I wanted to because it was a church outing. That's kind of what I'm talking about. It's harder to do that all the time working as an employee in a secular organization. I speak out when God opens a door, but if the whole operation were Christian, then I could always speak openly of God."

"You mean you'd run a camp for teens? One with a climbing program? I've thought about doing that myself."

David shook his head. "No, not just for teens. People would book just like they do an outfitter. They could book groups of teens or just come with some non-Christian friends. A lot of people are looking for experiences that challenge them, somewhere they can test themselves, learn a new skill. They're looking for something to bite into in a bland, overregulated world. I'd like to give them the chance to meet the One who can make their whole life an adventure."

As Julie listened, her excitement grew. "I like it! The emphasis on false spirituality is everywhere: New-Age stuff, native religions, eastern religions, everything except the truth. There are lots of outfitters around here who tie native spirituality into their programs. I think the rafting company Seth works for must do that with their sweat lodge. People are open and hungry for spiritual understanding. We could give them God's truth. It would be so cool to be able to be open about God—his power in nature, his strength within us. I think if the ads were worded right, we could draw as many non-Christians as Christians."

David's eyes were fixed on her; his gaze sparkled with intensity. "You said *we*."

"What?" Julie blinked.

"You said, 'We could draw as many non-Christians as Christians.'"

Julie nodded. "That's right. People would come

from all kinds of backgrounds. Hey, maybe we could use the poems of Gerard Manly Hopkins as a takeoff—mystic poetry and rock climbing in the wilderness."

David smiled as if she'd said something wonderful. He looked like he'd just won the lottery or been given the Nobel peace prize. As far as she could tell, she'd said nothing that remarkable.

"You like Hopkins too?" Julie looked at him uncertainly.

He paused, almost as though startled by her question. Then he shrugged. "Hopkins? Actually I do like his poetry." He stopped and stood, his hands behind his back, and quoted:

> Nothing is so beautiful as spring—
> when weeds, in wheels, shoot long and lovely and
>   lush;
> thrush's eggs look little low heavens, and thrush
> through the echoing timber does so rince and wring
> the ear, it strikes like lightning to hear him sing;
> The glassy pear tree leaves and blooms, they brush
> the descending blue; that blue is all in a rush
> with richness; The racing lambs too have fair their
>   fling.
> What is all this juice and all this joy?
> A strain of the earth's sweet being in the beginning
> in Eden's garden.—— Have, get, before it cloy,

before it cloud, Christ, Lord, and sour with sinning.
Innocent mind and Mayday in girl and boy..."

The well-loved words in David's deep voice flowed over Julie like a sweet fragrance. She shut her eyes and let the glory pour though her. David paused, and she felt his gentle finger under her chin as he lifted her face to look at him. "Most, O maid's child, thy choice and worthy the winning."

There was a long silence. Their eyes locked, and Julie thought she would be consumed by the emotion swirling inside of her. She could gladly drown in the steady depth of David's gaze. Gently he took her into his arms. For a second she leaned into his embrace. His strength enfolded her. The warmth of David's breath touched her cheek as he bent his head. His lips brushed her skin in a gentle kiss. A rush of response swept over Julie and left her shaking. David gently lifted her chin to face him and bent to kiss her again. Julie felt like she was falling into a well of ecstasy and longing, a well so deep that she could drown and lose herself forever.

"No!" The word was torn from her throat. She twisted away. This couldn't happen! It wouldn't work!

"Julie, what's wrong? Don't!" David reached for her, but she spun and ran, sprinting hard across the packed-gravel flats and up the bank. David called again, but she didn't look back. Driven by desperation, she kept running out onto the side of the road and beyond. Three miles down the road, shaking with exhaustion, she staggered to a halt. Gasping for breath, Julie turned and walked toward home.

Within minutes, she was in agony. She'd behaved like an idiot! David hadn't done anything wrong. The poor man had simply tried to kiss her!

God, what's wrong with me? She choked back a bitter laugh. The answer was painfully clear. Everything. Everything about her was wrong.

If that's so, then why does a man like David Hales seem to care so much for you?

"He cares about everyone." She was ashamed to hear the acid in the muttered response.

Does he take everyone in his arms? Does he kiss everyone?

She had no answer for that. Only sorrow. Bone-deep sorrow at the way she'd behaved. He may have wanted to kiss her then, but she was pretty sure David wouldn't be all that keen on the idea any longer.

She thought about finding David, talking to him and apologizing, but what could she say? *Sorry, David. Nothing personal. I'm a misfit.*

Maybe a note would be easier. After all, she was leaving tomorrow for a week-long hiking trip. Julie bit her lip fiercely, refusing to give in to the wave of weeping that threatened to overtake her.

Yes, a nice, impersonal note would be best. She

would write it, mail it, and get on with her life. Her miserable, alone-forever life.

Back at the apartment, Julie sat down to write David a note of apology. After she'd shredded her fifth try, she jumped up and paced the room. It had been so awesome when he'd quoted Hopkins's poem.

She froze in midstride. "'You said *we.*'" At the whispered repetition of David's words, she suddenly understood. "I said *we.* I acted like I was going to do the Christian-outfitting thing with David." Julie swallowed hard. She'd said that without thinking, as if it was the most natural thing in the world for her to work with David Hales.

Well, it wasn't!

After the way she'd acted, how could she explain without telling him her entire life story, her humiliation with Kurt—she closed her eyes—her fury with God? Julie sat back down and tried again to write him a note. This time she told David that he was more special to her than any other man on the face of the earth. With sweating hands, she tore the paper into chunks. He didn't need to know that. No one did! With a muffled sob, she threw the whole pile into the garbage, then ran to take a shower. She scrubbed hard as if she could wash the confusion out of her system.

But all that did was leave her feeling as raw on the outside as she felt on the inside.

Laurel came in near supper time. In a fit of nervous energy, Julie had cooked a full meal: fried chicken, potatoes, salad, and broccoli with cheese sauce.

"Wow!" Laurel surveyed the spread wide-eyed. "What inspired you? Is David coming over?"

"No!" Julie thumped the potatoes so hard with the masher that little bits flew all over the counter. "Look, if he calls while I'm gone, tell him I'm sorry."

"Sorry for what? Did you have a fight?"

"Just tell him I'm sorry." Julie refused to elaborate. "What time did you leave this morning anyway?" Laurel just stood looking at Julie. Julie fought the urge to turn her back on that questioning gaze. "Well? Were you chasing poachers today or watching your baby bears?"

"Baby bears." Laurel gave her a repentant look. "I'm sorry I asked David to take my place without telling you. I wasn't trying to set you up, really. I couldn't find anyone else at such short notice."

Julie sighed. "It's not your fault."

Laurel snagged a cucumber out of the salad and munched on it. "How was the river? Did the kids have fun?"

"The whole day went really well as far as the kids

were concerned, and the river was awesome." Julie had a vivid picture in her head of David grinning at her as the raft plunged into a haystack. She shut her mouth tightly, and tears stung her eyes. Determined not to break down, Julie turned the attention back to Laurel. "What happened that you couldn't come?"

"Alex brought a man out who was visiting from the States. He's one of the best-known animal-behavior scientists alive today, and Alex wanted me to take him around and show him the bears."

"Hey, that's great! You guided one of the top men in your field." At least someone had something to celebrate. "How did it go? Were you able to get close to the bears?"

Laurel grimaced. "Not really. Most of the other bears are shyer than Samantha was. Anyway, it was interesting. The scientist and Alex spent a lot of time talking about the global situation for bears. I learned a lot. I knew that bears were under pressure, but I didn't know how bad it was. Generally we've got it good in Canada."

"Has the poaching slowed down, then?"

"I wish I knew. The thing is, most bears live in remote places. Poachers could operate for quite a while before anyone would notice. The RCMP haven't exactly given it top priority, either. They still haven't done the computer search for the brown Ford."

Julie put the potatoes in a bowl. Taking her attention off herself had loosened the pressure in her chest a bit. Now she put the last dish on the table. Laurel prayed, and they tucked in hungrily.

Laurel savored a spoonful of broccoli and cheese. "Mmm, this is a feast. What inspired you anyway? Are you getting more interested in the domestic arts for some reason?"

"No, I am *not*." But even as she denied it, Julie wondered if that had been her unconscious motivation. Had she been trying to make herself more acceptable? She shook her head. This train of thought was getting her nowhere. "Did I tell you I'm going to be gone for almost a week? I'm taking two hikers through part of the Great Divide Trail way down in southern Alberta."

"That's what you meant when you said you'd be gone?"

Julie nodded. "It's going to be good to get away." She made the assertion as firm as she could, determined to make herself—and her heart—believe it.

Fourteen

JULIE FOUND MARTHA AND LIONEL HANSON DELIGHTFUL company. Martha was small and rounded, while Lionel was a tall and lanky dentist with a matter-of-fact manner. Both were in their late fifties and glowing with health. Martha and Lionel were slow, steady hikers, comfortable with each other and with her. It made for a pleasant walk.

Lionel stopped and paused to breathe. "You know, I didn't realize there was anywhere in the continent, south of Alaska, this remote." They were two days out of the campground at Dutch Creek. "Just how far are we from help if any of us would break a leg?"

Julie sipped water from her sports bottle. "With the satellite phone I'm carrying, I could have a helicopter here in a couple of hours. If the phone doesn't work, maybe a bit more than a day. If I pushed hard, I could get back to Dutch Creek in a day and try to get a ride to Blairmore or find the forestry guys."

Martha leaned on her alpenstock and gazed out over the pleated landscape. To the west, the land rose in a high, jagged crest that marked the divide and the border between Alberta and British Columbia. To the east, the land fell away in long ridges. "Even out here, it's not unmarked by humanity." Martha pointed. "Aren't those rectangles I can see on the far ridges areas that have been cut by logging companies?"

Julie looked to where Martha pointed. "That's right. This area is remote now, but oil and gas interests, lumber, the rights to pasture cattle on government land, and recreational use are all after the space." Julie hadn't sorted out how she felt about that. As a rancher's daughter, she'd grown up with the idea that land was to be used but not harmed. Most of her guiding friends wanted only recreational access. It seemed like everyone wanted the whole pie for themselves.

"Well, I'm glad we're here while it's still wild." Martha crossed her arms, tilting her chin up. "As far as I'm concerned, humanity is a cancer on the face of the earth, metastasizing, engulfing, and destroying everything."

Lionel chuckled. "With which cell were you planning to start the eradication? Me, yourself, or Julie? Aren't we part of the recreational use?"

"Oh, you!" Martha rolled her eyes but couldn't quite keep from cracking a smile. Despite Martha's playful rebuke, Julie had the sense that Martha meant business.

Julie couldn't help but pursue this discussion, though she didn't want Martha's fire aimed in her direction. "Isn't the problem more human greed than anything?"

"Not that simple." Lionel stared at Martha with a frown darkening his brow.

"Oh, I don't know." From Martha's quick response, it was obvious they'd had this discussion before. "Greed is a big part of it, along with the Judeo-Christian philosophy that humans own everything. But I'd better shut up. There's no reason to let my hobbyhorse ruin a beautiful day."

Julie had jerked back like she'd been slapped when Martha blamed the destruction of the earth on people who followed the Bible, but when Martha dropped the subject, Julie didn't follow up. She couldn't. *Lord, give me the words to help this woman see the truth.*

That night Julie set up her tent but chose to sleep outside under the stars. At midnight, Julie still stared at the sky, her thoughts racing. Oddly enough, they were not about Martha but about the condition of her own heart, her position at the crossroads. She yearned to be able to give her love to David, but how could she? Nothing had changed. She closed her eyes as pain seared her heart and tears burned her eyes. *Lord, grant me peace....* When she finally opened her eyes, she noticed there was no moon, and the stars were pinpricks of vivid light in the bottomless velvet of a black night sky. She kept staring at them, pondering God's glory reflected in nature. As the hours passed, a deep calm invaded her soul.

"The heavens declare the glory of God." God's love was as close as an embrace and as huge as the universe. How could she have ever mistrusted him?

Because you don't trust anyone but yourself. Not David. Not God.

Julie rolled on her side as the tears flowed. It was true. And it had to change. She had to open herself, to become vulnerable. There was no other choice. She'd certainly proved that she wasn't cutting it on her own.

"God, I give up. I'll be whoever you want me to be, and I'll praise you in it. I'm sorry I've been so angry. Help me live for you with the same joy I see in David's life, and help me explain to him why I ran. He loves you too, Lord. I surrender to you all my feelings for David. I don't think you want me to get married ever. So I'll try to trust you with that. Please don't let me or David get hurt. I just want to live your way no matter what."

Julie sighed as a deep peace flowed over her. It was a new day inside and out. Secure in God's love now, she knew she could never really be alone.

In the northeast a ghost of blue-green light hazed the stars. Slowly it brightened, sweeping the night sky in swaths of vertical bars, like a theater curtain made of light sabers. The sawtooth ridge of the divide stood out in stark relief against the northern lights. Julie watched in a kind of praise-filled ecstasy. A verse came to mind that made her chuckle: "He has taken me to the banquet hall, and his banner over me is love."

As a confirmation of his love for her, God was painting the whole of the earth's northern hemisphere with this banner. She'd seen pictures taken from space where the aurora glowed like a crown of flames around the arctic circle. No man's love could ever compare or compete with God's majesty. Whatever else happened to Julie, she knew she was God's child first. She could trust God in a way she could never trust any man. Any man. Even good men like her father failed or misunderstood.

Julie's eyebrows shot up. Was that the source of her mother's serenity? Was she trusting God first? If that was the case, married or single, Julie's true anchor had to be God himself. She smiled. Climbing had taught her a lot about anchors, about how important they were. They kept you secure. But her security didn't come from being tied into chocks and bolts on a rock face, or even from another human being. Her anchor was God himself. Looking up she watched the light ripple and sweep across the diamond-studded sky.

Oh my gosh! I'll bet Martha and Lionel would love this.
Julie ran back to the tent where the Hansons were

sleeping. "Martha. Lionel. Wake up! You've *got* to see this." Martha was the first to emerge. "Oh!" She stopped partway out of the tent. In the dim light, Julie could just discern the look of awe on her face. "Lionel, hurry—you must see this."

"I would if you'd let me through." He chuckled. "Honey, you're blocking the entrance."

"Sorry." Martha moved aside and grabbed his hand. "Come quick!"

Lionel's laughter stopped when he, too, saw the sky. The couple stood together, almost at attention. Lionel put his arm around his wife.

Julie had never mentioned her faith to the Hansons. She'd spent too much time on this hike tied in knots. Now she took a deep breath and quoted the first few verses of Psalm 19:

The heavens declare the glory of God; the skies proclaim the work of his hands. Day after day they pour forth speech; night after night they display knowledge. There is no speech or language where their voice is not heard. Their voice goes out into all the earth, their words to the ends of the world.

Martha looked at her sharply. "Are you a Christian?"

"Yes, I am."

"I can see we'll have to have a talk."

Julie smiled at Martha, then turned her face back to the glory of the night sky. As David had said, Big Foot was not a Christian organization. Julie needed to be careful what she said, but if Martha asked questions, the door was wide open for her to answer. That God would honor Julie with the opportunity of speaking as a witness for him seemed even more of a confirmation of his love than did the glorious night sky.

The next morning, Julie's sense of awe wasn't broken even though they woke up to a gray sky that quickly developed into wet snow. They trudged through a half inch of slippery slush as rocks and ridges appeared like apparitions in the mist. At noon the clouds broke up. Sunlight burst through in great shafts of light, and the world shone as if it had been newly polished. Snow melted into glittering water drops. They stopped for lunch on the top of a scree slope. A marmot whistled. The sunlight, caught in a fine mist, arched a rainbow across the landscape.

Lionel laughed. "What a melodramatic place."

"It is rather," Martha said. "Look at the colors, dear. Each of the spruce trees is gilded. See, the drops on the tips of the needles catch the light." After a long moment, Martha turned to Julie. "You think all of this—all the beauty around us—speaks of God?"

Julie praised God as the words of Romans chapter 1 came to her: "'For since the creation of the world God's invisible qualities—his eternal power and divine nature—have been clearly seen, being understood from what has been made.'"

"You don't think it's the goodness of the land itself?"

"I can see why people feel that way. It is so beautiful. It's easy to make the mistake of worshiping the creation, instead of the Creator."

Lionel grunted, but Martha said nothing for a long time after that.

Over the next few days, the friendship between Julie and the Hansons deepened. Whenever Martha brought up God—which was often—Julie was able to explain some of the things God said about taking care of the land. It was odd how their frequent talks about God brought David to mind. She frowned as she hiked along the rocky ground. If God wanted David out of her life, why did God let thoughts about David intrude now when she'd finally come to terms with God's will?

On their last afternoon together, Martha fixed Julie with an intent look. "After what you've said, I don't see how you can support the Christian doctrine that man owns the earth."

"I *don't* support that idea, but then, it's not a biblical idea. God owns the earth. 'The earth is the Lord's, and everything in it, the world, and all who live in it.'

Genesis says that he created it and found it good. We're to tend it for him. He'll judge us for the job we do."

Martha laughed. "If that's the truth, a lot of people who call themselves Christians are going to have a shock when they face their God."

In spite of her initial antagonism toward Christianity, Martha took Julie's Bible home with her and said she'd read it and think about things. Lionel seemed interested as well. Julie grinned as she watched the couple drive away. David was right. When you spoke freely and without pretense, God could do amazing things.

Back in Canmore, Julie knew she had to talk to David, but he was out all day with clients. After a long trip, she usually had a day off. The apartment was quiet. Sun shone through the windows. Julie sat at the table and wrote to David. She felt she had nothing to hide now. God was her keeper, the tower where she ran for sanctuary.

She clenched her teeth as she wrote about her breakup with Kurt and a little about the issues with which she was struggling. She fiddled with the pencil.

David, I don't think God wants me to get married. It's not that I don't like you. I just don't want to be

the cause of hurting you. I want to face issues head-
on and live my life for God, whatever that takes. I'm
sorry I ran.

Julie stared into space. She knew God had good things in store for her. It would be the realization of a dream if she could work with David on his Christian climbing outfitter idea, but that would be crazy, given the way she felt about him. Julie shook her head, then left to deliver the letter. She knew that David picked up his mail at Big Foot.

Sheryl was at her desk when Julie came in.

"Oh, Julie, it's a good thing you came in. Brent wants to know if you're free on Friday evening and during the day on Saturday. Two people are coming for a climb, and David is going to have to take them up that multipitch, the Mother-in-Law. Brent wants you to scout it with David."

"He's going to pay me for that? I can think of ten climbers who would do that for fun at the drop of a hat."

"David asked for you, insisting that you be paid." Sheryl's face tightened into a frown.

"Oh." Joy fizzed up her spine. *David wants me to be with him.* Julie swallowed hard. She shouldn't be with David, not the way she felt. Slowly she walked over to put the letter into David's mail slot. Julie felt

Sheryl's eyes on her every step of the way.

"Well, are you free for those days? You'll have to go out and meet them at Brent's campsite the night before."

Julie *was* free those days, and lying to Sheryl wasn't right. But there was no way Julie was going to explain to Sheryl why she couldn't spend more time with David. She would just have to find another climber to go with David, but that wouldn't be a problem.

Julie nodded. "Sure, I can do it."

From the look on Sheryl's face, a storm was brewing. If there was one thing Julie didn't need right now, it was more conflict. So she made as graceful—and quick—an exit as she could.

Fifteen

WHEN DAVID CAME BACK TO HIS APARTMENT THAT evening, Tommy lay on the bed, staring at the ceiling. Tommy had gotten off of work half an hour earlier, but he'd done nothing to clean up the mess from breakfast or start supper. David had asked permission from his landlord for Tommy to stay until he could find another place. The landlord hadn't been happy. Reluctantly he'd agreed, but only after he'd increased the rent by 50 percent. Tommy had been there almost two weeks and had made no move to look for other quarters. David bit back his irritation and put some frozen pizzas in the oven.

His initial feeling that Tommy was depressed enough to commit suicide hadn't left him, but the boy seemed determined to see the month out. Besides working, Tommy did virtually nothing but lie on the bed and stare at the ceiling. He only ate when David put food in front of him.

David had quit trying to get the boy to talk. That only seemed to upset him more. He prayed for Tommy again as he watched him mechanically down the pizza. To David's surprise, Tommy actually stayed and helped to clean up. *Maybe he's snapping out of it.* But after the cleanup was done, Tommy retreated to the bed.

David looked at the phone. *Julie should be home by now. She'd probably like to know what's happening with Tommy.* Then he sighed. She should have come out of the bush yesterday. It was Tuesday, a day they'd often worked out together in the evening. The muscles at the corners of his jaw clenched. He had wanted to go after her when she ran from him, but he'd stopped himself. A physical pursuit could hardly lessen her fears, whatever they were.

Then he'd wanted to call immediately but figured that would amount to the same thing. He'd decided to wait until the next day and give her time to calm down before he called. That was one of the longest nights of his life.

When he finally did call, Laurel had answered. "Julie is out on a five-day hike——"

"Gone for five days?" David's heart sank.

"She told me to tell you she was sorry."

"Laurel, do you know what is bothering Julie?"

There was a short silence. "Um, I can't say."

"Is it something I did? Did I offend her in some way?"

"No, it's not that. Look, David, don't give up on

her. Maybe she'll tell you; then you can deal with it."

"Tell me what?" But Laurel had already hung up.

Now the five long days were over. Julie should have been home yesterday. He'd wanted to call right away but found himself uncertain as to what to say. He decided just to go to work, but throughout the day she consumed his thoughts. Those moments by the river had been so special. He could tell that she shared his dream. They even liked the same poetry, for Pete's sake.

God, help me. David swallowed hard and reached for the phone. Julie answered on the second ring. David's mouth was dry, but he found himself speaking as if nothing had happened between them.

"Julie, it's Tuesday night. Would you like to go work out?"

Silence was his only answer.

"Julie?"

"Um, David? I'm sorry for running from you. That was dumb. Did you get my letter?"

"I didn't get any letter."

"I left it for you at Big Foot."

"Okay, I'll go over and get it, then call you back." David frowned. He'd checked his mail that afternoon. Sheryl had asked him if he was looking for anything in particular. She'd stood very close to him. He shook away that uncomfortable memory. Maybe Julie had dropped the letter off after he'd been by the office. He looked up to see Tommy watching him.

"Something wrong between you and Julie?"

"I hope not. I've got to head over to Big Foot for a few minutes."

"Uh, look, David, I know I've been really out of it. Thanks for putting up with me. I've been doing some thinking, and...when you get back, c-could we talk?"

David blinked. Here was the opportunity he'd been praying would happen for weeks. Why did it have to come at the same time he was hoping to finally work things out with Julie? Well, Julie wasn't a child, and she'd been praying for Tommy too. He'd call her from the office.

"Sure, Tommy. I'll be back in about twenty minutes."

The doorbell rang just as David reached for the handle. A hard-faced, middle-aged Asian man faced him. "Is Tomosuke here?"

The Japanese name confused David for a second. "If you mean Tommy Oshikawa, yes; he is here. May I ask you who you are?"

"His uncle." The man tried to push past, but David stood squarely in the way. This man was part of the family that had reduced Tommy to an almost clinical depression.

David crossed him arms and glared at Tommy's uncle. "Hold on a minute. I want to say something to you. Looks to me as though the pressure you're putting on Tommy is destructive. Let him choose what he feels is right and wrong."

The uncle's hard eyes were full of malice. He took a short step forward, and David braced for a blow, but only menacing words came. "This is family business. Who are you to come between a youth and his elders? Tomosuke!"

A bleary-eyed Tommy shot to the door. When David tried to remain between the two of them, Tommy's eyes widened. "No, I have to talk to my uncle. It's okay, David."

David looked from one to the other. He still wasn't happy with the situation, but he had to respect Tommy's feelings. With a shrug he left the apartment. At Big Foot, there was nothing in his mailbox. He looked around but could find no evidence of a letter from Julie. Quickly he dialed her number. "Julie, I'm at the office. I can't find your letter. Look, Tommy asked me to talk with him just after you called. I've been praying for this chance for weeks so I didn't feel free to say no. I told him we could talk as soon as I got back. His uncle turned up just as I was leaving."

"You'd better get back there, then. We can talk later."

"Thanks, Julie."

"I'll be praying for you both."

"I know you will."

When David got back to his apartment, Tommy and his uncle were gone. David blinked and looked again. All of Tommy's belongings were gone too. He crossed the room in three strides and reached for the phone, but he hesitated. It wasn't going to be easy to convince the police that Tommy Oshikawa was in trouble. Tommy had been depressed, eager to escape from the pressures of his family, but David had no evidence that they'd actually done him harm.

His only recourse was prayer. Instead of the RCMP, David dialed Julie's number. She answered on the second ring.

"Julie, Tommy is gone. None of his stuff is here. His uncle moved him out."

"Moved him out? Where to?"

"I don't know. If he doesn't turn up at work tomorrow, I'm going to phone the police. I don't have a good feeling about this." David paced around the room, running his hand through his hair.

"Me, neither. David, I know I'm changing the subject, but I left that letter in your box. Sheryl watched me put it there."

"It wasn't there. Maybe it fell down behind something or one of the other guides stuck it somewhere. I was too worried about Tommy to search for long. Don't worry about running away from me. We all have things to work out. Maybe you could just tell me about it. If we don't talk tonight, we'll have to wait until Friday night. Sheryl said you agreed to come climb with me."

There was a long pause. "Okay, we can talk then." Julie's voice was tight. David frowned. Was she crying? "Bye, David. I'll pray for Tommy."

He slowly put down the phone. *God, I'm losing her, and I don't know why.* That night he slept very little. He got up before dawn and walked for hours, hardly thinking about where he was going. The sun came up, and David was vaguely aware of warm light touching his face. He'd better hike back into town if he wanted to search the office again for Julie's letter. Sheryl came in in the middle of his search and stood in the doorway watching him.

"What are you doing?" Sheryl's question startled David.

"Sheryl, you're here. I need your help. Julie said you saw the letter she left for me, but I can't find it."

"If there's nothing in your box, maybe she lied to you."

Swift anger swept over him. He turned to let Sheryl know what he thought of her comment, then paused at the mutinous look on Sheryl's face. He took a deep breath. "Julie wouldn't lie. Maybe it fell out—" he fixed her with an intent stare—"or was misplaced." *Would she do such a thing, Lord?* No, he couldn't believe Sheryl would go so far.

The mailboxes were above a filing cabinet. Maybe the letter had fallen? David braced his shoulders and pulled the filing cabinet away from the wall so he could see behind it.

He looked up to find Sheryl beside him. "Here, I found it on my desk."

David reached for the envelope, then hesitated. Sheryl's eyes were so sad—and he knew. She had hidden the letter, jealous and still hoping he'd switch his attention to her. *Lord, give me the right words...*

Before he could speak, Sheryl shrugged. "I'm sorry." The apology was tight with emotion. "I know it was wrong, but—" She shook her head, her lip trembling. "First Brent. Now you. What is it about me that scares men away?" She looked away, swiping her hand at her eyes. "I'll never understand it."

David's heart swelled with compassion. "Sheryl, no man on earth can make things right for you. Only God can do that. It's *his* love that matters."

She gave him a wry smile. "God doesn't keep a girl warm at night. I tried reading the Bible like you said, and it was really boring."

"Try again. Only this time, do it for yourself, not to make me pleased with you."

"You just think Julie is prettier." Sheryl ducked her head. "I suppose she is."

David blinked, but then he wondered if it was just

another play for attention. "That's not the point. Look, neither of us is right for each other. It would do both of us harm. I'd be taking advantage, and you'd be looking for affirmation and security in the wrong place. Only God can fill the voids and supply your needs."

Sheryl gave him a hard look and turned away. "Okay, preacher man, I hear what you're saying. I read Julie's letter, and I don't think you're going far with her, either."

David's fury at Sheryl's nerve almost overwhelmed him. *I can't believe she read my letter!* He had to get out of there before he did something he'd later regret. With the letter clenched in his fist, he walked into the storeroom. Shutting the door behind him, David began to read. When he'd finished, he stared out the window. Various emotions tumbled through him, the strongest being rage at this Kurt Julie mentioned. *How dare he hurt Julie so badly?* He took a deep breath, acknowledging that jealousy was part of his rage against Kurt. Julie had obviously cared for the man.

David reined in his emotions and reread the letter. Julie said she planned to be who God made her to be and dedicate her life to God. She said she was sure she should never marry...yet the letter was full of pain. The one thing he'd hoped to see—a declaration of Julie's feelings about him—wasn't there. She never said she cared for him, but she never said she didn't, either. *Was she right about not marrying?* His whole being reeled at the possibility. David stood up abruptly. *God, if we're meant to be together, please do what you have to do to make that happen.*

David could hear Brent's voice in the other room. Someone answered him in a low voice. *Tommy?* David opened the door and stepped out. Tommy stood by Brent's door. David sighed. Tommy's uncle hadn't harmed the boy, at least not physically. David walked toward Tommy, but the boy moved away.

Brent watched Tommy's reaction to David with curiosity. "What were you doing in the storage room? You're here early."

"Reading a letter."

"You're a weird duck, Hales, and you're a bad influence on Julie too. The people she hiked with said they appreciated her religious insight. She was preaching at them."

"Did they call it preaching?"

"No, but why else would they say what they did? You're no better. I've heard you talking about God to climbers. I want no more of that, do you hear?"

David leveled a hard look at Brent. "I hear."

At the tone of David's voice, Brent's chin jutted out. "Yeah—" the response was full of challenge—"but are you gonna knock it off?" His eyes narrowed. "Or am I gonna have to find myself a guide who appreciates working for this kind of outfit?"

David felt the heat rise in his chest and travel into his face. He clenched his teeth so hard his jaw ached. *Please, Lord, let me do it. Let me tell this jerk just what I think of him. You know he deserves it for the way he treats his people...not to mention the way he treats women!*

His answer came swift and sure. *"In quietness and trust is your strength."*

David didn't like it. Not one bit. The last thing he wanted to be right now was quiet. But he had no choice. Not unless he wanted to go against what he knew was right in God's eyes. And that was one thing he would never do.

Drawing a calming breath, he searched for the right response. To his surprise, Sheryl cut in. "Oh, leave him alone. He's only going to be here another couple of weeks. Asking David to quit talking about God is like asking him to quit breathing."

David cleared his throat. "Brent, I had no intention of offending anyone. If you need me to quit because of this, I..." Brent wasn't paying the least attention. He was staring out the window at the parking lot. David turned to see two RCMP officers striding toward the Big Foot office.

"Hey, Chuck!" Brent met them at the door with exaggerated enthusiasm. "So are you finally going to book a climb with us?" He turned to David and the others. "This is Chuck Olson, and I don't know his partner."

"Bruce James." Chuck's partner tipped his hat. "Brent, we need some information. We understand that you have a brown Ford pickup crew-cab."

"That's right. It's an old beater. Did somebody steal it? Is that what this is all about? It was out back last time I looked, um, about five o'clock yesterday afternoon."

"No, we have no reports that it was stolen, but we would like to have a look at it. It matches the description and partial license plate of a truck seen near several bear kills."

"What?" Brent's face contorted with astonishment. "Chuck, tell this partner of yours he's nuts. My clients are people who *love* the wilderness. I'd be out of my mind to get involved in poaching." Brent spit out the last word as if it had a foul taste. "You guys can check for residual bear blood or whatever you want. Tommy, show them the truck. You've got the keys."

Tommy didn't move a muscle. He looked as if he were made out of wood. David wondered at the blank look on Tommy's face. The boy jerked into movement like he was being manipulated by remote control. Brent followed Tommy and the officers. "You'll see; you've got it all wrong. You only have a partial license plate. It's someone else's pickup, not ours. The idea is ludicrous!"

Tommy reached for the back door and glanced

over his shoulder at David. His look was a pure cry for help. David responded by following quickly. Outside, Bruce James went to work on the truck, scraping at the corners of the truck bed and putting samples into vials.

Chuck Olson focused on Tommy, asking him for his name, his residence, and so on. "Tommy, could you tell me what you think of poaching?"

Tommy lifted his chin and stared straight into the man's eyes. "You want to hear what I think of poaching? Well, I'll tell you. It's a filthy business and totally wrong." Tommy's voice had the ring of complete conviction. "I know this woman who studies bears. She knows each of the females and their cubs by name, and she showed me a picture." Tommy bit his lip, his eyes squeezed shut as if to shut out the memory. "It was a mother bear, dead and cut up by poachers. I want nothing, ever, to do with poaching in my whole life!"

The officer blinked. "Thank you, Tommy. Ready to go, Bruce?"

Bruce nodded, and the policemen left after thanking Brent for his help.

Brent snorted. "They're crazy to look here for poachers."

Sheryl nodded. "No kidding. Way to tell them, Tommy. You did great!"

Tommy turned and looked away.

Brent clapped his hands together. "Enough! We've

still got to pick up our climbing party and get going. Tommy, you'll drive us out; then I want you there on Friday before supper. Our clients want to stay out in the wilderness as long as they can, so I want you to bring in a good meal. You can stay overnight and take us out the next morning.

"Sheryl, tell Julie she'll need to bring her car to base camp. Let's go." Brent started for the door. David and Tommy followed, but again Tommy avoided David.

There was no doubting the fervency of that speech Tommy had made. David frowned. Could Tommy's uncle be forcing him to help with poaching in some way? That would fit Tommy's extreme reaction, but the idea seemed crazy.

Now, more than ever, he longed to talk it all over with Julie, to hear what she thought, to watch as the emotions washed over her face. He shook his head, almost angry at the desperation that pulled at him. *Jesus, what am I supposed to do with all of this?*

He was just going to have to trust that God was working out the details of who they would be to each other.

But soon, Lord, please. He closed his eyes. *Because I don't know how much more of this roller-coaster ride I can take.*

Sixteen

AS TOMMY DROVE BIG FOOT'S BROWN FORD, HE COULD feel his uncle's angry glare. He jumped as Atsuko banged his fist on the dashboard.

"You have ruined my plans. There were important things for me to do that would increase our family's wealth and prestige. You have forced me to sit in this small town baby-sitting you because you cannot be trusted!"

"Uncle, we shouldn't be doing this. It's wrong. People care about the bears. Now that I know something about them, I care about the bears, too. Besides, I've told you the police are suspicious of this truck." Tommy knew even as he said it that his uncle wouldn't listen.

Uncle Atsuko looked straight ahead, his arms crossed. "You also told me the truck was clean. Did you or did you not wash it carefully after the last time as you had been ordered?"

"I washed it."

"So the authorities could find nothing! They will be

less suspicious now than they were before. Especially since you told me you argued so well against poaching. In spite of being a fool, you occasionally do something wise."

Tommy's body stiffened. "I meant every word, Uncle. Our family should not be doing this. I know it is wrong. I tried to quit, but you stopped me."

"I stopped you from being a fool! I went to great trouble to arrange this job for you—"

"For *you,* you mean." Tommy couldn't hold back the angry outburst. "For you and your bloody business!"

His uncle's features hardened. "A business that has given you everything you have, Tomosuke. You dishonor your family with such talk."

"Family!" Tommy all but spit the word out. "It isn't family that you do this for. It's money."

"Money means nothing to me! It is a tool. A much-needed tool to make our family strong and powerful. You took the job I told you to take because of family. I arranged our contacts when you secured the job— because of family. Do you think it was easy to find those who would deal in the bear bladders you received from poachers? But I found them."

"You've involved my friends in criminal activities!"

Atsuko's smile was mocking. "It is convenient that your company has so many international clients. Their luggage has been the perfect tool for getting our prod- uct through customs to our contacts."

"And what if one of those people had been caught? They were innocent—"

"They are unimportant! They are not family. What do I care if they are apprehended?"

Tommy shook his head, fighting the desperation that welled up within him. "It is wrong, Uncle."

"It is business, Tomosuke. When will you learn that? This work has enabled us to build useful bridges with an internationally powerful consortium. It has made a great deal of money for them and for the family. That is all that matters."

Tommy rubbed his now-aching temples. "Allow me to quit now. I've already given my word I will ask for nothing more from the family. Let me go. Please."

His uncle seemed unmoved by Tommy's plea and continued to stare straight ahead. "First we will finish this contract. Other avenues are arranged after this month, but they will not help the Oshikawas. You have lost our family contacts and prestige with the powerful men who run this operation! Do you think this is only about bear gallbladders? Those important men have many other businesses. You have shamed me!" Atsuko finally turned to look at Tommy. "You will finish this job, and then I will leave you be. I will protect your parents and your siblings as I am able. If you quit now, Tomosuke, I will find a way to bring your shame to my brother and his wife."

Tommy's body was rigid. Only two more weeks; then he'd be free. *No matter what, I must not allow Uncle Atsuko to bring shame on my parents.* Whatever else he was, Tommy's uncle was a man of his word. He would let Tommy go in two weeks. *Only two more weeks. Surely I can hang on that long. Then I'm out.*

"You should continue working for Big Foot, Tomosuke. Even after our contract. Tell that man Brent that you will keep working."

Tommy frowned. "No, I'm quitting at the end of the month. You agreed!"

"My brother was a fool to raise you in Canada." Atsuko banged the dash with his fist. "You are a disgrace, a weakling who puts his own foolish scruples first, before his family. What kind of person cares more about the life of some animal than the wealth and status of his own family? Because of you, my own brother questioned my decisions."

Tommy looked at his uncle with sudden interest. Had some of the things he had said to his parents gotten through? "Dad actually argued with you?"

Atsuko snorted. "Only a little. But the conflict was your fault. You hurt family unity. I had to remind him that the penalties for poaching are not large. Only a fool like you would think that the government of Canada really cares. The authorities are not a serious threat to us. It is that man you were staying with, David

Hales. He knows something."

Tommy came to full attention. Uncle Atsuko was capable of almost anything if he thought family honor was threatened. "He knows nothing! David is a good man. Leave him alone!"

"He climbs rocks; is this right?"

"Yes, and he teaches others to do the same. He is no threat to you."

His uncle's lips tightened. "I have seen such climbing on television. They wear a harness. Is this correct?"

"If you know that, why are you asking me?"

Tommy didn't like the look on his uncle's face. They were well into the mountains now, near Brent's base camp. He felt fear tightening its hold in his gut. Surely Uncle Atsuko wouldn't...

He closed his eyes, unable to finish the horrible thought.

Things were not going well. Tommy and his uncle were to meet the man who'd been killing bears for them. To Uncle Atsuko's disgust, the hunter had nothing for them. The thin, dirty, red-haired man cringed from Atsuko's anger. "I've got a bear coming in to bait. I'll have her by tomorrow morning. I promise. Give me a chance, man. I *need* this money."

Tommy wanted to punch the man and walk away.

Remembering his parents, he stood still and watched his uncle bargain. Atsuko's face was twisted with disgust as he agreed to meet the poacher early the next morning. As soon as the poacher was gone, Uncle Atsuko turned to Tommy. "Tomosuke, take me to the place where David Hales is camping."

Alarm shot through Tommy. "Why, Uncle? There is nothing to interest you in the Big Foot camp. Besides, Brent told me they were going out on a day hike today. No one is going to be there."

"I wish to see it."

Tommy shrugged and drove to base camp. He couldn't see any harm in it, especially since the camp would be deserted and he had no intention of leaving his uncle alone there. At his uncle's prompting, Tommy showed him around. Uncle Atsuko peered into each tent as if he were making anthropological notes. *Why is Uncle so interested?* Tommy was sure he would never completely understand Atsuko Oshikawa. Back at the brown truck, he got in and started the engine, tapping his fingers on the wheel. It seemed to take his uncle a long time to walk around to the far door. Tommy glanced back to see him beside the left rear wheel.

They had driven only fifty yards when that tire went flat. "I will go and sit in the folding chair at camp while you fix this. I do not wish to remain in the truck while it is jacked up."

He walked away before Tommy could stop him.

The fear in Tommy's gut was now full-blown. Atsuko was up to something. He knew it as surely as he knew anything. He hurried to fix the tire, ignoring the trembling in his clammy hands. There was a huge nail in the tire. Had Atsuko placed it by the tire when he bent down? In his rush to get the tire changed, Tommy seemed to be all thumbs. The faster he tried to go, the more uncooperative everything seemed. He finally finished with the knuckles of both hands bloody and ran up the trail to camp.

His uncle sat innocently enough in one of the folding chairs by the fire. *I shouldn't be so paranoid.* Surely his uncle wouldn't have tried to do anything to the Big Foot camp. In minutes they were on their way back to town. They were more than halfway there when Julie Miller passed them going the other way and waved.

Julie looked in her rearview mirror. That had been Tommy driving the Big Foot crew-cab. *What is he doing out here now?* She'd called Big Foot earlier that week and found out that Tommy had been coming in to work. This morning Sheryl had said he'd taken the day off and wasn't due at camp for another four hours. There had been another man with him. She had the impression it was that uncle she'd met. She wrinkled her nose. That stiff and proper man didn't seem the type for wilderness adventures. Still, if Tommy wanted to drive his uncle around in the mountains, there wasn't any crime in that.

Sheryl had also told Julie that the French clients had wanted to camp in the wilderness for as long as possible. Even after the three-day climb, they didn't want to come in but planned to stay at the remote base camp and do another day hike on Friday. Sheryl gave Julie careful directions to the campsite three hours northwest of Calgary and said that it was remote enough that Brent figured he'd leave things set up during the day while they were gone.

It turned out that Laurel had been working near that area for the last three days. That morning Julie had left early to meet her friend for a couple of hours. Julie had learned that whenever Laurel was out in the bush, her mind was completely absorbed by her bears. At least talking about bears should take Julie's mind off the discussion she was going to have to have with David tomorrow.

Laurel met her as arranged where the smaller road branched off the forestry trunk road. As soon as they both got out of their vehicles, Julie could tell there was something wrong. "What is it, Laurel? You look positively haggard."

"I came out to help with Alex's work, tracking the range of the boars. Well, he can't find Igor."

"One of his male bears?"

Laurel nodded. "Igor is only three. Alex has tracked him for two years now."

"Couldn't the bear just have left the area?"

"Maybe. I'm driving down any track I can find and searching the zones around his home territory. I don't really want to quit. Do you mind parking your car and coming with me?"

"I can do that." Julie ran to move her car off the smaller track and out of the way. Back in Laurel's truck, they drove in silence for a while. Usually Laurel was a talker, bubbly and communicative, but now she was gnawing her bottom lip. She was pale and seemed to be fighting tears.

"Um, look, Laurel, you said Igor might have just left. That means he's probably okay. Why are you so upset?"

Laurel's white-knuckled hands gripped the wheel. "The thing is, there was no pressure on him to move. The older bears here have disappeared. Alex thinks they've been killed because they haven't turned up anywhere else, but we don't have any evidence. Now Igor is gone too. It makes me so mad I could spit!"

"So Alex thinks the poachers are still operating?"

"Yes. He's asked around. There were some oil and gas surveyors in here last week, and they saw a brown Ford pickup."

Julie's heart sank. Tommy was driving Big Foot's brown Ford pickup. She forced the thought away. There was no way Tommy would be involved with poaching. Just the sight of a dead bear had made him pale....

Julie suddenly felt sick. *Would Tommy react that way because he was feeling guilty? No, that just can't be right.*

Both women were unusually silent for several hours as they drove the perimeter of Igor's range, waiting for the signal that would indicate the bear was nearby.

Julie's mind reeled at the possibilities. Should she say something to Laurel even though she didn't have any proof? Julie rubbed her hands on her pants. Maybe she just had a suspicious mind. Tommy was their friend. They'd all been praying for him. It seemed disloyal even to suspect him.

The peaks were shutting the late evening sunlight out of the valleys when Julie finally reached out to touch her friend's arm. "I hate to say this, but I really do need to get back to my car."

Laurel gave Julie a startled look. "I wasn't thinking. What time is it?"

"Eight-thirty."

"I'm so sorry, Julie. Here I am taking up all your time with my problems."

"Don't worry, Laurel. I know you're upset about the bear. I don't mind getting in late. Really, I don't."

For the first time, Laurel really looked at her. "That wouldn't be because you don't want to have to talk to David tonight, would it?"

"Got it on the first try. It's going to be so hard."

Laurel turned the truck around and drove without saying anything for a while. Finally she sighed. "I don't know what to say. I haven't got an easy answer for you, but please just listen, really listen, to what he has to say."

Julie nodded and bit her lip. "I promise, but I don't think anything much can come of it."

They stopped beside Julie's car, and Laurel gave her a quick hug. "I'll be praying, and you pray about getting the poaching stopped too, okay?"

Julie's stomach knotted as she thought about Tommy again. She stepped out of the truck. "I'll do that." Julie ran to her car. After she started the vehicle, she didn't leave. She just sat there watching Laurel's truck disappear. She would certainly pray about the poaching, and for Tommy, too. Her suspicions had to be wrong.

Sheryl's directions to the campsite proved to be harder to follow than Julie had hoped. After several false turns, Julie finally found the spot, but not until after dark. She could see firelight flickering on the faces of seven or eight people gathered around a campfire.

"Julie, you came!" David jumped up from the campfire and came toward her. Even in the dim light, she could see the pleased look on his face.

Brent wasn't far behind David, but the look on his face was different. "You're late."

She wasn't really. He'd just told her to get there in time to leave early in the morning, but he must have been waiting, watching for her. Several of the other people had stood up from their seats on logs near the fire. A woman Julie didn't recognize laughed and came closer. "These men, they've been worried for you, looking for you to arrive as if they were jilted lovers. You must be kind to them both now."

"Julie's cute, but she doesn't hold a candle to you, Louise." Brent laughed as he put his arm around her shoulders and steered them back toward the circle.

The people around the fire laughed with Brent as the woman called him a flatterer. David, standing close to Julie, didn't laugh. "I set up one of those little dome tents for you."

The intimacy in David's voice made her heart race. This was going to be worse than she had thought. She forced herself to focus on something besides how close David was standing to her. "Is Tommy here?"

"He brought supper, then left immediately. Brent has the van here, but Tommy is supposed to come back tomorrow at ten with the truck to haul out the camp gear. Julie, he wouldn't even look me in the eye, much less talk to me. I wish I knew what is going on with him."

If Tommy was involved in poaching, it was no wonder he wouldn't look David in the eye.

254

"Come join us." One of the men by the fire called to Julie. "I want to see your pretty face in the firelight." The group had obviously been drinking just enough to think themselves very witty. "Come and sit by me. I'm lonely. Louise is abandoning me for our handsome guide."

Everyone laughed and called for her to come over.

Julie glanced at David. He had his fists clenched and was frowning at the man by the fire. Deliberately he moved to put his arm around her shoulders. Julie's heart lifted, but she stepped away and walked quickly to the fire. Until she knew her heart and his better, she didn't dare let him make that kind of claim on her in front of the others.

Both David and the other man motioned for Julie to sit by them, but she pretended not to notice. Instead, she rolled a four-foot-long log closer to the fire and sat on that. Brent introduced the climbers. It turned out that the man who'd been flirting with her was called Marc. Euphoric with success and wine, the climbers talked excitedly about the last several days. Julie gathered that the whole group had made the peak. Julie had to admit it—despite his faults, Brent really was good at his job.

She glanced at him. He sat very close to Louise, a wicked grin on his face. Julie looked away with a shake of her head. She found it difficult to pay close attention to the conversation. Her mind slid like an out-of-control car, veering between what she would say to David and her fears about Tommy.

By eleven-thirty the group began to break up. Brent got up, dragging Louise with him, and turned to the other climbers. "Nothing is happening until Tommy gets back at ten to pack up camp, so sleep in if you want." Brent walked toward the tents with Louise swaying by his side.

David watched Brent's grand exit, then continued to talk quietly with one of the men. Before long David and the man walked off together, engrossed in their conversation. Julie continued to sit near the fire. She could hear everyone's voices as they got ready for bed. Her eyes were full of the flickering pattern of the flames, and her mind was full of David. Everything about him was right. He stirred her in ways Kurt never had. Kurt had talked about supporting his family and being a good provider, as if she were looking for some kind of business deal; David talked about serving God together.

Julie's eyes blurred, and the flames became weaving blobs of light. She blinked back tears. *God, help me to trust your goodness, your love for me.*

The log she was sitting on jerked a bit. Julie turned her head to see David sitting down beside her. "A penny for your thoughts?" His voice was warm and quiet.

She looked away, trying to gather her courage. The camp was silent. She must have been sitting there longer than she'd thought. David was only a few inches away. She could feel his nearness as acutely as if she had a special radar set on David Hales. She wanted him to touch her, to put his arm around her. Julie clenched her fists on her knees. "I can't..." All the words fled from her mind, her heart pounding.

"Julie, I need to tell you first that I did get your letter. Sheryl found it." Julie looked at him, startled. His eyes were so dark in the firelight. Warm highlights touched his hair and cheeks. "I'm sorry Kurt hurt you so badly. No one should be hurt like that."

Emotion tightened her throat, making it hard to talk. "Those things happen sometimes. I-I'm sorry I ran away from you. I acted like an idiot."

David's form was outlined against the fire, his dark hair and powerful shoulders backlit by red gold. The firelight gilded the plane of his cheekbone and jaw. A sudden longing to lean against him, to let him hold and protect her, swept over her. She bit the inside of her lip fiercely. Why was God taunting her like this? If she was really meant to be single, where was all this emotion coming from? And why did it feel so...so right? She turned her head away and looked up at the dark, ragged line of spruce trees standing still against the stars. More than anything she wanted to take his hand, to go to him and feel his strength surround her. She shut her eyes for a second, resigned to the way things had to be. Then she stood.

"Good night, David."

His gaze held her immobile with the longing—the *love*—she saw reflected there. "Sleep well, Julie."

How she pulled herself away from David's gaze, she'd never know. But later, alone in her cold, dark tent, Julie crawled into her sleeping bag while hot tears coursed down her face.

Lord, when will I ever find peace? I am drawn to him so. It was a long time before Julie slept, but she didn't sleep well. Even her dreams were haunted by the image of a dark, intent gaze that drew her relentlessly...a gaze so filled with tenderness and love that it threatened to break her heart.

Seventeen

BIRDSONG OUTSIDE HER TENT WOKE JULIE. SHE ROLLED over with a small groan. Dawn always came early in Alberta in the summer. She closed her eyes, but she couldn't go back to sleep despite the fact that she knew it must be around four-thirty. Julie lay in her sleeping bag, listening to the birds and thinking. Someone was snoring in one of the other tents.

She propped herself on her elbows and bowed her head over her hands. "Holy Father, my life is yours. I'm really confused. I'd like to believe that David and I could be partners, but what if I'm just letting my emotions carry me away? What do you expect of me?" She wanted to scream, but she just prayed in a very soft whisper. She knew how sound carried in a quiet camp. The last phrase had come out in a tear-strained squeak.

Only silence and the calls of the birds answered her. Julie lifted her face and saw her Bible. Was Laurel right? Had she misunderstood what God expected of a wife? Her mother had said it never occurred to her that she could have had marriage *and* adventure. But now she was going to take flying lessons. Julie hadn't fit in with any of the guys in high school, and she certainly hadn't suited Kurt, but what if her temperament would actually fit with someone like David?

Quickly Julie wriggled into warm clothing. Grabbing her Bible, she climbed out of her tent and set off to find a place with the space to think. Dew-wet grass squished against her boots. The first sunlight of the morning was kissing the peaks high above her head, turning their snow fields a rich peach color. Long mare's-tail clouds of the same color streaked the sky.

Walking quickly, Julie moved away from the camp and upward through a stand of lodgepole pine. A sharp crack stopped her in her tracks. She listened but didn't hear the sound again. Had that been a rifle shot? She shook her head and moved on. Probably an old, dry tree had broken. Climbing hard, she crested a ridge. As the ground got rockier, the trees gave way to tough golden grass and Alpine wildflowers.

Julie knelt beside a dew-damp boulder. Sharp gravel bit into her knees as she opened her hands to the dawn. "God, the land is shouting your glory. Help me to walk in step with you so my life gives you glory too. You made me a certain way, and I don't want to hurt David. Please show me your will."

Other than her great love of the land, she felt no answer. Sitting on the boulder, she opened her Bible to the concordance in the back. *Manger, manna*—there it was—*marriage*.

Again she read the passage in 1 Corinthians 7. She finished even more confused than before.

Then she read the passage in Ephesians chapter 5. It was very clear that there was an order of authority in marriage. If she married, she would need to be under her husband's authority. But instead of the near-panic that had always filled her when she thought about submitting to Kurt, this idea actually felt...right. David's character, goals, and values seemed to suit her so perfectly—she could trust him.

On the next ridge to the west, sunlight was beginning to sweep down from the rocks onto the dark woods. As Julie watched the scene, a longing started to build from within her heart. It grew slowly, like the dawn, increasing in intensity. *Lord, I want...* She frowned. What did she want? *I want...* Her eyes widened as the truth hit her, and her throat choked with quick tears. *I want to be here, in a place like this, with David. I want to be with him, to work together in that Christian guiding company he described.*

Julie turned back to the concordance. She needed to find that passage that Kurt had quoted. The one that had convinced her she could never be anyone's wife. She frowned. It wasn't listed. Maybe it didn't have the word *marriage* in it. She bit her lip, trying to remember another word that might help her find the place. It had said something about older women teaching younger women. She tried those words and finally found the passage in the book of Titus.

Chapter 2 was giving a list of things to be taught to different groups of people. Older women were not to drink or gossip but to teach younger women to love their husbands and children and to be busy at home. The Bible she had was her mother's old NIV Bible. Something was written down the side of the page with an arrow that turned into a loop circling the words, "busy at home."

Julie turned the Bible and squinted to read the faded ink. "Actually one word, *oykoros,* from the Greek for 'home,' means something like 'home guard.' I'm to guard the welfare of my home, not house, but home, make sure my husband and children are well and well cared for."

Julie touched her mother's words with one finger. "'Not house, but home.'" As understanding dawned, regret washed over her. She should have talked to Mom long ago. Obviously they faced some of the same struggles.

She read the penciled words again, and joy surged through her. Even if she lived in the wilderness with her husband—and maybe children—someday she could be this kind of home guard. It was the old theme of not putting her own interests first. God asked that of each of his people. It was asked of wives and mothers in a special way, but it wasn't the horrible trap Kurt had made it sound like.

A huge weight seemed to lift off of Julie's chest. She wasn't doomed to be single, not if God sent the right man.

But God has sent the right man...David.

Julie blinked through tear-blurred eyes as the sun came into view. It was bathing her in golden light, so full of joy and hope. Julie shut her eyes and felt tears track down her cheeks. Would David still want her? He'd read the note. He knew she'd been thinking she shouldn't marry. What if he thought she was right? He hadn't said anything last night. David wouldn't interfere with God's will for anyone. It would be humiliating to tell him she'd changed her mind only to find out he wasn't as interested as she'd thought.

Resolutely Julie stood and started back to camp. With God's help she could face this day. After the long walk out, she realized she was thirsty, so she slid and scrambled down the far side of the ridge toward the creek she could hear below.

On a level stretch partway down, a heavy, rank smell made her hesitate. She stood still and sniffed. *Bear!* She'd smelled that before when she was out with Laurel. She sniffed again and wrinkled her nose. She sure didn't want to surprise any bear, and it had to be close to smell that strong. She licked her finger and held it up. The wind was coming from the left. The bear would be in that direction.

Surely the animal must have heard her coming, but there was no reason to take chances. Edging to her right, Julie walked cautiously. "Hello, bear. It's me, bear."

Half a dozen ravens flew up, croaking out their bubbling cry. Julie kept moving backward. She could see a dark mass on the ground now in the shade of the trees. A kill. It had to be. The bear was on a kill. She'd have to tell Laurel. Maybe it would be her bear Igor. More ravens flew up, definitely coming from that dark heap. Julie frowned and stopped. No bear would tolerate ravens on the kill if he were there. She squinted, trying to see more clearly. Was that an outline of a round ear on this end of the heap? Whatever it was had dark fur. A dead bear?

If it was a dead bear, she should go and look, if only for Laurel's sake. Julie shouted again and listened. The ravens were beginning to circle back. One tilted down through the trees and landed. With a jumping bounce it hopped forward onto the dark heap. Nothing was guarding that carcass.

Julie moved closer as quietly as she could. Her foot caught on something. She looked down to shake her foot loose and let out a startled squeak. It was a collar, one of those tracking collars that Laurel used. Julie had seen them in the apartment many times. She bent and picked it up, then nearly dropped the thing. It was cut through and streaked with bright blood. The radio had been thoroughly smashed. Laurel would definitely want this. Holding it between two fingers, Julie picked up her pace.

The ravens took off again and perched in the trees overhead. Julie walked up to the dark, shaggy heap. She was looking at the back of a bear lying on its side, obviously dead. It wasn't very big. She moved forward, and the rest came into view. Julie averted her face and ended up looking at the collar in her hand. She looked closer, and a buzz of fear went through her.

The blood on that collar was still wet. With two quick strides, Julie moved and laid her hand on the dead bear's back. *Warm!* That crack she'd heard, it *had* been a rifle shot! Julie turned and ran back toward the camp. The poachers couldn't be far away, and there was a radio phone at camp. Slipping on pine needles and jumping deadfall, Julie tried to take a shortcut. It didn't work. Instead of coming straight into the campsite, she ended up at a road about a quarter of a mile out.

Gasping for breath and holding the bloody collar away from her, Julie ran down the road. Tommy had come in last night, and now there was a dead bear. Could he really be using Big Foot's brown pickup to poach bears? He didn't seem enough of a woodsman to be successful. Besides, wouldn't someone have noticed a gun or a skinning knife or whatever?

The sight of a brown pickup parked in the bush brought Julie to a full stop. If Tommy had anything to do with this bear kill, there would be evidence in that truck. She ducked into the trees at the side of the road. Panting from her run, she stood and stared at the vehicle. No one seemed to be around. She looked at her watch. It was only six in the morning. Tommy wasn't expected in camp for another four hours. There was no innocent reason Big Foot's truck should be here.

Maybe this wasn't the Big Foot truck. Maybe the whole poaching thing had nothing to do with Tommy. Julie shifted from one foot to the other. This close to the Big Foot camp, that didn't seem likely, though. Did she dare investigate? If that was the truck the poachers were using, they could turn up any second. They could put their filthy trophies in and drive away.

Julie started running toward the truck again. The radio collar whipped her in the leg as she stretched out. As she came closer to the truck, she could see that it was the Big Foot vehicle. The license plate was covered with mud, but the dent where Brent had slid into a tree last summer was there.

If Tommy had left the keys in the truck like he often did, she could simply snatch the vehicle and drive it into camp. If its presence was innocent, it wouldn't be a big deal. The thing belonged to Big Foot anyway. If it was the vehicle poachers were using, she would have left them stranded. All this went through her head in a flash. Julie turned toward the truck. She would run by and see if the keys were in the ignition. If they weren't, she'd just keep going.

The keys were there! Julie skidded to a halt, jerked the door open, and jumped in. By force of habit she pulled the seatbelt over her shoulder and fastened it. Concentrating on not flooding the quirky old engine, Julie pumped the gas once and turned the key. Just as the engine caught, a male voice spoke in a foreign language right behind her. Shock went through her spine with a jolt, and her hand jerked, yanking the keys out of the ignition. Someone was in the vehicle with her! He must have been lying down in the backseat. The voice demanded something, still in another language.

Was that Japanese? The keys had fallen onto the floor. Julie scrambled for them. If she could get out and run with the keys, they'd still be stranded. She glanced over her shoulder—only to come face-to-face with Tommy's uncle, who had reared up from behind the front seat like a genie. He let out a loud expletive and disappeared again. Julie's hand closed on the truck keys. Tommy's uncle reappeared with a pistol in his hand and a deadly look in his eyes. Julie looked into the round, black hole of the gun barrel and froze.

"What are you doing here?" The man growled.

Julie gave him a wide-eyed look and forced incredulity into her voice. Of course, that wasn't hard to do. She'd never had a pistol in her face before. "I can't believe it! You're pointing a gun at me."

"Why did you get into this truck?" He gave a good imitation of a bear growl.

It was amazing how that pistol focused her thought process. Julie talked fast. "Why shouldn't I? It's Big Foot's truck. I went out for a walk and saw it on my way back. It seemed to be deserted, so I figured I'd better drive it back into camp." Julie could see the bloody radio collar on the seat beside her. If Tommy's uncle saw that, any chance she had of being thought innocent was gone.

"Is that why you're pointing that pistol at me? Because you thought I was trying to steal the truck? If so, then we can both relax." She smiled, hoping she looked more convincing than she felt. She moved her hand slowly toward her seat-belt latch. It wouldn't open. The idiot latch had chosen this of all moments to jam. Julie rattled on, hoping against hope to gain some time. "I'm sure Brent will appreciate that you're looking after his vehicle."

The man said nothing. Julie glanced at him. His expression was baffled and angry, but the muzzle of the pistol had wavered away from her. She didn't get the impression that he was eager to hurt her. The backseat squeaked as he shifted—then he gave a startled exclamation. He'd seen the collar!

Hard and cold, the pistol was suddenly against Julie's neck. "Start the truck! Drive!"

Shaking violently, Julie obeyed.

"Those keys were in your hand. You were going to leave with them. And the truck. You intended to leave us stranded, did you not?" He nodded. "It was a good plan. How unfortunate for you that I caught you." His tone hardened. "I do not enjoy what I must do now, but you should never have tried to interfere with the Oshikawa family."

Julie didn't have to ask what he meant by "what I must do now." She knew, as clearly as if he'd said it aloud. He was going to kill her.

Jesus, be with me. With that, she threw the truck into gear and accelerated. If she was going fast enough, he'd be crazy to shoot her.

"Slow down!" he bellowed. "I *will* shoot you, and if I get hurt, it will not matter."

He sounded fanatical enough to do it. Julie slowed down, but she was furious with this man. "You were so obsessed with honor before! What honor? You're a filthy poacher!" They were almost at the dirt track that went into Big Foot's camp.

"Shut up! I am an exporter. If a hunter wishes to sell me bear gallbladder, then that is only one more valuable thing to export."

Julie looked at him with disgust. "It's illegal."

"Laws are meant to be circumvented. Only a fool obeys blindly." The muzzle of the pistol dug harder into her neck.

Julie slowed down even more, but her mind was racing. This area was so remote they wouldn't have to drive far for Tommy's uncle to shoot her, then leave her body where it would most likely never be found. She had to do something. Her eyes scanned the situation…and she caught her breath.

She had a seat belt on, but Tommy's uncle did not. On the rural roads where she'd grown up, a rolled truck was one of the most common accidents. Her father had repeatedly drilled it into her: She was always to wear a seat belt because most people with belts on came out of that kind of accident with only bruises. With a sudden twist of the wheel, Julie sent the pickup over the edge of the road. Tommy's uncle shouted. The truck bucked violently, and the pistol went off inches from her ear. Julie yanked the steering wheel to the right as hard as she could. The horizon spun as the truck rolled.

When the wild motion ceased, Julie hung in her seat belt. The truck had landed on the passenger's side.

Her head was still ringing from the sound of that shot. This time when she poked at the release on her seat belt, it opened. She didn't think the truck had rolled more than once, but the windshield was gone. Julie scrambled through the hole and ran for the trees.

She threw herself down behind a log and lay there panting. The only sound was the popping of the hot metal of the truck's engine. She could smell gasoline. Except for a cut on her leg where she'd bumped the window glass, Julie didn't feel like she'd been hurt much. Her father had been right. She peeked cautiously over the log. No one was moving. Was Tommy's uncle unconscious? Hurt badly? What if the truck caught fire from gas on the hot engine?

Julie said a quick prayer for courage, stood up, and walked back to the truck. The back window of the cab was broken. Inside she could see Tommy's uncle sprawled against the lower door. There was blood pouring from his head. Had she killed him? With a wildly beating heart, Julie crawled back into the vehicle. Her hand touched the pistol. Picking it up, she threw it as hard as she could out the window and into the bush.

Using her first-aid training, she checked the man's vital signs. There was a gash at his hairline that was bleeding enough to make a big mess, but it didn't look life-threatening. His pulse and breathing were good. The smell of gasoline was overpowering. Holding his head and neck steady, she pulled him out of the truck. As she laid him down, he began moaning and starting to move. Julie thought about tying him up in some way, but there was nothing at hand. She needed help, and she couldn't be more than three or four hundred yards from the camp.

Julie started up the hill to the road but found that her legs were shaking too hard to let her run fast. When she wasn't far from Big Foot's camp, she cried out.

"David!"

It came out as a croak. She clenched her teeth. That call had come from deep inside. She was in trouble, and she instinctively called for David. Tears stung her eyes, and she forced herself to go faster.

Eighteen

JULIE BURST INTO CAMP, AND THE FIRST THING SHE SAW WAS David's startled face.

"David!" This time it came out strong and clear.

He dropped the pot in his hand into the fire. He and the Frenchman, Marc, were the only people in sight. Marc jumped away from the steaming water as David took two quick strides toward her. His arms came around her, and she sagged against him, relief flooding her every pore.

"Julie, you're all scraped up! What happened? Sit down before you collapse."

"It rolled." She let him lead her to a log seat. "They shot Igor. At least I think it's probably Igor, and the truck rolled. Tommy's uncle was groaning, and, David, I should have talked to you about Tommy—"

"Is she mad?" Marc raised his eyebrows.

"Julie, look at me!" David's voice was like a lifeline. "Now take a deep breath, and explain it from the beginning. We can't help you until we know what has happened."

273

She looked into his eyes, and the care and strength she saw there steadied her. "I got up early to read the Bible and to pray. Oh, David, I should have talked to you about Tommy last night, but I didn't, and now..."

David rubbed Julie's back, calming her. "Slowly. Just tell us one thing at a time."

She took a deep breath and tried to do as he said. "I was going down the far side of the ridge and found a dead bear. It was still warm, and there was a collar, one of Laurel's tracking collars, all bloody and broken, but I picked it up." She looked down at her hand as if expecting to find it there. "I left the collar at the truck!"

"The truck?"

"Big Foot's brown Ford. Tommy's uncle was in it and——" Julie shut her eyes, remembering the feel of that cold gun barrel against her neck.

David grabbed Julie's arms. "Tommy's uncle? He *is* involved in poaching!"

Julie's eyes snapped open. "You knew? David, he was going to kill me. He put a gun to my neck." She started shaking so hard it was difficult to speak.

David ran his hands down her arms and took her hands. "Steady, Julie. Just tell us what happened."

She clung to his strong hands and swallowed hard. As quickly and clearly as she could, she told them everything. "Tommy's uncle was going to take me somewhere and shoot me." Her voice rose as she fought for control. She swallowed and forced it to be level. "I had a seat belt on and he didn't, so I rolled the truck and ran back."

David squeezed her hands, causing her to wince. "You did *what?*"

"She *is* mad!" Marc gestured wildly.

People were crawling out of tents all around them now asking questions. Suddenly Julie's attention was focused on the sound of a vehicle on the road. She could see nothing through the trees. It came to a screeching halt, and she could hear voices in the distance shouting.

"Someone is down at the truck!" Julie dropped his hand and started running.

"Julie, wait!"

She didn't pause. She should have never left Mr. Oshikawa. What if he'd found his gun and shot at the people who stopped? She could hear David's footsteps behind her. Brent ran after them both, loudly demanding an explanation.

Julie stopped and spun around. "If you don't call the police, the poachers will get away!"

"Poachers?" Brent stopped and stared at her as if she'd lost her mind.

"Call the police!" David said fiercely. Brent nodded.

David had almost caught up with her, but when he

reached for her arm, Julie turned and ran again. "Julie, wait! You could get hurt!"

That didn't matter. All that mattered was that if Mr. Oshikawa hurt someone else it would be her fault. The packed dirt on the track made loud slapping sounds under her feet as she sprinted down the road. Knowing David was right behind her gave her courage. In a few seconds she could see a small, red sport utility parked just in front of the truck. Two men were helping a third into the backseat. One of them was slight, with a jacket like—

"Tommy!"

The boy gave her a hunted look. The uncle yelled something, and Tommy hesitated. The other man, a redhead, shoved Tommy into the backseat and leaped into the driver's seat. David caught up with her and grabbed her arm, as the vehicle accelerated away, tires kicking gravel.

"Julie, you may have the bravest heart in the world, but what did you think you could do against three men?"

She tried to pull away from David. "They have Tommy. We've got to get him away from that man."

David shook his head. "Tommy left my place of his own free will, Julie. He wasn't kidnapped. He's been coming to work and going back to his uncle."

Julie was not convinced. "I can't believe he's

involved in this terrible thing. Not without being forced into it."

There was the sound of more running feet, and Brent arrived with some of the climbers. He went straight past them to stare over the edge of the road. "My truck! It was *my* truck that got rolled? Who did this?"

Julie blinked. "I did. He was going to kill me."

"Tommy Oshikawa was going to kill you?" Brent's expression was incredulous. "Has everyone lost their minds? What was he doing here now anyway? If I get my hands on him——"

David ran his hands through his hair. "It wasn't Tommy who threatened Julie; it was his uncle. But if you want to stop either of them, get back on the phone to the police. They were in that sport utility that just left."

Brent shook his head. "Look, I have no idea what is going on here. Somebody better start talking."

Again Julie told the story of her morning. Brent motioned toward his truck. "All I see is a truck that shouldn't be here that's been rolled off the road, and you have this wild story of poachers and men with pistols."

"Look in the truck if you don't believe me." She shuddered. "The bear collar is there."

Brent strode over and looked in through the broken window. "I don't see any collar. What color was it?"

"Yellow. It was right on the seat..." As realization dawned, Julie shook her head. "He took it. Tommy's uncle or one of the others took it." Brent just looked at her. "So go look at the dead bear, then. I'll show you."

Julie turned to walk toward the carcass, but Marc stopped her. "I believe you, but I have one question. If all the poachers were not in that red truck, there are armed criminals in the woods. Is that right?"

Julie nodded.

Louise moved closer to Brent. "Can we please leave here? Perhaps they will try to steal the van."

Brent shot Julie a look of pure frustration. Obviously he thought she was getting the clients worked up for nothing. "Look, we'll pack up and get out of here in the van. Without the truck to carry gear, it will be crowded, but we can do it. We'll call the police as soon as we get to a phone."

"Okay." Julie started walking to her car. "It's going to take you time to pack and leave. I'm going right now."

"I'm coming with you." David quickly followed her.

"What about the scouting climb?" Brent's peeved voice followed them as well. "I've got people coming in on Monday to climb, and I need you ready."

Julie didn't stay to listen to David's answer. She was already heading back toward camp at a run. With or without David, she was going for help. Last night she'd been distracted by her interest in David and hadn't talked about Tommy. First Corinthians was right. She'd be better able to serve God without being distracted by a man. Half blinded by tears, she started pitching gear into the trunk of her car. She knew she wasn't thinking logically, and she fought for control, but things only got worse as the shock of the morning caught up with her. Shaking from head to foot, Julie leaned her forehead against the cool metal of her car's roof.

David gave her shoulder a gentle squeeze. "Are you okay?"

Julie spun to face him, too upset to watch her words. "I've never been so mixed-up in my life! Last night I should have talked about Tommy, and now I'm shaking so hard I don't know if I can drive safely. I should be able to do what's right, but I'm so confused!"

"Julie, you know as well as I do that two are stronger than one. And there's no way I'm letting you drive." He dumped his armload of gear into the back-seat and held the passenger door open for her.

She bit her lip, but she was simply too shaken to argue. She climbed in. David got in on the driver's side, reached into the backseat, and handed her his sleeping bag. "Cover up with this. You're shivering."

As they left, Julie huddled into the corner of her seat, her arms holding the sleeping bag tightly around her. Gradually her shivering stopped. David's words echoed in her head. *"Two are stronger than one."* That wasn't what Paul had said in 1 Corinthians. She pulled the sleeping bag like a cowl over her head so David wouldn't see the slow tears that trickled down her cheeks. *Lord, be with Tommy wherever he is. Please let us reach him before his uncle can harm him.*

They saw no evidence of the red sport utility. As they got closer to Sundre, Julie felt calmer but still weak and shaky inside. Instead of heading for the police station, David turned off at a hamburger place.

"What are you doing?" Julie frowned.

"You're so pale your eyes look like huge holes in a white mask. You haven't eaten today, have you?"

Julie shook her head. "There's no time."

David, who was just pulling up to the drive through, didn't answer but placed an order. As the first sip of hot, sweet coffee hit her system, Julie realized he'd been right. On the short drive to the police station, she wolfed down most of a hamburger. Forty-five minutes later, she and David were in a police vehicle on their way back out to the mountains.

Julie knew she would never have gotten through the rest of that morning without David. He was with her as she led the policemen and a chunky, gray-haired Fish and Wildlife officer to the dead bear. He stayed close as they walked her through what had happened with Big Foot's truck. There were smears of blood on the truck seat where the smashed collar had been. The police took samples of that, and they found Mr. Oshikawa's gun where Julie had flung it into the bush.

"Lady, you've got more guts than 99 percent of the men I know, and that includes police officers." The Fish and Wildlife officer stood there shaking his head. "You are one tough woman."

Julie's stomach sank. There it was again. She hadn't meant to be tough or gutsy. She'd only been doing what seemed logical. David put a gentle hand on her shoulder, and she looked up at him with startled gratitude.

When the police had finally taken them back to Sundre, it was nearly suppertime. "Stay in touch. We may need you to answer further questions."

"I may be doing an all-day climb tomorrow." David looked at the officer. "Is that a problem?" Julie's eyebrows shot up. Tomorrow was Sunday. David never climbed on Sunday if he could avoid it.

The officer assured him that it wasn't; then they were on their way out to the car, alone for the first time that day. "Brent talked you into doing that climb tomorrow?"

David nodded and smiled ruefully. "It was obvious we weren't going to get it done today like he wanted. I don't like to work on Sunday, but I had to agree with him so I could follow you. I thought you were going to drive off without me."

"I was going to." Julie yawned. "I would never have survived today without you, David." She sighed and shoved her hand through her hair. "What time are we heading out to climb?"

"Uh, Julie, I don't think that's a good idea. You got knocked around when the truck rolled, and you're going to be very stiff. I'd rather you stayed home and rested. There'll be other climbs."

She bit her lip. Did she have to fight for everything? Her emotions were so jumbled. "Thanks for your concern, but I'll be okay, David. I'd really like to go with you."

He studied her in silence for a moment, then nodded slowly. "If you want to climb with me, you're more than welcome. I know you'll do fine even if you are sore." He reached out to touch her arm. "Julie, I've been doing a lot of thinking this week about what you wrote. Maybe we can do some serious talking tomorrow."

She looked at him anxiously. What kind of thinking had he been doing? What if he'd decided he agreed that she shouldn't marry? He said nothing more until they were in Canmore, but she could see the tension in his jaw. "Could we pray together?"

Julie nodded and bowed her head.

"Jesus, please be with Tommy. He must be very frightened." He paused, and his voice was rough when he continued. "Julie and I are both your children. You know what I want, but, God, just guide our lives."

A wave of hopeless longing swept through Julie. David was such a good man. When he finished speaking, she found her voice was too tight to say anything at all. Finally she managed a whispered Amen. She kept her head down as he gathered his gear and left the vehicle.

Tomorrow would be a day that would change her life one way or the other. And she was not sure she was ready.

Nineteen

TOMMY WAS A HALF MILE FROM THE HIGHWAY BETWEEN Calgary and Edmonton. He sat hidden in the tall, scratchy wheat—and even there he felt exposed.

The scene in the poacher's vehicle was vivid in his mind. Tommy and the poacher had come back to find the brown truck gone. At first the poacher, a man Tommy knew only as Red, wanted to simply dump him off with the goods, but Tommy insisted his uncle wouldn't have left, not without the goods in any case. Finally Red drove up the road, and they found the rolled truck. Tommy could still hear Julie's voice as she called after him. When he had moved out of David's place, he'd felt like he was betraying both of them and Laurel, too.

His uncle had promised to let him go at the end of the month. Now the things he feared—the disappointment in his parents' eyes, the shame to his family—were likely going to happen anyway.

That wasn't why he was in this wheat field, though. Tommy had been intending to stick with his uncle, especially since he was hurt. He had never seen Uncle Atsuko so angry. Tommy stayed in the backseat trying to make him comfortable, keeping pressure on the gash on his head until the bleeding stopped. His uncle demanded a cell phone and was disgusted when the poacher didn't have one. He then demanded that they stop at the first possible pay phone. Tommy got the impression that Red would have gladly dumped Atsuko Oshikawa off beside the road.

While Tommy tore up his T-shirt and bandaged his uncle's head, his uncle proceeded to give him a lecture on standing up for his family's honor no matter what the circumstances.

Goaded beyond endurance, Tommy finally interrupted. "How can you talk about honor? If the police aren't looking for us now, they soon will be."

"Ha, the Canadian police! Once I call my associates, we will get on a plane to Vancouver and be gone from here in no time. I am too conspicuous covered with blood, but you will call them and arrange for someone to book tickets and meet us at the Calgary airport with clean clothing. When we stop, you will get paper towels and clean my head. I will wear this man's hat." He jerked with his chin, pointing at Red. "Everyone wears western hats in Calgary."

There was an argument as Tommy's uncle told the poacher he needed his western hat. Red protested that he liked that hat. Atsuko finally offered him five hundred dollars. The money and the hat changed hands, but both men were obviously furious. Tommy looked at his uncle. If he could actually get them out of here, Tommy would go. But once they were in Hong Kong or wherever, he intended to live his own life. No more being managed by family for him.

Uncle Atsuko began to rail against Julie, venting his anger and blaming the situation on her. Suddenly the words came that froze Tommy in place. "I should have shot her. No, better, I should have done the same to her as David Hales. That man will soon trouble us no longer, and it will not be traceable to me."

"What did you do?" Tommy looked at his uncle with horror in his eyes.

Uncle Atsuko only looked at him, his blood-streaked face complacent.

"I will not make that phone call unless you tell me what you did."

Atsuko shrugged.

"You did put that nail where it would put a hole in the tire!" Tommy glared at his uncle.

Atsuko nodded. "A man needs to be able to think, especially when he can't trust his own nephew."

David Hales was in danger. Tommy didn't know how or why, but he knew it was true. His uncle had done something, that much was clear. Fear clawed at him. *If David hadn't tried to help me, this wouldn't have happened.* He would have no chance to help David if his uncle knew what he was thinking. With an effort, Tommy kept his face blank.

Tommy almost felt dizzy. He couldn't let David die, but how could he warn him? He could call David before he called the number his uncle would give him. No, that wouldn't work. David wouldn't be back yet. Maybe Laurel would be home at Julie's place. At the gas station outside the town of Olds, Red went in and got the key to the men's room since Tommy's hands were covered in his uncle's blood. In the washroom, Tommy scrubbed his hands clean, then soaked several stacks of paper towels. After handing those to his uncle who was lying out of sight in the backseat, Tommy headed for a phone.

Tommy could feel Red's eyes on his back. Putting his body between Red and the phone, Tommy called directory assistance, but no number was listed for Julie Miller. It had to be in Laurel's name, but he couldn't remember her last name.

A wave of revulsion swept over him as he began to dial the number his uncle had given him. He couldn't leave the country, not if it meant risking David's life. Tommy turned and walked away. He could still feel Red's eyes on him. When he heard the truck door open, he sprinted, running hard through the truck parking area, off the pavement, and into a wheat field. No one followed.

Crouched in the wheat, Tommy tried to figure out his options. Red and his uncle didn't dare make much of a commotion. That would draw attention, the last thing they needed. He had some money and his uncle's calling card. Tommy figured he had a bit more than a day to find a way to warn David. After all, David wasn't booked to work this Sunday.

For hours Tommy simply lay there, too numb to do anything. Around dusk, he finally stood up and looked toward the gas station. All the years of training in loyalty weighed heavily on Tommy now. He had abandoned an injured family member. Red and his uncle might have left, but Uncle Atsuko would probably try to get Red to make the call and take him to the airport. Red was greedy enough that it would probably work. He was pretty sure that Atsuko Oshikawa could take care of himself. Still, Tommy felt uneasy.

After several long moments, Tommy turned and walked toward the lights of the town of Olds. The waist-high wheat swished harshly against his jeans. It began to hit him that he'd just divorced himself from his family. Suddenly the night felt very empty. He was alone as he'd never been before in his life. Without family, just who was he? Would he even be able to continue at college? He was taking prelaw because his family wanted him to, but what did he, Tommy, want to do?

An image suddenly filled his mind. His father used to keep an aquarium. Once, when Tommy was about four, he had walked into the living room to find one tiny fish flipping around on the rug. Lint stuck to its sides, and its gills gasped as it lay there all alone. The other fish in the tank didn't seem to have noticed.

Tommy felt just like that little fish.

The buildings in Olds were getting gradually closer. Tommy frowned. Julie had tried to explain how she felt like part of a bigger family because of her trust in God. He stopped, threw back his head, and looked at the deep, blue sky. Was there a God out there? What Julie had talked about sounded so good.

He had intended to find a motel in Olds. He could stay there and keep trying David's number from his room. A sinking feeling hit his gut as Tommy realized that his uncle's contacts could be looking for him. He turned away from the motel, buttoned his jeans jacket to cover his chest, and walked down the main street of Olds. He could call David from anywhere. A truck was pulling out onto the highway. Tommy waved it down.

"Can I have a ride?"

"Where you going, kid?"

"Wherever you are." Tommy held out a fistful of bills.

The trucker shrugged and motioned him in. "I'm

289

heading for Vancouver. That okay with you?"

"Sure, whatever." As the man worked his way upward through the gears, Tommy stared blankly out the window. He felt as disconnected from his past as if he'd just boarded a spaceship for Mars.

"You look beat." The trucker jerked a thumb at the bunk behind the seat. "Get some shut-eye if you want."

Tommy glanced back at the bunk. Sharing that motel room with his uncle, he hadn't slept properly in days. Besides, the idea of getting out of sight, shutting his eyes, and hiding for a bit sounded good. Nodding his thanks, he crawled into the bunk. Within minutes he was deeply asleep.

Back in his tiny apartment, David stood in the shower and scrubbed off a week's worth of grunge. He wished he could scrub the confusion out of his mind as easily. He and Julie belonged together. Would she ever really open up to him? David clenched both fists in the heavy damp material of the towel, then threw it violently into the corner of the room. He had spent hours going through Scripture, reviewing passages on marriage, drawing together a case with which he hoped to convince Julie. He'd wanted to talk to her, but yesterday just hadn't been the right time.

Though he lay in bed and tried to force himself to

relax, going over each muscle group and willing the tension away as he'd learned to do before competitions, David could not sleep. As soon as one area relaxed, another tightened up. All the events of the day kept spinning through his mind.

Julie had deliberately rolled that truck. His stomach clenched as it hit him again. *She could have been killed!* He forced the muscles to relax again. Julie wasn't dead; she was just fine. She was an amazing woman. When she came into camp, she'd been shaking from head to foot but still determined to act. All the time she'd been worried about Tommy.

Tommy! Bolting out of bed, David reached for the phone to call the police. He tried to find out if Tommy had been picked up yet, but the woman who answered the phone said she wasn't authorized to give him any information. The boy must be scared. Pacing the room, David prayed for Tommy.

Even with all the worry about Tommy, it didn't take long for David's thoughts to return to Julie. What if she rejected him tomorrow? He found himself sweating like he had just before a big climbing competition. David wiped his hands and face on a towel. He'd never been this nervous, not even before the biggest competitions. There was so much at stake, so much he hoped for, yet he could end up rejected and alone. David pulled on some clothing and set out to walk until he was more at rest with himself and God. It was nearly two in the morning before he came back, crawled into bed, and slept.

God, it's in your hands, but I ask you in Jesus' name to open Julie's heart to me.

Twenty

TOMMY HAD SPENT MOST OF THE NIGHT IN RESTLESS, dream-filled sleep. In one, his uncle turned into a bleeding bear. In another, David welcomed him to an honored seat at a huge family gathering, then fell dead. Around 2:00 A.M. he had climbed back into the front seat of the truck and sat staring blankly as the mountains unfolded under a full moon.

The trucker geared down as he came into the town of Golden, British Columbia. "I've got to stop here for a four-hour break. You going to go on with me?" He turned the wheel and pulled into a truck stop.

Suddenly the thought of going farther in that truck seemed unbearable. Tommy shook his head. "No, but thanks for the ride, man." He climbed out of the truck. He walked aimlessly down the side of the road, the noise of the Trans-Canada Highway on one side of him. Maybe he shouldn't have gone so far. He should have tried to call David again. He shouldn't have slept so long. Tommy hugged himself against the chill mountain air. His stomach hurt.

The flashing vacancy sign on a motel front caught his eye. Would they let him in at this time of night? No harm in trying. Thankfully, they were willing. The room stank of stale smoke, but it had a phone and a bed. In a few minutes, Tommy was under the welcome warmth of a hot shower. Out of the shower, he stood wrapped in a towel, staring at the phone. Feeling defeated and battered, he sighed and lay down on the bed. Tomorrow morning would be soon enough to call. No use to bother David in the middle of the night.

Tommy couldn't sleep. He had already slept for too long in the truck, and his mind was in turmoil. Had his uncle gotten safely out of the country? Did his parents know what had happened? What if he missed David Hales tomorrow? If he didn't turn himself in, would the police look for him in British Columbia? Did he want to live anywhere but Canada? He'd never killed a bear but had acted as a link in the chain of dealers in bear gallbladders. How harsh would the penalty be if he turned himself in? Could he do that without ratting on his family?

After half an hour, Tommy bolted out of bed and put his clothes back on. He was going back. It would be stupid to quit school and go on the run now. His uncle would either be out of the country by now, or the police would have picked him up. No one else in his immediate family had been involved, and Tommy didn't know his uncle's contacts. The only thing he could give the police was information about the man who'd actually shot the bears, and Tommy felt no loyalty to that man at all. Besides, he had to make sure David Hales was safe.

Golden was on the main Trans-Canada truck route, and Tommy still had money in his pocket. It didn't take him long to find a truck going the other direction. He ought to be in Canmore by nine on Sunday morning. He'd find David at church.

Julie's evening hadn't been easy, either. Telling Laurel that Tommy Oshikawa had been involved in bear poaching wasn't fun.

"So that's why he hated that picture of the dead sow so much. I should have stuffed it up his nose!" Laurel's gentle face twisted with anger.

"He tried to leave, to run away from his uncle."

"But he went back, and he was out there today. He chose."

Julie nodded slowly. "That's what David said."

Laurel shook her head. "At least what happened today should slow down the poachers for a while. I can't believe you rolled a truck on purpose and got away. Julie, you are amazing."

"One tough woman." Julie looked down at her folded hands.

"Oh, Julie, I didn't mean it that way. You're not weird or anything. I bet David didn't act put off, did he?"

Julie didn't answer Laurel's question. Instead she told Laurel she was going with David on a climb called the Mother-in-Law and needed to get to bed early.

The next morning, David seemed more remote than usual. If she'd known him better, Julie would've thought he was acting nervous, almost shy, but David Hales was never shy. Wasn't he the person who was so at home with himself and God? Besides, why would he be shy with her? Julie's stomach tightened as her fears of rejection grew. They'd picked up coffee and doughnuts on the way out of Canmore. As she drove, she could see David fiddling with his empty coffee mug. It didn't take them long to reach the base of the climb. Julie began to get out gear, but David stopped her, putting a hand on her arm. "Julie, we need to talk."

Her hand slid off the shoulder strap of the pack she'd been lifting. Slowly she turned to face his direct gray eyes. "I know, David, but could we please do that at the end of the day? Can't we just enjoy being climbing partners for now?" Her voice sounded pleading, even to her. She swallowed and said more steadily, "Besides, we should have more time at the end of the day than we do now. I mean, isn't it usually better to leave extra time for a multipitch climb? Things can happen to slow us down."

David's gaze never left hers. Again she felt that he could see straight into her very soul. His hand was warm on her arm. She blushed and turned her head away.

"Okay, climbing partners it is." David's voice sounded tense, but then he smiled. "I know we climb together well. You've come a long way in both skill and confidence this summer."

"Thanks." Julie thought about what he'd said as they hiked to the base of the climb. David was right. She had learned a lot about climbing.

"Remember the climb at Acephale? I almost hated you that day."

"What? Why?" His eyebrows were raised, and his gray eyes twinkled. "What did I do?"

"It was who you were. Who you are. A top-level climber from Europe, a person who had already made his mark. I felt outclassed and very threatened." She looked at him seriously. "What you just said made me realize that I am going to be okay. I've got my Association of Canadian Mountain Guides rock-guide certification. Big Foot isn't my only job anymore. God has opened doors for me to work in the mountains, and that's partly due to your help. I'll always be grateful to you for that."

"That sounds a little too much like a farewell speech." David's hands were clenched on the straps of his pack. Was it her imagination, or did he look pale?

"I was just saying thank you. It's not time for farewells yet." As she said those words, Julie felt suddenly like her body was made of lead. David would be leaving soon. And she would be alone...again.

Julie led the first pitch, feeling the rough rock, still cool from the night, under her hands. She took her time, placing protection carefully as she moved upward. As she concentrated on climbing, she began to feel better. The sky shone clear blue against the hard edge of the rock high above her head. She was going up there, up high into the light, where the ragged edge of the mountains touched the sky.

At the top of the first pitch, she set up anchors. "Secure!" she called down, letting David know that she was tied in to the anchor now. There were ledges to stand on at the belay points most of the way up this climb. That was a lot more comfortable than belaying another climber while hanging from the anchor. She gathered in the loose rope until it wouldn't come anymore.

"That's me," David's voice floated up, letting her know the rope was taut between them.

She moved to put him on belay. David climbed smoothly and quickly. Even removing the protection she'd put in place didn't take long. He didn't falter, and the rope never tightened to his harness.

David came up the last few feet smiling. "This is a beautiful place." He gestured out across the valley. The ledge was too narrow. David's arm touched hers, and she found it difficult to think properly.

David's breathing was uneven, but she assumed that was from the climb. His pupils were dark, almost hypnotic, as he looked at her. "Okay, tell me about the next pitch."

Forcing herself to concentrate, Julie looked up at the rock face. "There is a bit of an overhang—see, just there?" She pointed. "The route goes around the west side, and there's not much place for decent protection. Once you get on top of that, there's a very nice crack to follow."

"Right." David checked that he was on belay and began climbing.

Julie tended the belay rope automatically and watched David climb. He moved with smooth, graceful power around the overhang and up out of sight. He never faltered, and the rope never tightened to his harness. It seemed only minutes before it was her turn to climb again.

Three pitches later, they were high above the ground. Both of them were climbing well. A sound far below turned her head. Down there, in the scree, she could see two tiny figures. They seemed to be yelling and gesturing wildly. David was above her, in the first hanging belay. She looked up, but she couldn't see him as the cliff blocked her view.

Julie looked down and squinted to see better. Only unintelligible wisps of sound came up to her, but those people were yelling. Looking straight down on the tiny figures, she couldn't see much detail. One had on a red shirt or blouse or something. That's the one she'd seen first. The other had on inconspicuous green or brown clothes. What could possibly be wrong? Julie squinted harder. Was that Laurel? Laurel and someone with dark hair? She shook her head. Laurel would be in church now, so it couldn't be her. Maybe the two people were in some kind of trouble. Well, she couldn't do anything about it now. She'd tell David when she caught up to him.

As Julie climbed upward around the overhang, David came into view about forty feet above her. He sat in his harness, taking up rope as she climbed. "Julie, when you get up here, can you help me tighten my harness? It seems to be loose around the middle."

Julie gave him a puzzled look and forgot all about the people far below. She had seen David put on his harness the same way he had hundreds of times. Why should it be loose? Her pulse quickened. Something wasn't right here.

"If you're secure, could you stay there a minute, Julie?"

"Just a second." Julie got both hands and feet into a solid position. "Okay." She watched anxiously as David tried to take some of his weight off the harness, balancing on small footholds. He couldn't use his hands as long as he had her on belay. Neither could he tighten the harness or check it properly without taking her off belay.

"David, something is wrong with your harness, isn't it?" Julie could hear her voice shaking.

"I think so. I'm going to tie your rope off."

"Get the rope around yourself first. I'm okay."

He ignored her. Moving evenly and slowly he tied her rope separately to the anchor webbing. He had to do it one-handed since the other hand held her brake rope, keeping her safely on belay. He was balanced precariously on small footholds. Just as he finished the knot and reached for the rope with his left hand, one of his feet slipped. He fell into his harness, and it came apart in front of her eyes.

Julie screamed as David began to fall, then dropped to the end of the slack. He held his weight for a split second with his hands on the rope; then he swung in, smacking the wall hard and jarring his hands loose. Julie was still tied in. If she could just catch him.... She lunged at him and snagged his body as he fell past her. Julie clung to him with her right arm, and they fell together for a fraction of a second until she hit the end of the rope. His weight threw her sideways and smacked them both against the wall. The jerk of David's weight threw her upside down, and her arm was ripped from his body.

She watched horrified as he grabbed at the cliff, turned sideways, and thudded into the narrow, V-shaped, horizontal ledge above the overhang. His helmet struck with a crack, and he just lay there, his body motionless. She started to call his name but choked off the sound. If David heard her and even stirred a finger, he was going to fall farther.

Julie tried to think as her body quivered uncontrollably. *I have to get to him!* She hung in her harness at the end of less than half of the climbing rope. The balance of the rope was hanging just to her right. A rush of fear slammed through her. *What if my harness fails too?* Putting her feet on the rock wall, she swung sideways, grabbing the loose rope and wrapping it around her body. She wanted to stay there, momentarily safe, but she had to get down to David.

God, please help me! Don't let him die.... If David hadn't tied her in first, she would've fallen with him. The anchor and her rope had been connected to his harness. If he hadn't tied her in first, he could have gotten a rope around himself. Maybe he wouldn't have fallen at all. *Oh, David...* Julie looked at her harness and tugged hard on it. Nothing seemed to be loose. She had to trust it if she was going to rescue David.

Slowly she unwound the rope from her body. Julie

was shaking so much she could barely get the figure-eight device off of her harness. *Why won't my right arm work? What did I—*

Stop it, Julie! You don't have time to think about that now. Get busy! David is your first priority. To reach David, she had to unhook herself from the shorter end of the rope and fasten herself to the longer half of the rope. She was almost prepared to rappel down but found it very difficult to untie the knot that held her on the short end of the rope. She fumbled desperately at the unwilling lump with her left hand. It seemed like ages before she was free. Julie painstakingly rappelled down to David's limp form.

When she got to him, she quickly tied herself to her rope. David was so still. Had his chest just moved? *He isn't dead!* Before she did anything else, Julie needed to tie him to the rope somehow, fear dogging her every move, so he couldn't fall farther. What if his back was broken and she made it worse? Well, a broken back was better than death. His left leg was twisted like a pretzel.

Gritting her teeth, she slid the loose end of the rope under his back and tied it solidly around his waist, then around each thigh. Now neither of them would fall. Julie leaned her head against the rock as the world swam around her. *No, I won't faint. Not now. I'm a rock guide, for Pete's sake. I've been trained for this.* Julie forced her mind into the patterns she'd been taught for rescue.

Okay. Good. She'd done the first part and removed both of them from immediate danger. Now she needed help, and she needed to make sure David wouldn't die of something she could prevent.

She checked to make sure that David was still breathing. His heartbeat was rapid but steady. She ran her hands under him. There was blood on his arms and legs, but he wasn't bleeding profusely. He seemed to be out cold...shock. She had to keep him warm against shock. She fumbled in her pack, jerked out her jacket, and laid it over him.

People! There had been those two people at the base of the cliff. Julie looked down. If they had stayed where they were, they wouldn't have been able to see her once she went over the overhang. They wouldn't have seen David fall, either. Her eyes frantically searched the area she could see, but no red shirt was in sight, no small people. Maybe they couldn't see her and David.

"Help!" Julie took a deep breath. "Get help!" Her voice sounded so tiny in the huge valley.

Movement caught her eye. The tiny figure in green was there in the trees. It was waving wildly and pointing downhill. Maybe the red shirt had seen the fall and had already gone for help. *I'd better be sure.* "Get help!"

Again the figure pointed; then it headed rapidly downhill. Still no figure in a red shirt, so either Red Shirt was still below or he had already left. Leaning back against the rock, Julie closed her eyes, drawing in deep gulps of air, willing her pulse to slow, her heart to stop pounding.

She wanted to look at David, to touch him, but she didn't dare do either. Touching him could startle or hurt him...and looking at him, well, her heart just couldn't take that right now.

"God, don't let me lose him."

The whispered prayer seemed to hang on the wind, and she opened her eyes, staring in front of her, taking in the expanse of the sky, the movement of the clouds. *"The heavens declare the glory of God; the skies proclaim the work of his hands...."*

Peace, sweet and all-consuming, settled over her. She was not alone. God was there. With her. With David. And Julie knew as she'd never known it before. That was enough.

Twenty-one

JULIE WAS SHAKING FROM HEAD TO FOOT AS SHE TRIED TO think of what to do next. What if David had a broken back? What if the people she'd seen at the bottom of the cliff hadn't gone for help? Julie swallowed. It would be better for David if she didn't have to lower him off this cliff by herself. That would complicate his injuries. But she didn't want to leave him and go for help, either.

Julie shut her eyes and fought back tears. *Dear God, please let help come soon. I'm so scared.* Her mind seemed to calm down, and she was able to think more clearly. Okay, she had another six or seven hours of daylight. She would wait two hours; then if help hadn't come, she'd make David as secure as she could, climb down, and go for help.

Again, she ran through her safety checklist. The first thing was to get David tied in more securely. The anchor above them had stopped a hard fall when she'd tried to catch David. The bolts could've been jerked loose. Taking several chocks and nuts off her sling, she wedged them into the crack above the overhang. Again her right arm was making a nuisance of itself. Rigging the anchor took longer than normal since she had to work nearly one-handed. Using nylon webbing, she tied David securely by both his hips and his shoulders. He moaned and stirred, almost gaining consciousness, then went limp again. His legs had moved. *Hallelujah!* His spinal cord wasn't cut.

Julie shook her head. It was too soon for celebration. The fact that he could move his legs now didn't mean the bones in his back were sound. It just meant any break hadn't hurt his spinal cord yet.

Julie put more nuts in place and tied herself into the new anchor. It wouldn't help David if she fell. When they were both secure, she looked at the leg that was twisted. She gently lifted his right leg off of it. The twisted leg was definitely broken just below the knee. If only she had some way to immobilize it, but she had nothing. His backpack was underneath him, so maybe it had protected his spine, but the back of David's helmet was smashed. No, she wouldn't take off his helmet. She had no ice to put on his bruises there, and the helmet was still some protection. She stroked his cheek, feeling the roughness of his beard under his pale skin.

"Oh, David, I hope you'll be okay. You have to be. I love you."

His face twisted with pain, and he moaned.

"David? David, can you hear me?"

There was no response. He didn't seem to be aware of his surroundings, but he was conscious enough now to feel pain. Julie bit her lip. *I wish I could do something to reduce his pain!* Again she checked him over, nervously looking in case she'd missed something. His elbows and hands were torn, scraped, and ragged. She sucked air through her teeth. *If only I could take your place....* A gash above the knee on his good leg was bleeding steadily. Julie ripped off the sleeve of her T-shirt, folded it into a square, and applied pressure to stop the bleeding.

"God, after I caught on that maybe I could marry the right sort of man, I wanted David. I wanted him for my husband. I'm sorry I acted so selfishly. Please just let him be alive and able to heal so he's healthy. He is such a special man." Her voice caught in a sob. "I love him; I really do. Please, I don't care where he goes or what he ends up doing to serve you, just help him to be okay."

David stirred under her hand, and Julie looked quickly at his face. Was he coming to? His eyes stayed shut. She could see the muscles at the corner of his jaw starting to work. His breathing was faster now and uneven from the pain. She turned back to the gash. The worst of the bleeding seemed to have stopped. Julie looked for something soft to tie the pad in place. She ripped off her other sleeve, which was more difficult since her right hand wouldn't grip properly. Finally she got a decent grip and pulled it off with her left hand. When she finished tying it in place, she looked back at David's face and found his eyes on her.

"David!"

"Julie?" It came out in a hoarse whisper. His hand reached toward her, and she took it with her left hand.

"I'm here." Her voice quivered, and she tried to steady it. "I'll make sure you get help."

"Stay with me." His voice was strained, and he held her hand tightly.

Julie had an urge to laugh. Where was she going to go? They were both tied to the same rope high on a rock face. She swallowed hard, realizing she was close to hysteria. At least David was conscious now. That was a very good sign. She forced her voice to be steady. "I'm here, David. Hold still, okay? I don't know how badly you're hurt."

David's eyes were dark with pain, but he managed a faint grin. "I'll be okay. Just stay with me."

Julie nodded as tears sprang to her eyes. Was he asking not to be left alone while he was hurt, or did he mean more than that? David's grip on her hand suddenly tightened. He had shut his eyes against a wave of pain, and his face was even more pale. Julie gripped his hand, trying to give him something to hang onto. Beads of sweat stood out on his forehead, and little rivulets were running back into his hair.

"Oh, David!" Julie's breath came out in something close to a sob.

His eyes opened, and again there was that cocky half smile, but it didn't quite reach his eyes. "Hey, no tears. You're the brave one, remember? What happened?" His gaze traveled up the cliff face to the ropes and anchors. "How did I fall?"

"Your harness—" Her voice wobbled, and she swallowed hard. "Your harness came apart."

A sound brought her head up. A helicopter! *Please, please, let it be help!* The sound got rapidly louder, and a helicopter swung into sight. A rush of relief washed through Julie as she saw the blue circle of the mountain-rescue symbol on the side. The people *had* gone for help. Her bones seemed to give way. For a split second, she leaned limply against the rock.

No! She had to get their attention. David held her left hand, so she tried to wave with her right. *Yeow!* Julie clenched her teeth and forced herself to wave anyway, but her arm just wouldn't behave.

"You're hurt!" David's voice was filled with concern.

"I'm hurt?" Julie gasped. "Look who's talking!"

David had let go of her good arm, so she waved with that. The helicopter swung close and hovered. She could see the people in the cockpit looking the situation over. Julie pointed at David and waved more wildly.

Suddenly a man was on the skids, then hanging underneath them. She could see the first-aid symbol on his huge pack. The rope that connected him to the helicopter spooled out, and the helicopter rose.

He was now hanging thirty feet in front of them. Gently the helicopter got closer to the cliff and deposited him next to her. Julie reached out to catch him.

"Hold still!" he commanded, yelling over the noise of the copter.

The helicopter held him in place while he quickly set up an anchor for himself. He unclipped from the rope and motioned the copter away. The noise lessened, leaving the three of them together. The man, who introduced himself as Doug, had deep blue eyes and a freckled face. His competence reassured Julie. She wanted to cry with relief. Instead she forced herself to give a quick, professional summary of what had happened to David.

David focused on Doug. "Julie is hurt too."

"I'll look at her in a minute; don't worry." Doug pulled the radio off his belt and called for a Bowman bag. "I don't think his back is hurt, but I'm not going to take any chances."

Julie couldn't hear the reply, but Doug nodded, clipped the radio to his belt, and pulled off his backpack. He clipped his backpack to the anchor and pulled out splinting material to immobilize David's leg. He didn't try to move or straighten the leg. Even so, David whipped his head to one side. The muscles stood out in his neck. Julie reached for his hand, but he was clutching at the rock underneath him.

"Can't you do anything for his pain?"

"I can't—" Doug kept working—"but the ambulance personnel will as soon as we get him down."

Julie looked away. No one's pain had ever hurt her the way David's did. The helicopter was coming back. She could see another man on the end of the rope and something that looked like a very shallow bathtub inside a sack. She knew that was a Bowman bag. The men were going to need space to work, so Julie stood up.

"Hold still; we'll work around you." Doug looked up at her. His eyes were kind. They had a calming influence. "You've done a good job here. Just relax."

"She's fantastic." Pride shone from David's eyes as he gazed upon Julie.

Doug gave him a startled look and laughed. He didn't have time to comment before the other rescuer was beside him, tying in to Doug's anchor. Julie felt like a child in the way as they moved around her, efficiently sliding David into the Bowman bag and strapping him down tightly.

"Take care of her!" David insisted again as they

312

clipped him to the helicopter's rope.

"I will; don't worry."

Seconds later, David and the second rescuer disappeared upward on the rope. Julie watched anxiously until they were deposited gently on the ground. There was an ambulance down there, a police car, and several other vehicles. She had a sneaking suspicion that Brent wasn't going to be very happy about this kind of publicity, when a touch on her arm drew her attention. Doug was calling her name, had been for several seconds.

Now that David was safe, everything seemed to come apart. The ache in her shoulder swelled into a dreadful, pounding pain. Even Doug's voice didn't seem to matter. "Julie, your shoulder is dislocated. I'm going to strap it down. Do you hurt anywhere else?" He was working as he talked.

He had to repeat the question twice before she answered. "No, I don't think so. I tried to catch him, but—" Suddenly Julie was crying hysterically. She shook her head back and forth. "I couldn't catch him. He fell." She was wailing and couldn't stop.

"Julie! Look at me!" Doug's tone of command was not to be ignored. Julie gulped and tried to focus. "Your friend is going to be okay. Do you hear me? Let's get you into this harness so the helicopter can take us down."

Shaking she tried to help. Pain was like a loud, harsh noise in her head, muddling coherent thought. David wasn't dead, and Doug said he was going to be okay. Julie held onto that knowledge as the helicopter swung Doug and her up and away, then gently lowered and set them on the ground. Many hands were around her, taking the harness off, helping her toward the waiting ambulance. Through the haze of her pain, Julie looked around for David but focused on another face.

"Tommy!" Her startled eyes went past him. "And Laurel. How——?" The hands urged her forward. Tommy had on a red jacket, and Laurel was in her olive dress. They were the people she had seen earlier...the ones who went for help.

"Go with them, Julie." Laurel brushed tears away from her eyes. "They want to take you in the ambulance with David."

"But why is Tommy——"

"Don't worry about that now. I'll come and talk to you." Laurel's tears kept coming. "Oh, Julie, I'm so glad you're both alive!"

Julie looked back over her shoulder as they helped her into the ambulance. People gently pulled her into the ambulance, and the doors shut. Julie saw David lying there, still strapped into the stretcher. He watched her with an intent, anxious look.

"You okay?" His words came out thick and slurred.

His pupils were huge. He'd obviously been given something for the pain.

Julie nodded. "I'm okay." David closed his eyes, and Julie let herself relax. A wave of dizziness ran through her, and her vision blurred and then went black. She was only vaguely aware of her surroundings as hands caught her and laid her down. Someone gave her an injection. Gradually the pain from her shoulder became more bearable. Her vision came back, but everything seemed distant. Strapped to the gurney, she swayed slightly with the movement of the ambulance. The siren wailed overhead. Julie turned her head to look at David. He was very pale, and his eyes were tightly shut. Doug had said he would be okay, but he looked—

"David?"

"He's going to be fine," a firm voice said over her head. Julie looked up at the face of a bearded man. "He was worrying about you; now you're fussing about him. Both of you relax and quit fretting. We'll be at the hospital in no time."

The man sounded so certain. Julie sighed and let her eyes close again. At the hospital, Julie lost track of David as they wheeled her into a small, curtained space and gave her another injection. Muscle relaxant, she was told. It increased the floating feeling. A nurse surprised her when she fussed with a wound on Julie's forearm. Julie hadn't even known she was hurt there.

In a few minutes, a doctor who looked to be in his late fifties appeared. He was frowning so hard his bushy eyebrows nearly covered his eyes. His mouth was tight. Without speaking, he had her sit up and put one hand on her shoulder and another on her arm. There was a click, and the pain in her shoulder disappeared. The doctor spun on his heel to leave when the nurse interrupted him.

"Her forearm needs stitches."

The doctor grunted and came back, muttering about people who did foolish things. In her drugged state, Julie felt like a small child. She cringed from the angry man.

"Don't worry." The nurse prepared the sutures tray. "He just doesn't like risk takers."

"Bloody right I don't!" Despite his angry countenance, the doctor's hands were gentle as he injected a local anesthetic and stitched her arm. "Crawling around on some cliff is a fool reason to be here." Then he left.

The nurse stayed and looked at Julie carefully. "There's an RCMP officer here who would like to talk to you. Do you think you could manage that?"

Without the pain in her shoulder, Julie felt much better but very odd from the drugs. "I think so." Her tongue seemed too big for her mouth. More than anything she wanted to lie down, but Julie managed to give the officer a more or less coherent account of what had happened.

"His harness came apart. Is that right?"

Julie nodded. "That's why he fell. Did you talk to David? Is he all right?"

"I will later. He's in surgery now."

After the policeman was gone, Julie lay back down. For a long time nothing happened. The nurse seemed to have forgotten about her existence. Feeling like a piece of left-behind luggage, Julie lay there. Was David's back okay? They'd taken him in that Bowman bag, so in spite of what Doug had said, he'd been worried. When would David be out of surgery? She could hear activity in the rest of the emergency room, but her curtain stayed drawn.

Julie's head was getting clearer by the minute as the drugs wore off. Slowly she sat up and took stock. Her shoulder ached, so did her forearm and knee, but nothing was unbearable. She thought about walking out to find someone, but they were probably all too busy. She was in good shape. She could wait. All that was wrong with her was a couple of bruises and a cut that was already tended.

Not like David. The picture of how he had looked, pale and unconscious, came back to her. *He could have died!* Her desperate prayer—and the flood of love she'd felt for David——came back to her. She'd been so desperate. Julie could remember praying, telling God that she wanted David for her own and giving him back to God. She sucked in her breath. She had prayed aloud! David had been conscious shortly afterward. Could he have heard her? Her face burned at the thought.

Laurel's voice outside the curtain brought her head up. Laurel was not far away asking for Julie Miller. "In here!" Julie climbed down off the bed.

The curtain opened, and Laurel came in with a nurse. "Oh, Julie!" She rushed toward Julie as if she was going to embrace her, then stopped abruptly. "You really are okay? They said I could take you home."

"I am." She gave her friend a hug. The nurse seemed concerned that she was standing up and quickly put Julie into a wheelchair.

"I want to go home." Julie looked up at Laurel. "But first I have to know how David is. I want to know if his back is okay. If there is any permanent damage."

"I don't know. I just got here." Both of them turned to the nurse. She didn't know either and suggested that they call the hospital later.

Julie shook her head. "I'll wait." She began to get out of the wheelchair.

"No, stay there." The nurse gently pushed Julie back into the chair. "I'll go call and see if I can find out anything."

As the curtain swished closed behind the nurse, Julie turned to Laurel. "David *has* to be okay. He has to. I don't think I could stand it if he wasn't."

"I've been praying like mad for both of you ever since Tommy—"

"Tommy! You were with Tommy. What happened? Where is he? Did the RCMP—"

The nurse came back into the room. "Your friend's back is fine. He's still in surgery for his leg, but they don't expect any trouble from that." She took the handles on the wheelchair and pushed Julie past the curtain and through the hospital's double doors.

"I don't want to talk until we get home, Julie, or I'm not going to be able to drive. I've never been so upset in my life as I was on the way to that cliff."

"Laurel! How did you—"

"Julie Miller, you be quiet and let me drive!" Laurel reached over, put on one of her favorite tapes, and cranked up the volume. Julie smiled at her friend's determination, leaned back, and let the music wash over her. Slowly, but irresistibly, her eyes closed.

Julie frowned. Someone was calling her name. She forced her eyes open and turned to look for the source of the voice, then winced.

"Ooooooh." She couldn't stop the soft moan from coming out. Every inch of her body was sore. She blinked and tried to get her bearings.

"Wake up, Julie. We're home."

Julie stared in wonder. Laurel was right. She must have slept the entire hour-long ride home. As Julie climbed out of the car, Laurel chuckled wryly. "You're moving like you're ninety-five years old. Come on, I'll help you into the house. You can take one of those painkillers the doctor gave you."

Julie turned her face to the cool wind. It felt so good to be in the open air. She turned back to Laurel and smiled. "You're right; I ache. But I'll take the painkillers only on one condition. You have to tell me how you ended up at the bottom of that cliff."

Her friend grinned. "Deal. Now let's get you inside."

As they went in, Julie's stomach tightened as she realized just how important Laurel's help had been. "If you hadn't been there——"her knees quivered——"I don't know what would have happened to us." She sat down on the couch with a bump. "How come you were there? How did God send you? Was it really Tommy Oshikawa I saw with you? I don't understand that at all."

Laurel sat down across from her with a laugh. "One question at a time, okay? Yes, it was Tommy. He came here about an hour after you left this morning. I wouldn't let him in. I was going to call the police."

"But you were standing right beside him, and you came to the cliff together. That was you and Tommy I saw, wasn't it?"

Laurel nodded. "It was us. See, when I started to call the RCMP, Tommy yelled through the door that he had to find David because he was in danger. That stopped me halfway through dialing. I opened the door to tell him that you and David had gone climbing. He went crazy. He grabbed me by the shoulders and shook me. He was yelling something about his uncle killing David. It took me a few minutes to understand what he was saying. Julie, his uncle sabotaged David's harness."

"He *what?*"

"Sabotaged David's harness. That's why David fell."

A vision of David's harness coming apart filled Julie's mind. For a second she was blind with rage. It slammed through her, making her shake. *I should have killed Atsuko Oshikawa when I had the chance!* Julie shut her eyes, shocked by her violent response.

"Julie, you told me where you were going to climb, remember? Tommy climbed into my truck, and I was hurrying too much to pay him any attention. Tommy kept apologizing, but I didn't answer him. I think we did over a hundred getting there. Then I couldn't find the exact place at first. My dress pumps aren't exactly designed for running on scree. Tommy came with me. He saw you two first. When I finally found the place, you were too high to hear us. That's when we saw David fall."

Laurel stood up and paced the floor. "It was horrible! Tommy turned and ran. I didn't know if he was running away or what. You yelled for help. I went back to the truck, and Tommy was there, on the cell phone to the police. Julie, the police took him into custody."

"Good! Serves him right."

"I know. I feel the same way. Still, I heard Tommy tell the police that he'd gotten to Golden, British Columbia. He left his uncle as soon as he found out what he had planned. When he couldn't reach David on the phone, he came back and got me. The RCMP let him stay at the scene of the accident until he saw that David was alive; then they took him away."

Julie covered her face with her hands. She knew she should pray for Tommy, ask God to be with him, but. . .

Lord, I'm sorry. It's just so hard to forgive anyone who would put David in such danger. He could have died!

Shame filled Julie, and tears trickled down her cheeks.

"Julie?"

"I want to forgive Tommy. I really do——" Her voice cracked, but she made herself go on. "But David could have died."

"He could have, but he didn't."

Julie kept her head down.

Laurel touched her shoulder gently. "I'm sorry. I didn't mean to upset you. You must be exhausted and hungry."

Julie shrugged. She knew what she needed to do. She didn't want to do it, but she would. Because it was right. "We should try to go see Tommy, or I should anyway."

"What you should do is get something into your stomach and then get some sleep. I'll stick some soup in the microwave; then you can take one of those painkillers the doctor gave you and go to bed."

Laurel was such a mother, Julie thought as her friend headed to the kitchen. *Mother!* What if her parents saw her name on the TV news? The accident was sure to be in the news. Julie grabbed for the phone and punched in the number. No one was home. They must have gone to Sunday-evening service. Julie left a message to say she and David were fine and she'd call back with more details. The smell of the soup made Julie realize just how hungry she was. Her right arm and both knees were aching now. With the painkiller and warm soup in her system, sleepiness swept over Julie with overwhelming insistence. She heard Laurel through a dopey haze.

"I'm going to take tomorrow morning off. We've

got to get your car; then I'll take you to see David."

See David? Julie flushed, the warmth spreading across her body. How was she going to face David not knowing if he'd heard what she had prayed? She swallowed hard and got to her feet. "If Mom calls, will you tell her what happened?"

"Sure, Julie, meanwhile I'll stand in for her. Come on, lets get you into bed."

"Thanks, you're a real friend." Julie barely got the words out as Laurel tucked her in. Instead of falling asleep, Julie hovered in a dreamlike state. Over and over she tried to find the right words to say to David, but she couldn't find them anywhere.

Twenty-two

AT ABOUT THE SAME TIME JULIE WAS FALLING ASLEEP, DAVID was waking up. Disoriented, sick to his stomach from the anesthesia, the first thing he knew was that he was freezing cold and his leg hurt. Someone mercifully put a hot blanket over him, and he was out again. He became more lucid sometime later. This time he knew he was in a hospital. His leg still hurt, but his overwhelming emotion was of happy anticipation. As if he were a child waking on Christmas morning.

I don't get it. Why do I feel so euphoric? The pain in his leg came in great throbbing bursts. His head banged like there was an anvil choir in residence, yet the feeling of well-being showed no signs of leaving. David tried to remember what had happened. He had been climbing with Julie. The pitch hadn't been difficult, yet he had fallen, and his protection must have failed. How else could he have ended up in a hospital? He glanced down. His leg was in a cast that went from his thigh to his ankle. David frowned. How could he have been that careless? It didn't make sense at all.

He could remember nothing at all about the fall or about the time immediately after it. He knew that forgetting events close to the time of an injury wasn't unusual with a concussion. So why did he feel like a kid on Christmas morning when he should be miserable? He had an unshakable certainty that something good was going to happen. What was he forgetting? David tried again, going back to the beginning of the day and reviewing everything he could remember. He shook his head, then grimaced. That had been a mistake.

It seemed he had far more reasons for gloom than for happy anticipation. He could remember clearly the tension he'd felt at the beginning of the day. Julie had talked like she was saying thank you and good-bye. He could remember how hard it had been to be so close to her at the belay points. How much he had wanted to touch her, to tell her he loved her.

Even thinking about that made him sweat. David shifted uneasily on the stiff hospital sheets. He dreaded her rejection more than he ever had any physical pain. When they were climbing, he'd been in emotional turmoil. Was that why he had fallen? His first clear memory after the fall was of another man swinging through the air and of grinding pain. He had seen Julie. She wasn't hurt badly. David could remember the relief he felt and the deep joy. Deep joy? Was that just his pleasure at finding out Julie was okay?

He remembered hands on his body as they strapped him into some kind of sling...swinging... dropping...faces...then the ambulance and blessed release from pain. Faces? David frowned. Had he seen Tommy Oshikawa's face? Was that the thing that made him happy? Had Tommy come back? If that was true, it certainly was good news.

David sighed, inexplicably disappointed. Was there something else he should be remembering? It seemed to hover just at the edge of his mind.

A policeman came in and questioned him briefly. The pain in his leg made it hard to think, but David was able to give him reasonably clear answers. The man kept asking about the harness failing. To his relief, a nurse bustled in, shooed the policeman out, and asked David to swallow several pills.

"Can you tell me how Julie Miller is? She's the one who came into the hospital with me."

The nurse smiled. "They told me you'd ask about her. She went home last night."

"Home? Home to Canmore or home to her parents' house?"

"I'm sorry; I don't know. We're short staffed this shift, so I have to run. Maybe tomorrow you can find out what you need to know."

What I need to know...If only he could remember. The pain in his leg receded as the pills kicked in. David dropped into a troubled sleep in which he was endlessly pursuing something he couldn't grasp.

The next morning, David found himself watching the door. Would Julie come in to see him, or was she too battered to travel? Time seemed to drag by. With the pain in his leg and the noise of hospital routine, he'd wakened very early. He'd wanted to call Julie but didn't want to wake her if she'd been able to sleep in. When he finally decided it was late enough to call, there was no answer.

Each time the door opened, he looked up, hoping to see Julie. He had just poured himself a glass of water and nearly dropped it when Tommy Oshikawa walked in.

"Tommy!"

Tommy stayed near the door as his eyes looked David up and down. "You're going to be okay?"

"I'm going to be fine. Now come and tell me what on earth happened! Do the police know where you are?"

Tommy nodded. "They released me on my own recognizance. I've got to go back for the trial." The whole story poured out of the boy. David listened, looking up sharply when Tommy told him his uncle had sabotaged the harness. So that's what the cop had been getting at. By the end of the tale, Tommy was fighting tears.

"David, if your God is real, I'd like to belong to his family. I've lost my own, and I want what you and Julie have."

A shock of joy went through David's system, but before he had a chance to respond, the door opened and Laurel walked in. "Tommy! You're here!"

David's heart turned over as Julie appeared in the doorway behind Laurel. She took one look at Tommy, and her features turned to ice. "What are you doing here?"

David had never heard her sound so cold.

Tommy stood and faced her, though from the way his face paled, David could tell how much the action cost the boy. "Julie, I'm sorry. I'm so sorry I didn't come back in time." He looked over at Laurel, who stood frozen by the door, then dropped his eyes. "I should have left my uncle long ago. I'm sorry about your bears, too, Laurel."

David watched Julie carefully, seeing the emotions that played over her expressive features. Anger...shame...grudging compassion...then she sighed. "No, Tommy, I'm the one who is sorry. I'm sorry for being so angry with you. I...I'm just glad you came back at all." She clenched her hands together, as though willing the anger to leave her body. "Without your help and Laurel's, David and I could've been stuck on that cliff for hours. I might've had to leave him there and try to get down to get help on my own."

David thought he had never seen a more beautiful woman than Julie at that moment. She was so clearly trying to be merciful and forgiving, which he respected. But he couldn't deny the rush of pleasure at her anger with Tommy on his behalf. Surely she must care for him after all. *At least a little, Lord?* "You would have managed it." He grinned and folded his arms.

Julie looked at him warily. Her eyes searched his as if she was looking for some kind of information. She turned her head away and looked back at Tommy. "So, did the police let you go?"

Tommy made a wry face. "Only until the trial."

"Actually, Julie, you and Laurel got here just in time."

"In time?" Laurel looked from David to Tommy curiously. David couldn't stop the grin that filled his face. He didn't even try. "Tommy just told me he'd like to belong to God's family with us."

"Wow!" Without hesitation Julie went to hug Tommy. "I'm so glad for you! David and I have been praying all summer. Laurel has too." David felt a huge rush of love for Julie. She had put Tommy's decision above her own anger. Julie turned and looked at her roommate; so did Tommy.

Slowly Laurel came forward. "I'm sorry, Tommy. I was so angry about the bears. I didn't answer when you apologized yesterday. I forgot that all of us are sinners.

Christ died for you. If he offers you forgiveness, how can I do less?"

Tears stung David's eyes. The others were crying openly.

"Let's pray." David found that his voice was rough as he thanked God for Tommy. Julie and Laurel prayed; then with halting words, Tommy asked Christ to forgive him. After the prayer, they merged into a celebratory group hug. David struggled upright to join in. But even in the midst of his joy, he noticed that Julie had moved to the far side of the group.

A nurse walked in. "Sorry to break up the party, but visiting hours are over."

As they walked away, Laurel and Tommy promised to come back and visit.

David stared at the door after they left. Julie hadn't said she'd come see him again. He had sat up to protest, but she'd closed the door before he had a chance to say a word. Now he fell back in defeat. The pillow had shifted, and the corner of it poked at a bruise in his back. His pain medicine was wearing out, and his leg hurt badly. His whole being hurt.

In fact, he was almost as physically miserable as he'd been just after the fall. Something tweaked at his memory. Something to do with Julie praying. *Trust me and remember.* The thought was as clear as though God had spoken in his head. David's eyebrows rose in surprise, but he shut his eyes and let Julie's voice as she prayed replay in his head. Her compassion for Tommy had been so clear in that prayer. Julie was such a caring person. He didn't think he could bear to lose her.

He frowned. Something was coming back to him...about her voice calling on God. He shifted. A sharp jab of pain stabbed through his leg, and his memory clicked. His leg had hurt so much, and Julie had been praying.

"*Dear God*—" Suddenly it seemed he was back on the cliff, dizzy and disoriented, and her voice was there in his mind, praying. She was nearly sobbing, calling out to God...

"Jesus!" The joy-filled cry burst out of David as the memory of her voice came, clear and wonderful. "*I wanted him for my husband. . . . Please just let him be alive. . . . I love him; I really do.*"

"Oh, Jesus, thank you!" David sat up abruptly, set his teeth against the pain in his leg, and got out of bed. Julie Miller loved him! What was more, she wanted to marry him, if only he wanted her. *If only I wanted her!* He hopped across the room and pulled open the door. His eyes scanned the various walking figures. The elevator door was just closing.

"Julie!" David hopped into the hall, one hand on the wall. They'd promised him crutches later today, but he needed them now! The elevator doors finished closing.

There was no way she could have heard him. A middle-aged nurse ran toward him, scolding. He nudged her aside and hopped rapidly toward the elevator. "I've got to talk to Julie. She must think—"

"It doesn't matter what she thinks. You need to get back into bed, sir."

David kept going and firmly pushed the elevator call button. To his great joy, the other elevator door opened immediately. The nurse grabbed his arm.

With a sharp move that cost him more than he cared to admit, he pulled free. Grabbing the rail in the elevator, he hopped in. The nurse followed him, yelling for help. When the elevator door began to close, she reached to stop it. David didn't have time for that. With his free arm, he braced himself on the rail and pushed her away from the door as it closed.

On the first floor, the elevator door slid open. Julie, Laurel, and Tommy were walking down the hallway, nearly at the front door. "Julie!" Praise the Lord, she turned to look. He called again and hopped out of the elevator. This time the three of them ran toward him.

"David! What are you doing down here?"

"Are you out of your mind?" Laurel supported his arm.

A wave of pain made him dizzy. David laughed and leaned against the wall. "Julie, I just remembered. I heard your prayer."

David saw red flood Julie's cheeks. People were running toward them from all directions. He took her hands, wobbling unsteadily on his good leg. "Julie, come back and see me tomorrow. Say you'll come back."

"But—"

"Just say you'll come back, please?" Several nurses and an orderly were around him now. One was trying to convince him to sit in a wheelchair.

A nurse clamped onto his arm. "Hopping around the way you are doing simply can't be allowed. Please sit down."

With his eyes still on Julie, David slowly obeyed. Again he watched the play of emotions in her beautiful eyes...anxiety gave way to confusion, and then an emotion that made his heart soar. He saw hope reflected in the blue depths of her eyes. He was sure of it. "Do you wish to check yourself out?" The nurse was talking to him, but David ignored her. His full attention was locked on Julie.

"Julie?"

"Okay, I'll come."

Laurel and Tommy cheered, and David felt as if he were suddenly lighter than air. "Come pick me up. They said they'd let me out tomorrow."

Julie nodded.

"Thank goodness that's settled." The middle-aged

nurse chuckled. "Now can we get you back to your room?"

"Anytime." David could not keep the smile off his face. "Whatever you want." He was babbling, and he knew it, but he didn't care. Julie loved him. Nothing else mattered. "You name it and it's yours, dear lady. The moon, the stars—"

"Young man, I don't know what medication we have you on, but we need to either reduce the dosage—" her stern gaze gave way to a grin—"or pass it out to everyone else."

David's gaze never left Julie until she exited the hospital. As the nurse pushed him back into the elevator, he looked over his shoulder at her name tag. "Lois Taylor?"

She smiled. "That's right."

"Well, Mrs. Taylor, I'm not on drugs. Not like you think."

She chuckled. "Well, whatever you're on, I'd like a dose of it. It's been a long time since I've seen a man look as happy as you do right now."

Happy. David's heart sang. Yes, he was happy.... The woman he loved was coming to pick him up tomorrow.

Twenty-three

JULIE FELT ILL AS SHE APPROACHED THE HOSPITAL THE NEXT afternoon. It wasn't from the fall she'd taken, either. Well, not from the physical fall. Falling in love with David Hales was scarier and more painful than a dislocated shoulder.

Sheer rock faces...climbs that tested skill and courage...cliffs with seemingly bottomless drop-offs... she could face them all without so much as a tremble. But now?

She was terrified.

David had said he was happy. He had begged her to come back. He had escaped from his hospital room and hopped after her on one leg.

Laurel had told her not to be silly, that of course he cared. And when he'd come after her, Julie had found her heart wanting to believe it was so. He *had* to care, at least a little; didn't he? Why else would he have battled his way through doctors and nurses to reach her?

She closed her eyes. *Father, I'm so frightened! What if I'm wrong? What if he was just concerned for a friend?* She had yearned for David's love for such a long time, and it had seemed so hopeless. *But how can I dare to believe it? I don't think I can take being hurt like that again....*

Nervously, Julie had delayed going to the hospital. It was good to have Tommy around. It was fantastic that he was a Christian now. David had invited Tommy to stay at his place, and Julie had spent most of the day with Tommy. They took his belongings from the motel where he'd stayed with his uncle and moved them to David's apartment. While they moved, they spent a lot of time talking; then she took him over to visit with the youth pastor.

If she'd had to spend those hours with nothing to do, she would have gone mad. Tommy refused to call his parents. "Not until I find out what happened to my uncle." His mouth had a stubborn set to it. "I doubt they will even speak to me."

"Maybe you're wrong."

"Maybe I'm not."

Julie didn't push him. She knew a bit about how he felt. She was hoping her parents wouldn't call. Questions about the accident wouldn't be hard to answer, but her parents were almost certain to ask about David. *Julie, you're being silly. Your hope is in God, remember? You won't be alone no matter what happens.* Besides, no one ever died from humiliation and grief, did they? Her stomach was not convinced. She hadn't

337

been able to eat anything at lunchtime.

As she got closer to the hospital, her hands began to sweat. She walked into the building with her head held high, but her heart was beating wildly.

David looked up as she opened the door to his room. "You came! I thought you weren't going to."

"Sorry I'm late." She met David's eyes and stopped as if rooted to the spot. They didn't need words; the real conversation was happening in their gaze...and suddenly Julie couldn't seem to breathe properly.

"Excuse me." The voice behind her made her jump. Feeling silly, she stepped out of the way as a nurse pushed a wheelchair through the door. It was the same woman who'd assisted David in the elevator. "Ready to go, David?"

David grinned at the woman. "Julie, this is Lois Taylor. It was due to her grace that I escaped to catch you."

Julie shook the woman's hand, and David touched Lois's arm. "Could you give us a few minutes?"

She looked from David to Julie—and there was a definite twinkle in her eyes. "Sure, I've got to bring someone up from the recovery room to that other bed. I'll do that first, but you won't have long." She gave them a conspiratorial wink and went out.

Julie stayed by the door fighting an urge to run. She chanced a glance at David and found his gaze tender and amused.

338

"Julie, I can't come to you. Not very well." He reached out his hand to her.

Those steps from the door to his bed felt miles long. She didn't take his hand, and neither would she meet his eyes. Instead she rushed into speech. "Look, if you overheard me telling God I wanted to marry you, don't worry about it. I mean, I decided that God is my anchor. I'll be okay. I've learned so much from you, and I know you have your own life."

David drew both of her hands into his. "Julie, listen to me. I love you."

Her breath stopped in her throat. "You—"

"That's what I said. I love you, Julie Miller. I've been fighting the urge to tell you for weeks, but I thought you would run. The last six weeks have been pure torture. At your folks' place, I thought you were afraid of me. I tried to pull back to give you room so I wouldn't scare you off. It's been one of the hardest things I've ever done. I've never felt like this with any other woman. If God sends us in different directions, I don't know how I'm going to bear it."

"You, too?" Her voice was a whisper.

David swung his cast off the bed and stood beside her. His lips brushed her forehead, and she felt the shock right down to her toes. David bent to kiss her on the lips but staggered. "Drat this cast!"

Julie automatically caught and steadied him, and she

found herself with her arms around his solid, lean frame. David smiled down at her, and his arms enclosed her. They just held each other, neither saying a word. Julie felt like a lost child who had finally come home.

"Nice catch. It's a good thing you're strong." David kissed the top of her head.

"And one tough woman?" Her voice was a mix of teasing and tears.

David lifted her chin and looked straight into her eyes. "Tough, gutsy, impulsive, godly—" He punctuated each word with a kiss, nearly falling over with the last one. They both laughed a little breathlessly. "It's all a part of who you are, Julie. And it's what drew me to you." He touched her face with gentle fingers. "I love everything about you. Every wonderful, unique, God-given piece of Julie Miller."

He kissed her again, and when he lifted his head, they both were unsteady.

"I'd better sit down before I fall down. Obviously staying on my feet and kissing you are not two things I can do at the same time." David swung his leg onto the bed and leaned back. "I can't believe it. I'm in the hospital with a broken leg, and I've never been so happy in my entire life."

"You're crazy, David Hales." Their fingers were still intertwined. This seemed like an impossible fairy tale to Julie.

Suddenly the door banged open, and several people came in pushing a gurney. The patient for the other bed wasn't fully conscious. David's nurse, Lois, paused before she pulled the curtain around the bed, then smiled widely when she saw Julie and David holding hands. An orderly brought up the rear.

"Lois told me to take you downstairs while she gets the man in the other bed settled in."

Julie followed David and the orderly down the hallway. Her feet didn't seem to be firmly connected to the rest of her body, and she floated on a feeling of wonder. She watched, half dazed, as the orderly situated David crosswise in the backseat, which was the only way David could get his cast into the vehicle. On the drive back, Julie couldn't see David, but his hand gripped her shoulder. She twined her fingers around his, and they drove in silence, the warm touch evidence and reassurance of the new bond between them.

It wasn't until she had dropped him off and was driving back to her own apartment that doubts flooded her. David was going back to Britain. What would happen to them then? Could he really want her in his life? There must be hundreds of women who would love him. Look at the way Sheryl had chased him. Maybe this bond between them really was an impossible fairy tale.

Laurel met her at the door. "Julie, what happened?"

"He says he loves me." Julie could hear the confusion

in her own voice, but Laurel didn't seem to. She swept Julie into an enthusiastic hug.

"That's wonderful! I'm so happy for you." She stood back grinning. "I knew it!"

Julie just shook her head. "It doesn't seem real. Laurel, he's leaving in a week."

"Did he say that today?"

"Not today, but I've known that all summer. He's booked to go back at the beginning of September."

"And you remembered it. Of course you would. Oh, I'm supposed to tell you right away. Brent called. He wants you to call him at home. He said it was urgent."

Julie rolled her eyes. Whatever Brent wanted was always urgent as far as he was concerned. He answered on the first ring. "Julie! Look, I can't find anyone to take the climbers I'd asked you to take tomorrow. Is there any chance you could do it? I know you're a bit beat up...."

Her first impulse was to refuse. She wanted to be with David, and she was still stiff, but she hesitated. Brent had been good to her, and he'd found her other work when he hired David. He probably really was stuck, especially with David out of commission and Tommy—

Tommy! He had been worried about what he would do now without a job. Maybe she could help.

"Brent, if I come, will you give Tommy a second chance if he wants it?"

There was a long pause. "He turned himself in, didn't he?"

"Yes."

"Yeah, okay. The kid doesn't deserve it, but the way things went today, I'd hire a green chimpanzee if it had the proper license. I had to get Sheryl to drive, and she didn't like that one bit. If there is any more trouble, he'll be out on his ear. You tell him that for me."

Julie thought about calling David to tell him and Tommy the good news. She smiled knowing that she just wanted to hear David's voice. She'd just spent several hours with him, surely she could wait until tomorrow. Besides, if David felt anything like she had the first night home from the hospital, he needed all the rest he could get.

That's not why you won't call. You're afraid. Afraid of asking David about leaving. Afraid to find out that you're right...he doesn't really love you.

She pushed the dark thoughts away and held David's love for her close to her heart. Perhaps if she looked at it too hard or spoke of it too often, it might disappear. She went to bed, hugging the image of him, the memory of his arms around her, his lips on hers, in her mind. Even if nothing ever went right for her again, she had this day. *David Hales said he loved me!*

It was the end of the day when she got home, pleasantly tired and a little sun drowsy from being outside. There were messages on her answering machine. The first two were from her mother.

"You said you were okay, honey. We know you fell. We've been talking to Laurel. She said you'd be fine for Ben's wedding. Your dress is finished and waiting for you. I'll try to call back later, but we'll talk to you on Thursday when you come for the rehearsal. Is David still coming out with you? Don't forget Ben is counting on you to give Richard a ride."

Julie stared at the wall. *Ben's wedding!* She'd forgotten all about it in the confusion.

There were five more messages, all from David. At the sound of his voice, tingles shot through her. The first message made her smile. "Hi, sweetheart. Just wanted to hear your voice. And I wondered when you wanted to leave for your brother's wedding. Call me." By the fifth message, David's tone was decidedly anxious. Even a little frustrated. "Julie, where *are* you? Are you okay?"

Taking a deep breath, Julie tried his number. It was busy, so she gathered her courage and drove over. A big car was parked out front, but she didn't give it much thought.

Tommy opened the door. His face was happier than

she'd ever seen it. "Julie! I'm so glad you're here. Come in. I'd like you to meet my parents. Norman and Esther Oshikawa."

Julie followed him inside, wondering at the joy in his voice. Hadn't Tommy said these people had pushed him, almost forced him, to work with his uncle? What was going on here?

Mr. Oshikawa came forward and bowed slightly. "You have our thanks for caring for our son. We didn't realize exactly what Atsuko was doing until Tommy finally talked to us. Tommy thought I knew more." He shook his head. "Patterns are hard to break. Atsuko is ten years older than me, and the family leader. He's not an easy man to question, though I did try. I should have tried harder. This has made me begin to rethink many things."

Julie realized her mouth was hanging open and shut it. She looked at David, and he was smiling at her in triumph. Obviously God was doing something wonderful here. She focused on the Oshikawas and shook their hands. "I'm so glad to meet you, so glad you came to see Tommy. How did you find him?"

Tommy's mother reached out to rest a hand on her son's shoulder. "The police—Tommy had to give the phone number where he would be staying to the police. When we heard that the police were involved and Tommy was on the run, I thought I would go mad.

But he came back, and David is alive."

"Yes!" Julie watched David crutch his way across the room. When he reached her, he put both crutches under one arm and put the other arm around her. "I'm alive, and Tommy still has a family."

Julie put her arm around David's waist and lost her train of thought completely. Mrs. Oshikawa was talking, but Julie didn't hear a word she said. David's warm strength next to her, his solid arm touching her, filled her mind. She didn't really want to think of anything but David, especially since the time was so short, but wasn't there something she should tell Tommy?

Julie slapped her palm on her forehead. "Oh, Tommy! Brent said you can have your job back."

"But we want him to come home with us," his mother protested.

Norman Oshikawa shook his head. "Let Tommy decide. When we told him what to do, we made a bad mistake. He should choose."

"I'll stay and work here, then." Tommy grinned. "I've got two families now instead of none, and I want to learn more about the second one. David said he would teach me, and so will Julie and the youth pastor at their church."

"Two families?" His mother's brow wrinkled.

"I've become a Christian, Mom."

David squeezed Julie's shoulders. A quick elated

glance passed between the two of them as Tommy tried to explain. Tommy was publicly confessing his faith!

"This means a lot to me, but I don't want to make trouble for you and Dad. Uncle Atsuko will be even more angry with me, if that's possible, when he hears about this. Have you heard any news of him?"

Norman shook his head. "Not yet. I think he has left Canada."

Tommy nodded. "That's what he was planning. Maybe you shouldn't come around me. I made a choice to split with him. He has powerful friends."

"I don't think he'll make trouble for us." Norman put his hand on Tommy's back. "Besides, I've been rethinking some things. What will happen, will happen. Meanwhile, I want to hear about this business of being a Christian."

The Oshikawas stayed and talked until late into the night. Julie and David sat close, holding hands and fielding questions. Julie left when the Oshikawas did, since Tommy obviously wanted to get to bed. She and David needed to do so as well. There was no time for private words between them, only a quick kiss.

If only she knew what David's plans were. Surely he wouldn't just leave Canada. All her questions would have to wait.

Twenty-four

JULIE WAS BOOKED TO TAKE A FAMILY ON A HIKE FOR THE next two days. This was not a Big Foot trip but one she had booked herself. Now she would have given anything if she hadn't agreed to the trip. David had such a short time left in Canada that she didn't want to miss any chance to be together. Not only that, being away from him left a constant ache, as if she'd lost part of herself.

She'd left him the night before planning to find another guide to do the work for her. But after five calls she slammed the phone back into the cradle. Everyone she could think of was busy. Finally, though she didn't like to do it, she called the clients intending to cancel, but the mother answered. She sounded so excited about hiking and talked about how neat it would be to let their eight- and ten-year-old boys see the Rockies. They'd driven all the way from Alabama. Julie didn't have the heart to cancel.

She called David to explain. "You do what you know you should, Julie. We'll have time to talk on the way to your brother's wedding on Thursday."

"But I told Ben we'd give Richard a ride. That's one of his friends from vet school that lives in Canmore." She let out her breath in a sound somewhere between tears and laughter. "I did that when I was afraid to be with you. We're supposed to pick him up at eight in the morning. David, you're leaving so soon. Maybe Richard can find another ride or drive himself."

"Don't worry, whichever way it turns out—" David's voice was warm and reassuring—"I'll talk to you when you get back Wednesday night. Have fun hiking. I love you."

"I love you too." Her voice was just a whisper. Slowly she hung up. Next she tried calling Richard Wilkinson, but he wasn't home. Neither was he home the next morning.

For two days Julie hiked, was kind to her clients, and thought of David. Her mind played with the possibilities. Hiking down a long valley in the rain, she wondered what it would be like to live in Britain. It was supposed to rain there a lot, especially in Scotland and Ireland. Julie smiled. As if that made a difference. The way she felt at the moment, she'd live in Antarctica to be with David Hales.

He hadn't actually asked her to go to Britain, though. Julie hunched under her raincoat, suddenly cold. What if he didn't? What if he just left? The trail got steeper and more rocky, and she had to turn her attention back to her clients. "Okay, we're going to have to scramble a bit. Be careful. The rock is wet." The boys rushed ahead, competing with each other and not the least daunted by the dampness.

Their mom called after them anxiously. "Don't slip. You could get hurt!"

The words echoed in her mind. *Don't slip, Julie. You could get hurt.* She pushed her bangs back so the water wouldn't run down and drip into her eyes. If she slipped and misunderstood what God wanted of her, both she and David would get hurt. David had said if God took them in two different directions, he didn't think he could bear it. She was sure God had used this summer to bring them together. David didn't lie, and he had said he loved her.

That night Julie tossed and turned. She rose early and spent a long time in God's Word. There was mist in the valleys and in between the trees. Philippians chapter 4 spoke to her in a special way. She knew that Paul had been in prison when he wrote it, yet the whole book was full of joy. "Rejoice in the Lord always. I will say it again: Rejoice!" Julie looked up as the first full light of dawn touched the mist, turning it gold.

Rejoice. Julie closed her eyes. *Rejoice.* She let the thoughts fill her mind, opening herself to obey.... *Rejoice. Be glad. Give thanks.*

Prayer flowed from her heart in waves. *Thank you*

for David, for this love you've shared with us.... Thank you for the beauty of your world, of your Word.... Praise you, Most Holy God, for the ways you are working in my heart.

Opening her eyes, she glanced down to read again, and the words all but jumped off the thin pages, piercing her heart. *"Do not be anxious about anything, but in everything, by prayer and petition, with thanksgiving, present your requests to God.... I have learned the secret of being content in any and every situation...I can do everything through him who gives me strength."*

She sighed and let the tension flow out of her body. She gave God her love for David and thanked him again for the last few days, for the feel of David's arms around her, her hand in his. "Thank you so much that he didn't die, that you kept us safe on that cliff."

She had so much for which to be grateful! Tommy was a Christian now. David loved her. God truly was good. She shut her eyes. "God, I trust you, but please don't let David go away without some understanding between us. Help me not to be so full of fear. Help the trip to Ben's wedding go well tomorrow."

Julie was sitting where she could see the tents. When she opened her eyes, there still was no movement from the family members. But that was just fine. God was in control, and the day would follow his plans, not hers.

What in the world is God doing?

The day had had one of the most frustrating starts she'd ever had as a hiking guide. It was soon evident that no one in this family, except the youngest, was a morning person. Mom and Dad and the twelve-year-old dragged and grumbled. The eight-year-old tore around, getting in the way and irritating everyone.

They didn't leave the camping area until eleven in the morning. Consequently, Julie was late getting home that night. Laurel had left a note for her by the phone. "David called about five times. He says he loves you." There was a huge smiley face. "He also says he'll be looking for you at seven-thirty tomorrow morning. Richard Wilkinson called to confirm that you are picking him up. He said the transmission is gone on his truck so he's glad he's got a ride with you."

Julie sighed. So much for time alone with David. Would they ever get a chance to talk? There were only eight more days now before David left.

In any and every situation, be content....

She bit her lip. If there was one thing she was not right now, it was content. Afraid, definitely. Anxious and frustrated, you bet. But content—

With a sigh, she headed for the shower, wishing fear could be washed away as easily as the day's dust.

Seconds after Julie rang David's doorbell, she found herself in his arms. After a long, delicious kiss, David looked at Tommy Oshikawa over her head and waggled his eyebrows. "There *are* compensations."

"What are you talking about?" Julie pinched him on the waist when he wouldn't answer.

Tommy laughed. "David has been pacing the floor on crutches for forty-five minutes. I just told him if that's how a man in love behaves, I'm not sure I'm interested." He grinned at them. "Anyway, I'm supposed to be at work at Big Foot's office by eight, so I'm outta here. Have fun, you two." The door slammed behind him.

David fumbled with his bag, trying to handle it and the crutches too. Julie raised a playful eyebrow at him. "Time for me to do the strong woman thing again?"

"Right, I forgot who I was with." When she reached for the bag, David stopped her, turning her toward him for a long kiss. Their closeness made her bones feel like water. With a little groan he stepped back and had to grab for his crutches to keep his balance.

Julie giggled. "At least you caught yourself that time. David? David?" She waved a hand in front of his face. "What are you thinking?"

"About rafting with you, how you laughed at the wild water."

Julie grinned. "You laughed too. No one else ever shared that kind of fun with me. Not like you did." Julie's smile disappeared. "We'd better go. I couldn't cancel giving Richard a ride. The transmission is out on his truck. Sorry."

When they arrived for the rehearsal, Julie was swept into a warm family whirlwind. David wasn't really part of the crew, but they all made him feel welcome. At supper she sat next to him, holding his hand under the table. He seemed to need the contact as much as she did. When everyone started to leave the table, she and David lingered.

Ben walked by and gave her a huge smile. "Your turn next, Julie?"

She ducked her head and felt the heat warm her face. What if David didn't ask?

"Don't mind my teasing, you two." He looked straight at David. "You be careful of my little sister."

Julie kept her head down. Ben was only trying to keep her from being hurt again, but she didn't like David pushed like this. David's arm came around her shoulders. "I intend to be very careful of Julie. I love her."

Julie felt a rush of joy, but before anything else could be said, Dad's big voice overrode the noise in the room. "Okay, everyone that's in the wedding party, let's get this practice started. Ben, Amber, the rest of you, get over here."

Julie had a hard time concentrating on the rehearsal. All the other bridesmaids had turned to face the pastor, but Julie hadn't moved. David had put his arm around her and told Ben he loved her, but what good was that if he was leaving in less than a week? She was going to have to quit being so cautious and ask some hard questions.

The woman next to her, one of Amber's friends from back east, poked her. With a little start, Julie got into line. *This rehearsal is taking forever!* She glanced toward the back of the church—and caught her breath. David was gone! Was he just going to leave and go to bed? Julie bit her lip. She was being selfish. He couldn't be comfortable standing around in that cast. Her bruises still ached, and she hadn't been beat up nearly as badly as David had. She didn't look around for him again. *God, please calm me down. Help me relax and rest in you.*

The rehearsal ended in hugs and excited talk of the next day. Julie tried to participate, but all her smiles felt wooden. As soon as she could, she slipped away, ducking through the pastor's office and out the door. Slowly she walked to her car. David must have found another ride back. She probably should ask, but then everyone would notice. They might feel sorry for her again. Julie put her head down on the cool plastic of the car's steering wheel. *Stop it! You're being silly. David didn't have much chance to say anything, not with Richard riding with us. Then there was all the rush and excitement.... Just stop doing this to yourself.* She took a deep breath, started the car, and began to back out of her parking spot.

The headlights of the vehicle swept across someone walking rapidly toward her on crutches. *Crutches!* Julie slammed on the brakes so quickly she stalled the car.

David covered the last few feet in two big leaps. "Hey, trying to ditch me, eh?"

"I thought you had gone already." Her throat tightened, and the last word came out somewhere between a laugh and a sob.

David shook his head. "I sat down against the side wall in back. I had to get off my feet, and the pews don't work well for casts." He studied her face, and she saw understanding and compassion in his tender gaze. "Sweetheart, don't you know the only reason I'm here is because of you? I wouldn't leave without you." He glanced around then. "I do have one question for you, though."

"W-what?"

"Isn't there anywhere in this whole wide-open country that we can get away from your friends and relatives for just a short time?"

Julie's laugh was still a bit shaky. "There *are* a lot of people, aren't there? I know almost all of them, and I've still been feeling claustrophobic. Aren't you too tired to talk?"

"There are things that are more important than

sleep." David touched her cheek, and Julie rested her head on his hand.

She tilted her head up. "There's a decent track to the top of the slabs where I took you bouldering. I've got a kind of thinking rock there. Would that be okay?"

"Perfect." David touched her cheek one more time and began to lever himself into the backseat.

After a bumpy ride down a track usually used by four-wheel-drive pickup trucks, Julie parked the car. As soon as she turned off the engine, the stillness of the night swallowed them. It took a few minutes for her eyes and ears to adjust after the noise and light of the vehicle. The night was not silent, nor perfectly dark. No moon was up yet, but stars shone in a velvet sky. Toward the west, the sky shaded into a dark, glowing blue where the last light of sunset hovered behind the mountains.

Crickets chirped, and a distant coyote called. David's crutches made soft thudding sounds on the pasture grass. Julie walked slowly to give him time to maneuver on the rough ground. In a few minutes, they could hear the creek murmuring to itself.

"This is my thinking rock. I hope it's okay. Even though she spoke softly, her voice sounded loud in the quiet night.

"Just as long as there's room for you beside me."

She'd never brought anyone else here, not even Kurt or her family. Yet it seemed the most natural thing in the world to sit by David on her thinking rock. His arm came around her, and she felt complete in a way she never had when she'd sat there by herself. David didn't speak right away, but Julie felt no panic now. A glow in the east drew her eye. Together they watched the moon, about three-quarters full, slide over the edge of the world. At first it looked a deep rust orange from the dust of prairies; then it slid higher to reveal itself in silver splendor.

David turned from nature's splendor to look at Julie. "'The heavens declare the glory of God.'"

"'The skies proclaim the work of his hands.'" She looked up and raised her hands skyward.

David turned her face toward him, and she laced her fingers with David's and shut her eyes, expecting a kiss, but nothing happened. She opened them again to see David smiling tenderly at her in the silver moonlight. "Julie Miller, I love you with every fiber in my being. Will you be my wife?"

Julie stopped breathing. She swallowed hard and looked away from David, out at the night sky. She had been hoping for those words, but she had to be sure. "David, you know I thought I couldn't marry...."

"I thought about that for an entire week. I made about a thousand different speeches in my head and on paper proving you were wrong. I prayed about it over and over." He laughed. "I should have trusted God more. He didn't need my help at all. You decided on your own that you were free to marry."

"But I'll still be me." Julie took a deep breath, praying for courage. "Are you sure you want someone like me? I'll never be able to be the perfect homemaker. You're the most wonderful man, but I can't just cheer for you. I'd want to do things too. I'm competitive, not quiet and gentle—" Her throat tightened with emotion, cutting her words off. She forced herself to continue, but all she could manage was a tear-filled whisper. "Not even when I try."

David cupped her chin in his hand. "God doesn't even make two blades of grass or two snowflakes the same. Good marriages aren't all identical, either. What makes a good marriage for some doesn't fit others. Julie, I don't want a cheerleader, nor do I want a housekeeper. I want you to be my partner, to share the challenges, to laugh with me in the rapids. I want you to climb with me and reach out to people with God's love."

"But what if we have kids?"

"I don't know that children grow up best in stuffy suburbs. You're right. We'd both have to change our lives to make room for their needs. But there will be a time for that if God wills, and I'd like to be your partner in that adventure too."

Julie looked hard at David. He was, in many ways,

almost a stranger…and yet he was more familiar to her than even her own heart, more painfully beloved than she'd ever dreamed possible. His steady gray eyes looked back, waiting. He meant what he had said!

Julie's heart melted. "Yes, David Hales, I will be your wife."

David wrapped his strong arms around her, holding her close. He moved to kiss her, then pulled back, concern on his features. "Julie! Are you crying?"

"Just because I'm so happy!" And she was. Happier than she'd ever been in her life. Nothing, not even beating the most challenging climb, had even come close to what she was feeling right now. She couldn't stop her tears…or her smile. "Did you know that more than a month ago I told God to put my love for you where it wouldn't hurt either of us?" She gave a kind of nervous giggle. "I never thought that this, us together, was the best possible place of all. Even if you leave next week and I don't see you for months, I will be so happy!"

"But I'm not going. That's why I didn't ask you to be my wife when we talked at the hospital. I couldn't ask you and then just leave."

"You're—you're not going?" Julie could hardly believe her ears.

"That's what I've been doing while you've been out guiding the last couple of days. I spent hours on the phone; then Tommy drove me to the immigration office. I didn't want to say anything to you until I knew for sure. I've got a six-month extension on my visa."

Julie whooped and threw herself into his arms. His cast skidded on the rock, and they ended on the ground in a tangle of crutches.

"I'm sorry, David." Julie struggled to get off of him. "Are you okay?"

David laughed and wrapped her in his arms. "Never better. But if we are to be partners, I'm going to have to get out of the habit of falling over every time we get close."

She grinned through glad tears. "Especially if we're going to be climbing guides together. Are you absolutely sure you're okay? It's just that I was so happy, and I for-got—"

He laughed and gave her a quick kiss. "I already told you I like you the way you are. Impulsive, beautiful, strong, competitive, the works. Now you've got a wedding to help with tomorrow, and they're going to come out looking for us if we stay away much longer. Would you like to be my crutch on the way back to the car? That way I won't have to let go of you."

"You can lean on me anytime."

In the rush of Ben and Amber's wedding day, there was no chance for David or Julie to tell anyone their good news. Julie cherished it in her heart. As she walked down the aisle behind Amber's best friend, she felt like she was walking on air. Ben looked so joyful and solemn as he took Amber's hand and turned to face the pastor.

As she listened to the wedding service roll on, her heart filled with emotion and her skin tingled.... She caught her breath, aware as she'd never been before of God's glory and presence. Once she glanced back and saw David's eyes on her. Someday she would be making these same vows with David, but he wouldn't be going away, not for a long time. They'd have time to grow to understand one another, to plan together. Maybe she'd go and visit his family in Britain.

Unlike the rehearsal, the service seemed to take no time at all. It seemed only minutes later that they were clustered outside in the sunshine, ready for Amber to throw her bouquet. Ben said something in Amber's ear. She grinned and pitched the bouquet. Julie had to throw up her hands to keep it from hitting her in the face.

"Yeah!" Nathan jumped, his fist punching the air. "Now Julie has to marry David!"

David stepped through the mass of girls and put his arm around her. "Actually, she already said she would."

The whole party cheered, and people crowded around congratulating them. Julie found herself in her mother's arms. "Oh, Julie, I'm so happy for you!" She stepped back. "Did you know that David talked to your dad and me yesterday?"

"He did?"

Her mother nodded with a twinkle in her eye. "He did, and you have our blessing."

"Where are you going to get married?" Nathan danced up and down in between them. "Up in the mountains? Julie likes it there."

David laughed. "Maybe up a cliff. At least that way we won't have you jumping on our toes."

Nathan stopped jumping. His eyes were wide. "Are you really going to marry him up on a cliff?"

"Only if we're both tied in good and tight."

"To solid ground, to each other, but mostly to God. Right, Julie?" David's arm was around her again.

"Right!"

Being married to David was going to be a lifelong adventure. Julie couldn't wait to get started.

God really had prepared good things for her to do.

Dear Reader,

I've never found it easy to conform. I imagine you've felt that way at times too. No matter how we try, we end up feeling like round pegs in square holes. Sometimes I've even resented God for making me who I am.

In *Summit,* Julie isn't always comfortable with who she thinks God made her to be. She doesn't want to do wrong, but the right pattern of life for her isn't easy to find or follow either.

I've begun to learn that God has good things for each of his very different children to do. I hope you look for the joy of finding God's good will for you. No matter what situation you are in, or who you are, he has good plans for you.

I enjoyed writing a book in which the main characters are rock climbers. I'm no expert climber, but climbing is one of my favorite things to do. Getting high up in God's mountains is a thrill. Getting to the summit isn't easy—neither is living God's way—but both are well worth the trouble.

Jeremiah didn't live in easy times. Difficult things were going to happen, but this is the promise God gave his people in Jeremiah 29:11, 13: "'For I know the plans I have for you,' declares the Lord, 'plans to prosper you and not to harm you, plans to give you hope and a future.... You will seek me and find me when you seek me with all your heart'."

Take care,

Karen Rispin

Write to Karen Rispin
c/o Palisades
P.O. Box 1720
Sisters, Oregon 97759

Don't miss the other exciting spring Palisades releases...

HI HONEY, I'M HOME by Linda Windsor
ISBN: 1-57673-556-7
Available now!

Friday night traffic on the beltway was typical, but nonetheless horrendous, particularly if one had a deadline. Kathryn Sinclair did. A glance at the clock on the dash told her she had exactly one hour to deliver her prodigal son to her neighbor's home. Then she had to make like the devil for her own, where her assistant manager was putting the final touches on their promotional brain child—an intimate open house to display the Emporium's latest imports. At seven o'clock, not only would her choice customers fill the spacious living room of her historic Georgian manor, but her employers would be there as well.

One dilemma at a time, Kathryn decided with a sidelong glance at her small companion. He looked shaken by the parent-teacher conference. At least, she hoped he was! It was hard to tell. Jason was like his late father in that respect. He tacked off to more neutral ground rather than dwell on a troublesome matter. Drawing him back to the subject at hand required vise grips.

"There will be no television this weekend. I expect you to make up all the homework you excused yourself from." The computer-generated note, allegedly from her to his teacher, was a gem. He hadn't even used the spell checker!

"You already said that, Mom." Jason also possessed his late father's uncanny knack for undermining her momentum, which was amazing considering he'd spent a scant three years with the man. Most of the time Nick Egan had been a TV shot for thirty seconds here and there, hardly the real father a little boy needed and certainly not the husband she herself had hoped for.

"I did know all the material, Mom. Even Mrs. Himes said that," Jason reminded her, taking a stab at his defense. No afternoon cartoons was a serious penalty.

"Jason, you have to follow certain accepted rules." Kathryn held back the *unlike your father* that flashed through her mind. "You *must* do your homework!"

"Maybe if I had a reason to do it," the boy began, cutting cinnamon-hued eyes at her from beneath a forelock of sandy brown hair. It was the same color Nick's had been in his boyhood pictures, before it turned darker with maturity.

Jason was so like Nick, even down to the long dark lashes that set off his eyes in a way a woman would die for. They had a lazy, pensive look at the moment, one Kathryn recognized well.

She felt a familiar anguish tear at her chest as she looked away from the mirror image of her late husband. Although their divorce had almost been final when Nick was killed in a terrorist explosion in some third-world city she couldn't pronounce, she hadn't been prepared for the grief that overtook her. After all, she'd been about to have him legally removed from her life.

At least that's the way it had appeared. Actually, she'd prayed that asking for a divorce would shake Nick up enough to make him realize how he was neglecting her and Jason. When he agreed to it without a fight, she'd been so hurt and angered that she let it coast on its own momentum, against heart and reason.

Then he was taken from her forever.

She swallowed back the sudden rise of memories. Nick always invaded her thoughts more at Christmas. She'd both married him and said her final good-bye to him on Christmas Eve. With the same resolve with which she'd reassembled her life, borne Nick the second son he never knew about, and established herself as one of the lead import buyers on the east coast, Kathryn willed the gnawing ache away.

"I can think of a reason to do all that work," Jason spoke up, bringing Kathryn back to the conversation at hand. He obviously was up to something. "Soccer."

"I should have known." Jason also had Nick's tenacity, the ability to go after what he wanted if it took days, even weeks. It had made his father one of the top network reporters. He always got his story.

"Dad was a football captain. He could have gone pro! I want to be like him, but I'll settle for soccer."

Double wham! If Jason were any more like his father, she'd not be able to bear it. "Jason, we'll discuss this later, okay?"

"An' what am I going to do while the guys watch TV tonight?" Jason lamented, switching tactics smoothly. "I can't even go to my own room in my own house because of that dumb old party."

Why had she ever told the boys the house was really theirs, held in trust from their late father's estate? Dr. Spock never had a chapter on this situation. "But I am in charge of the house until you and Jeremy are twenty-one. Then you can kick me out and do what you will with it!"

Her knuckles whitened from her grasp on the steering wheel as she turned onto a county road boasting several swanky developments. She glanced down upon feeling her son's small hand close about her arm.

"I'd never kick you out, Mom."

The stricken look on Jason's face tugged at her heart. "I know, Jason. And you do have a point. A lot of the books you need to finish your homework are in your room."

"Does that mean I can play with the guys and watch TV?"

"Only if you give me your solemn promise to spend the rest of your weekend at home working on your catch-up work," Kathryn conceded.

"Cool!" Jason's smile was back in place.

As Kathryn maneuvered into the Anderson's driveway, Jason gave her a hasty peck on the cheek. "Thanks, Mom! Hope you have a good party!" Bundled in a down-filled jacket, he practically rolled out the car door and dashed for the house.

Grateful for good neighbors like the Andersons, Kathryn backed out of the drive and headed toward the far end of Brighton Heath's boundary where the original homestead, which belonged to the Egad family, lay on the remaining four acres still in that name.

Kathryn pulled her minivan into the garage. The last of the items they intended to show tonight were packed in boxes in the back of the car, but her assistant David and housekeeper Ruth Ann would have to get them out. She had to shower and dress in less than forty-five minutes!

The scent of the Cajun-blackened prime rib and its accompanying dishes being prepared by the caterers followed her as she scrambled up the servants' stairwell to the master suite. It reminded Kathryn that she'd missed lunch. Lying across the bed, à la David, was one of the Parisian designs she'd purchased for Mrs. Whitehall's fashion department at the Emporium. Coordinating shoes, purse, and gloves, as well as a short matching velvet cape, were beside the dress.

After a quick shower, she slipped the dress on. The dark green velvet fit her figure like a sheath. By the time Kathryn drew on the matching long silk gloves, a glance in the mirror told her she looked quite the princess, especially after she fastened a jeweled velvet comb in her hair to hold her upswept locks in place. With one last breathless look in the mirror, she hurried down the main staircase just as the walnut grandfather clock in the central hall struck six.

Six! But it should be seven! Kathryn stopped halfway in her descent and stared at the face of the elegantly carved Swiss timepiece in confusion; then it dawned on her that she'd been running on the schedule of the clock in the dash of her car. It had not yet been set back for daylight saving time. She was an hour *ahead* of schedule!

With a breath of mixed relief and exasperation over her unnecessary tizzy, she started downward again, drawing the attention of her assistant manager, David Marsh, and Paul Radisson, her attorney and fellow trustee of the children's estate.

"David, you're a lifesaver!"

"And you, Kathryn, are a work of art."

"I'm willing to come to your rescue anytime," Paul Radisson spoke up. "Especially if you wear that dress!"

She patted his cheek. "You already have come to my rescue by agreeing to act as my cohost. David and I will be frantically involved with sales if this works out the way we plan."

Paul had been Nick's best man at their wedding and for a while, he and his wife and she and Nick had socialized together. If only time could have stood still then—when they were all newlyweds and so much in love. Upon Nick's death, Kathryn discovered that Paul had divorced his wife, although it didn't come as a complete shock. Word drifted down along her mother's grapevine that Paul had become something of a silver-tongued devil with the women in the elite social circles about D.C. He'd tried his charm on Kathryn, but to no avail...yet.

Even if he had truly had enough of his *freedom* as he claimed, she was not ready for a relationship beyond the one they had as friends and occasional escorts to thwart well-intentioned matchmakers like her mother and friends. Sometimes Kathryn wondered if she'd ever be receptive to another man.

She humored Paul with an absent smile as he made a gallant show of lifting her hand to his lips. "I'd love a cup of the imported punch before the hoards arrive."

"At your service, madam." Paul broke into a toothsome grin and winked.

"You're a dear for putting up with me."

"Us," David injected at her side as Paul retreated to the bar

set up in the front parlor. "I was in such a dither, I asked *him* to help unpack the Venetian glassware."

Kathryn grinned at the last-resort implication in David's voice. Like her, he was very particular and preferred doing things himself.

Just then, the front bell rang. She grinned at David, feeling her face flush with anticipation. "You start the music, I'll get the door. It's probably the Whitehalls." As she walked into the marbled hall, her heels clicked crisply on the polished surface not covered by Turkish area rugs. "After this, you can take over," she added to Paul, realizing she'd promptly assumed her cohost's assigned task.

He touched his heels together in mock salute. "Yes, mein madame! It's now my one goal in life to be your man."

Kathryn let the innuendo slide. "Crazy!" she accused playfully, allowing Paul that out. Could she ever bring herself to take him seriously?

Brandishing a brilliant smile to wash away her doubt, she opened the front door. The wind had picked up, and the icy air rushed in to assault her back and shoulders, bared by the halter design of her gown.

Instead of her employers, however, she found herself face-to-face with only one individual. He stood, shoulders hunched in a beige topcoat. His brown hair whipped about his face, while his breath fogged the air before a mouth frozen in a thin white line.

Somehow an incredulous "Nick!" escaped her tightening throat as Kathryn stared at the mature version of her son Jason. Were it not for the fact that her heart seemed to have stopped cold, the expectant whiskey-colored gaze fixed upon her would have negated the icy air rushing in and warmed her from head to toe as it always had.

But it couldn't be! Kathryn felt her strength drain as quickly as the blood from her face, leaving a pinpricked trail of disbelief. *Nick was dead!* They'd sent home a few of his charred belongings, his body having been destroyed in the explosion beyond retrieval, much less identification. She buried them in his place. Pregnant with his second son, the one she hadn't told him about during the divorce negotiations, she'd wept at the small gravesite with guilt and grief until she could cry no more.

The memory reemerged with a terrible blow. Staggering a step backward, Kathryn blinked as if to erase this bizarre visitation of the ghost of Christmas past from her sight, but he remained there, studying her with an enigmatic gaze.

Suddenly he spoke, his voice as real as he appeared to be, the solemn line of his lips breaking in a poor attempt at humor.

"Hi, honey, I'm home."

ISLAND BREEZE by Lynn Bulock
ISBN: 1-57673-398-X
Available now!

Bree Trehearn had never realized how dark a night could be until now. Back in Indiana on the farm roads, the darkness had always had a velvety quality to it. Dark had been safe and friendly, a welcoming part of God's handiwork. The dark she was in now felt almost menacing.

Sanibel Island was mostly resorts, wasn't it? So why weren't there any streetlights? There had been plenty of light on that golf course she'd passed a little earlier. And the strip of restaurants along the main streets had been positively glowing with neon. But now, when she needed the light to try to figure out what was wrong with the car, it was as dark as the inside of a cow and just as welcoming.

She knew she should probably wait for someone to come along. Only problem was there hadn't been anybody else on this road in quite a while. No, she was going to have to get out and start trying to decipher what it was the car had been trying to tell her when all those little warning lights went on before everything quit.

Bree got out of the car, noticing that the inside light still worked. It was a comforting little glow in all the darkness. The foreign nature of everything around her came back again in the gusts of salty breeze on her face and the warmth of the air around her. She had to be crazy to be doing this. But then she'd felt a little crazy since at least Kentucky.

She walked around and opened the passenger door,

pulling the front seat back to try and shift a box or two. Her flashlight had to be here somewhere. "Now stay right there," she cautioned Gabe. It was the wrong thing to do. His wide blue eyes opened even wider and he was out of the car like a shot. For a moment he was a pale blur in the dark; then he was gone.

"Oh, Gabe, no. Come back here. You'll get lost! *Gabriel!*"

"Did you hear something?" Shawn asked, his headlight making a pool for Cody North to trace the bumpy path in front of their racing bikes.

"Yeah. Maybe gulls. Maybe a person. Couldn't tell."

They rounded the bend in the path and Shawn pointed to what Cody had already seen. A car, doors flung open and inside lights on. Although it seemed to be packed to the roof with stuff, there was no person inside.

"This doesn't look so good, sport." Cody coasted to a stop.

"I know. Want me to go look for a phone?"

"Not yet. Let's look around first. Together, okay?" Cody raised his voice to Shawn, who was already abandoning the bike to head into trouble. Cody winced at the thought. He hadn't gotten to be a thirty-two-year-old ex-cop by leaping into the face of danger.

He got off his own bike and walked around the car. No one was there, not even on the floorboards. A little way down the path, the sound they'd heard before came again. It was definitely human.

"Hellooooo!" In a moment, a pale shape came racing out of the darkness.

"Lost?" Cody asked.

The young woman *looked* lost. Her pale hair swirled around her like a demented cloud and her wide eyes looked panicky. "I sure am. But I'm more worried about Gabe. When I opened the door he jumped out of the car and took off. I can't find him."

"Is this an adult we're talking about?"

The woman shook her head. "No. He's a three-year-old white male—"

"We'll help you look." Cody cut her off. No sense in panicking her more by pointing out that this trail and road turned a hundred yards farther, opening onto public beach. If they didn't find this kid soon, he could be walking in the ocean. Or worse. "Can Gabe swim?"

He hadn't thought it possible, but she went another shade paler. "No. He doesn't even like water. But he isn't—"

Cody turned to Shawn. "You go down the street, calling. I'll go down the path toward the public access. We'll meet up there either way, okay?"

Shawn nodded. "Fine."

Cody got back on his bike and started pedaling slowly. He strained his eyes in the darkness, adjusting his eyes down to three-year-old height. Why did it have to be a kid? He hated looking for kids.

There was a rustle in the grass toward his right and he stopped the bike. "Gabe?" More rustling. Cody headed toward the waist-high grass. As he parted it, something screamed like a panther and a blur of white hurtled toward him, landing on his shoulder.

The momentum of the blow knocked Cody back on his seat, hard. Swearing, trying to hold on to twenty pounds of unhappy cat—with all claws apparently intact—he got up. The spotty clouds overhead chose that moment to give way to rain. Cody held up the furry face in front of him for inspection. "If you're Gabe, she's got some explaining to do."

By the time they got back to the trailhead, Cody and his squirming furry companion were both soaked. "Gabe!" The woman plucked him from Cody's battle-scarred arms. "Oh, baby, you're so wet."

She looked at Cody as if for an explanation. Cody bit his lip. Hard. "In case you hadn't noticed—" he ground each word out carefully—"it's raining." He narrowed his eyes. "And one more thing. Gabe is a *cat.*"

"I never said he was human." She cooed over the wet cat as she put him back in her car.

Cody tossed his keys to Shawn. "Go home and get dry. I'll be there as soon as I can." The kid was so wet he didn't argue for a change, just pocketed the keys, got on his bike, and left. Cody turned his focus back to the woman.

"You may not have said he was human, but why on earth didn't you tell me he was a *cat*? I could have broken my neck out there looking for that fuzzball." Said fuzzball had deposited himself in the car's back window well and was giving himself a thorough grooming.

"You didn't give me time. You just charged out of here before I could say anything." She stopped, running a hand through that impossibly pale hair. "Listen to me. I should thank you for saving my best friend. Instead, I'm getting caught in the same bad-manners trap you seem to find yourself in——"

Cody couldn't take it anymore. "Look, lady, I'm wet, I'm tired, and I've been chasing a cat. Manners aren't high on my list right now."

"I know, and I'm sorry for my part in causing you trouble, Mr.——"

"North. Cody North."

"And I'm Bree. I should be offering to pay you or something, except I've been driving since Yorktown, Indiana and I think I've spent just about everything I had on gas."

"Yeah, well, you didn't spend enough." A quick examination of the car when she'd tossed the cat in had told him that among other things, the car was out of fuel.

"And I feel really stupid about that. I guess I just got preoccupied." She looked up at the sky; rain was still coming down steadily. "Guess this dumps on my plan to sleep on the beach."

If Cody thought he'd been upset before, this pushed him over the edge. "Sleep on the beach? Lady, are you *nuts?* There are great big signs all over telling you it's illegal."

Bree stiffened. "Signs I can't even see, much less read, thanks to the lack of lights around here."

"Even without the laws, you'd have to be crazy to sleep on a public beach. Not only are there all kinds of animal predators out during the night, it's just not safe for a young woman." A beautiful young woman at that.

North! Keep your mind on business!

"I have my attack cat." She looked as defiant as anyone resembling a water sprite could look. "And God's protection."

Oh, great! She sounded like a trusting four-year-old. "Some attack cat." It was lame, but it kept him from berating her——or her Pollyanna concept of God.

Cody looked again to where Gabe was curled up in the window well. From this distance he reminded Cody of the business end of a dust mop. "Don't you have somebody to stay with? reservations somewhere?"

She shook her head. "I was just seeing how far I could get. It was supposed to be a little more organized than it ended up, but it seemed like a good idea at the time. The one night I stopped, there was this great rest area in Georgia. The wind in the pines was wonderful."

"You slept in a highway rest area?"

She bristled again. "I locked the car. And remember, it wasn't like I was alone or anything."

"Right. You had your attack cat and your guardian angel or whatever."

"I take it you have a problem with that?"

If he was smart, he'd ignore the sweetly sarcastic inquiry. But this woman was grating on his nerves like a piece of foil on a filling. She was what his mother would call an innocent. It was about time someone introduced her to reality.

It would be so much easier just to walk away, leaving her to whatever crazy fate she'd called down on herself. Who knew, maybe this Bree——he frowned——what kind of sprouts-and-granola name was *that,* anyway?——was one of those people that God actually took care of. There had to be some on the planet.

Besides, the image of his mother just wouldn't let him

walk away. Laura North would have taken her in. It was the *Christian* thing to do. And his mother would give him a hard time if she found out he did otherwise. He sighed and straightened his shoulders. "Wait here. I need to make a phone call." Shawn should just about be home by now, and he always jumped at a chance to drive the truck. Tonight was going to be his big moment.

An hour later Cody was still asking himself how he had gone from taking a quiet bike ride in the dark to sitting in the back of his own truck getting rained on while surrounded by a strange woman's belongings. When they pulled to a stop at the complex, he jumped out and started handing things to Shawn. "Put her behind the office." Cody watched Shawn's wide-eyed nod. So he thought it was a crazy idea, too.

Couldn't be helped. This girl was a menace, true, but from the looks of her there would be no harm in giving her the room behind the office until morning. Then he'd lend her enough for a tank of gas and she could be on her way.

She looked like a sleepy little kid standing there outside the truck on the white parking lot, holding the bedraggled cat.

"Come on, I'll show you to your room." She followed quietly enough as they went through the small office and into the back. "I know it's not much, but it's warm and dry. There are towels in the bathroom closet and clean sheets for the sofa bed."

"You're just letting me stay here? For nothing?"

"Overnight." Cody folded his arms and leaned against the office door. "Tomorrow we'll go rescue your car before the cops tow it away."

383

She looked up, a frown wrinkling her brow. "Aren't you a police officer? I thought from the way you acted——"

Cody shook his head. "Not anymore. And not here. No, I just run the condo complex here. I rent vacation units, not chase bad guys."

She set the cat down and it walked around the room, purposefully sniffing each new piece of furniture he encountered. Without the large furry creature in her arms, Bree looked even tinier. *Somebody ought to be looking after this woman!*

"Cody?"

He met her guileless stare.

"Thanks a lot. This is the kindest thing anybody's done for me in a long time."

And with that, she slid slender arms around his neck and hugged him. It was a warm, sisterly hug. But the contact, brief as it was, left him stunned. He never was certain afterward what he'd said to warrant it, but then did any man really understand women?

Knowing the answer to that, he chose the better part of valor and fled the room to take refuge in his own house across the yard.